ASTRO-FOCUS Y

A straightforward gui
planetary transits and pr
how to chart the future for yourself and those
important to you.

By the same author
ASTRO-PICK YOUR PERFECT PARTNER
HOW TO ASTRO-ANALYZE YOURSELF AND OTHERS

Astro-Focus Your Future

by

M. E. COLEMAN, B.A., LL.B.

THE AQUARIAN PRESS
Wellingborough, Northamptonshire

First published 1987

British Library Cataloguing in Publication Data

Coleman, M. E. (Mary Elen)
Astro-focus your future.
1. Astrology
I. Title
133.5 BF1708.1

ISBN 0-85030-522-5

The Aquarian Press is part of the Thorsons Publishing Group

Printed and bound in Great Britain by
Cox & Wyman Ltd, Reading

CONTENTS

FOREWORD

'Can anyone learn to forecast the future? *And* get it right?'

Those are questions many people ask nowadays and the answer is quite simply—'Yes'. To both. In a sense, it's just like the way meteorologists can forecast weather for weeks, months or even years ahead by the plain, scientific method of studying maps and local conditions. Modern astrological science shows you how to do the same for your own life (and those close to you) so that a 'spell of stormy weather' can be prepared for in advance and the problems thereby minimized. Or if 'sunny days' are coming along soon, you can plan ahead to make the very most of them, too.

There is no doubt that forthcoming events *do* cast their shadows before them. You'll find as you learn the techniques set out in this book that when anyone is teetering on the edge of disastrous mistakes, the future movements of the planets, called transits and progressions, switch on their warning beacons. Often years beforehand.

You'll see this process in action when you read the astrological histories of Edward Kennedy, youngest brother of the murdered US President and HRH Edward, Duke of Windsor in Chapter 7.

Take heed in your own life of what the planets are saying and you'll have the change to pull back from the edge of trouble. The same goes for great opportunities. When the planets give the 'green light', provided you rise to the challenge, you'll discover it's 'all systems go!'

Of course, in this book we're not concerned with clairvoyance, soothsaying or making fortune-teller-style predictions. Character is destiny and studying individual personality is the first step in mapping out the shape of things to come. Thus forecasting future life trends is a simple matter of *cause and effect*. The *cause* of everything that happens to us lies within our own personalities. Our special talents or defects. The people we attract, are influenced by, or reject. The *effect* of that unique blend of traits and needs in handling the events of the future determines their outcome.

The natal chart—commonly called the 'horoscope'—supplies us with a clear blueprint of each personality. This is our starting point for assessing what individual psychological needs and drives actually are and therefore in what direction they are likely to lead.

Certainly, some people are fearful of looking into the future. They say things like: 'You can't do anything about it, so why know about what's coming to you?'

That is a disturbingly fatalistic view as well as being wrong. You (and every other human being) have the free will to choose between right and wrong decisions within the framework of your own personality and the birth patterns which reveal it.

Preparing a map of the way ahead markedly cuts down the margins of human error. Try it and you'll see.

M.E. Coleman,
Sydney, Australia.

CHAPTER ONE

What Future Forecasting Should and Shouldn't Be

This book is designed to change your thinking about your future. To convince you that 'things just don't happen!' through some haphazard quirk of fate. To show you how future events can be anticipated, directed, and where desirable, avoided.

But this book is very definitely not about foretelling the future in the sense of clairvoyance. *Nor* the so-called 'predictions' which are churned out daily in newspaper 'stars' columns and which range in content from patently fatuous to the downright dangerous. Without doubt, it is these regular doses of mass-marketed fortune-telling (under the guise of astrology) which have earned the science its ugly image of fair-ground charlatans and 'mumbo-jumbo' star-gazing in the eyes of the thinking reader. Worse still, such varieties of 'predicting' foster the erroneous impression that everybody's future is pre-recorded (like a television commercial) and therefore human beings are pushed around in it like helpless pawns on the chess board of fate. I know of no person of academic background who has also trained in the principles and practice of astrological science . . . and today their number covers a very wide range of professions . . . who swallows that idea and neither do I.

From my own first experiments in blending what I had learned as a university-qualified psychologist with astrological theory, I found affirmation of the fact that you, I and every other human being have free will. The inborn capacity to choose between the right or wrong decisions throughout life within the framework of our own individual personalities and our own unique birth patterns.

Assuredly, the Future Life Trend Forecasting techniques set out in these pages *are* based on the individual horoscope chart. But individual is the operative word here. That is why neither personality analyses nor any form of future forecasting can be mass-produced—'pop' astrology style. A valid, worthwhile natal chart must be calculated and correlated exclusively for its subject. Not for anybody and everybody born around that person's date of birth. It is, in fact, as uniquely personal as a portrait or fingerprint! The same principles apply to valid and reliable future forecasting. This view is identical with that propounded by Hippocrates (the 'father' of medicine) and was also shared by Nostradamus.

Both men achieved fame which has survived for centuries and both insisted on the individuality of the natal chart (commonly called the 'horoscope') and further that it never—not to the slightest degree—denied human free will. Indeed, Hippocrates went so far as to frame on oath in which he required all astrologers to swear that they would teach a philosophy of free will and emotional self-control that was the antithesis of fatalism and predestination.

Nostradamus repeated this warning to anyone who sought to practise astrology and cited startling cases of captains and kings, lords and ladies of his own time to prove his doctrines right. (One in particular leaps to mind. That of a French monarch who rode to his death in a tournament because he *chose* to ignore the planetary warnings.)

Hippocrates and Nostradamus, in common with a long procession of great minds who have studied astrological science over the centuries, always maintained each indicated future event offers each person a clear-cut choice. Of dealing with the stated situation in a positive, constructive manner and thereby gaining optimum results. Or of handling it in a negative, destructive way and hence guaranteeing a dismal outcome. That is the approach to Future Life Trend Forecasting I also adhere to.

So that is the form of forecasting this book is designed to teach you. To show you how to *chart* the way ahead. For yourself. For anyone important to you. Without any variety of clairvoyance or psychic flashes, but by scientific method and relatively simple mathematical calculations. You will learn through these chapters to look at the future like a detailed road map, spread out on a table in front of you. As you look, you can see at once just where you'll find yourself if you decide to turn that corner, climb a steeper mountain or go back the way you have come.

That word 'if' is vital in this context and spotlights the vast difference between fatalistic prophesying or fortune-teller-style predictions and the methods set out in this book. Future Life *Trend* Forecasting is never intended to tell you what *will* happen. Only what *can* happen. *If* you let it. The choice remains yours. That is why I always include the word 'trend' when I calculate and advise on possible future event patterns. I suggest you do the same for the *Oxford English Dictionary* defines 'trend' as 'a general direction or tendency' . . . which is what we will be discussing in this book.

You'll also be interested to note that most leading astrological societies and associations firmly adhere to this view too. In its Code of Ethics, the Federation of Australian Astrologers states as follows:

> In view of the accepted meaning of the word 'prediction' by the general public as indicating a definite statement of coming events, as it would be from a fortune-teller, it is preferable to use the words 'indication', 'probability', or even 'forecast'.

Couching your analyses of future patterns in the above terms is not a cop-out. It is done to preserve the element of individual choice and to remind each client of his/her role in handling the astrological answers to future-oriented questions or decisions.

To illustrate: Let's imagine your chart shows certain future planetary movements are putting heavy pressure on your marriage. (These movements are technically termed 'transits' and 'progressions' and will be fully defined in Chapter two.) They are all the fortune-teller/astrologer needs—and many other species of soothsayers drag astrology into their act too—to announce you'll soon be on the Divorce Court doormat.

By contrast, the approach of future forecasting I suggest points up the risk areas in the relationship, indicates precisely where you and/or your spouse are going wrong and then shows you how to avert the breakdown. *Provided* you're both willing to work towards that end.

Or to put the technique in broader terms. Future Life Trend Forecasting as discussed here will teach you to:

1. *Foresee* the end results of whatever you're planning right now.
2. *Decide* if the goals you're pursuing are the right or wrong ones.
3. *Anticipate* which of your hopes, desires, ambitions are likely to reach

fulfillment at particular dates in particular years.

4. *Re-think* objectives (no matter how urgently sought and lovingly nurtured) which would be better set aside for now, changed or perhaps even abandoned.

The last No. 4—is of extra-special significance when you set out to change your future into what you wish it to be. For example, it's no good pushing all your energies into pursuing love affairs or marriage when your current chart patterns are offering career advancement. Or vice versa.

Just recently I ran across a story of the deadly disappointments which follow when chart indicators are deliberately ignored. The subject was qualified for a profession which his natal chart patterns favoured, although a marked lack of practicality and sustained effort also showed. During the years in question, his future planetary positions were strongly backing career progress . . . but he failed and badly. So badly, he decided to take a job as a clerk which was far below his qualifications and which he hated. What went wrong? He did. Because successes did not come instantly, he stopped trying, turned his back on persevering and insisted no worthwhile professional opportunities had come his way.

Careful probing revealed that valuable chances *had* come but future planetary movements only offer opportunities. They do *not* hand them to you gift-wrapped on a gilded platter. What's more, such offers have to be accepted through hard work and success-oriented thinking—neither of which our man was willing to apply. (It's a whole lot easier to fail in life or in love than it is to succeed.) Worse still, our man was fast approaching forty. A dangerous age both psychologically and astrologically as we'll see in later chapters.

So to compensate for his mounting terror at the thought he'd already lived half his life without getting anywhere and seemed to be going downhill instead of up, he decided his chart was 'all wrong' and the only mistake he'd ever made was to remain single. Within months, he became obsessed with the desire to marry. With the fixed idea that marriage would miraculously solve all his problems.

It couldn't, of course. And predictably, since his natal chart revealed him as a demanding personality which did not co-operate comfortably with others in intimate situations (the real reason why he was still a bachelor in his late thirties), and his future patterns were dead against successful relationships just then—that project failed too. The harder he tried to find a bride, the more his disappointments piled up.

That is the inevitable result if you push for the wrong objectives for the wrong reasons at the wrong time.

On the other hand, had our man followed the leads in his chart, he would not only have been much more satisfied with his life and himself but also become a far more attractive marriage proposition later on.

In my experience, deliberately ignoring helpful future planetary movements is tantamount to walking down a road . . . finding a signpost to where you're going . . . then pig-headedly marching off in the opposite direction. You may eventually wind up at your destination but you'll have wasted plenty of time and shoe leather in the interim.

Your Future Begins in Your Past

Future Life Trend Forecasting techniques are neither difficult to learn nor hard to use—even though some old-style textbooks make them seem so. In many ways, they boil down to simply applying the fundamental law of cause and effect.

From the psychological standpoint (as well as the astrological), there is no denying that the *cause* and *shape* of things to come in every life lie within the personality itself. Therefore, in that sense, the future is revealed by the past. The basic self of each individual *causes* a set of actions and reactions to be put in train. The future results follow from the *effects* of such actions and reactions.

If you take a detached view of your own life and those around you, you'll observe that—literally from the cradle to the grave—we each attract like magnets certain sets of circumstances and certain types of people which either block or assist our development and our hopes. For no other reason than we are *who* we are. Extrovert or introvert. Confident or fearful. Cheery or depressing. And so on.

Thus the prime cause of every success or failure we encounter is firmly and visibly rooted in the type of personality we were born with. Psychologically, this can be assessed through personality, intelligence and aptitude testing. Astrologically, personality type is set out in the natal chart as graphically as a blueprint.

Once you thoroughly grasp the psychological implications of birth patterns shown within it plus their combined effect on behaviour and life choices, you perceive at once *why* we are driven to do the things we do. Whether we are our own best friend or worst enemy. What specific traits and personality traits set our feet upon this path or that. (If you're a newcomer to astrological science, you can learn accurate methods of natal personality assessment and chart calculation from my companion book—*How to Astro-Analyze Yourself and Others*.)

Now, let's look at a set of famous names—we'll choose film actors because everybody has at least heard of them—and see just what drove them to succeed.

Explaining what set *his* feet at the age of fourteen upon the path which later led to international film fame lasting more than fifty years and wealth beyond his wildest dreams, Cary Grant once said: 'I became an actor for the usual reason—a great need to be liked and admired'. I suspect those words were spoken from his Capricorn heart. Grant was born on 18 January 1904 in Bristol, England, and like so many strongly Capricorn types worried that others did not easily warm to him. His comment therefore encapsulates his own very personal need and does not, in my view, represent the 'usual reason' why acting fame is both sought and achieved.

Compare comments made to interviewers by two other English actors—Laurence Olivier (born 22 May 1907) and Michael Caine (born 14 March 1933) and you'll observe their personal drives and priorities were not exactly the same as Grant's. The differences are subtle but they are nevertheless evident.

Piscean Michael Caine upon reaching the pinnacle of his career gave *his* reasons for striving in these words: 'I have all I ever wanted: to become a millionaire, to be a big film star, to become the best actor I could possibly be'.

Born on the Taurus/Gemini cusp, Laurence Olivier records he was 'not conscious of any other need than to show off'.

If you examine the natal charts of Grant, Caine and Olivier in detail, you will easily isolate the traits which led them to speak as they did and walk the paths they chose. The same goes for your own natal charts. The story of your future begins right there.

I stress this point heavily because virtually all mistakes made in future forecasting stem from the failure to correlate it with the individually-calculated birth chart. Thus when you sent out to plot your future by means of planetary transits or progressions, you must always:

- Seek out firstly your own, very personal reasons for wanting this experience or that relationship through a painstaking analysis of your own natal chart.
- Assess next what talents/capacities exist therein to achieve your chosen goal.
- Observe what planetary transits or progressions in the future are baulking or boosting that goal.

To correlate in this manner is the *only* way to find the right answers to your future-oriented questions. . .whether they concern future business/career decisions, love relationshiops or family affairs.

Never forget that future planetary transits and progressions are not separate, independent energies. They can only accentuate or obstruct potentials shown in the natal chart.

If you doubt the necessity of following all those steps, let's take another look at Cary Grant's career along with two other legendary Capricorns—rock singers Elvis Presley (born 8 January 1935) and David Bowie (born same day in 1947).

Read the life stories of the trio and you'll note a recurring theme emerges. The one-pointed ambition and perfectionism of the Capricorn personality. Natural talent plus the determination to apply it relentlessly in the pursuit of wealth and status. The steadfast refusal to give up or be daunted by set-backs. The shrewd utilization of each new opportunity as soon as it presented itself.

All the above are, of course, classic Capricorn traits. But why did these three make it to the top of the world in such spectacular and enduring style when millions of other Capricorn types are still plodding along? Were Grant, Elvis and Bowie just fantastically lucky? Not in my mind. Great successes in any life sector do not come from luck but from candid self-appraisal, hard slog and that most crucial of factors—'timing'. Put bluntly, 'timing' means making damn sure you're always at the right place with the right attitude at the right time.

Present Focusing and Future Timing—How They'll Change Your Life

To begin with, there's nothing mysterious, magical, clairvoyant or occultist about the concept of 'timing'. . .although it does involve the ability to see ahead. Any wartime general—who won a battle because he advanced at the right moment or lost because he did not—can testify to the paramount importance of 'timing'. And to the fact that he 'foresaw' the results of his actions rightly or wrongly as the case may be. That is true for all of us.

In everyday affairs, we all try to 'foresee', or 'forecast' what will happen if we do this or decide against that. Even in the smallest things. Will the boss be in the right mood today to agree to a rise in pay? Will tomorrow be fine for a picnic with the family? Will the person we love offer marriage soon?

Certainly, some individuals seem to be better equipped to forge ahead through a well-attuned, instinctive sense of 'timing' their actions and decisions, their advances and retreats. (It's rather like the sense of rhythm in music and dancing. To some it comes naturally. Others don't feel the beat at all.)

Those who do have and use this instinctive sense of 'timing' appear to get exactly what they want out of life without really trying. . always turning up in the role of winners, never losers. But what about the rest of us? If we haven't got it, can we develop it?

Yes, anyone can do it as you'll see in later chapters. But, first, you'll need to spend a little time working at what I've termed 'present focusing'. You'll arrive at a better understanding of what 'present focusing' means if you remind yourself that life's winners always know precisely what they want and go after it single-mindedly throughout their lives. No let-up. No side-tracks. (Which means they're trying a lot harder and a lot more consistently than you might think.)

To quote again from actor Michael Caine: 'To most people I was an overnight discovery. They all forgot what an awful long dark night it was'. In other words, Caine was pointing out that gaining any goal demands a long hard haul up the ladder without looking back till you make it to the top.

Or to use another analogy. Imagine yourself a scientist in a laboratory with a microscope. Think of your most deeply-desired future goal as a specimen slide that you're placing under the microscope. As you do, you'll have to adjust and readjust the microscope lens till you see the specimen in the sharpest focus possible. Obviously, in a laboratory that exercise is going to demand all your attention. The same applies to everyday life.

If you want to become a future winner—and naturally, I don't mean only fame and fortune—you must focus all your effort on accomplishing your goal *now*. (That's why I used the word 'focus' in the title of this book.) However, and this point is of enormous significance, your most important aim must be stated in positive terms.

Think for a moment and you'll soon realize it's far easier to say what you *don't want* than it is to say exactly what you *do want*. (The negatives usually come up well before the positives.)

Let's say . . . You don't want to be single?
Or you don't want to be lonely?
Or you don't want to be eternally short of money?

What are you actually doing about getting rid of those *'don't want* situations in the future? No use wasting time in futile daydreaming about lost lovers, missing friends or faulty finances. Or continually cursing your unhappy fate. Or blaming others for your own failures. Or even bemoaning those glum-looking planetary patterns in your chart. Instead, begin to change your future now by switching those negative *'don't want'* type questions into positive *'do want'* questions by focusing your mind like this.

Let's choose the first of the foregoing list and assume you *don't want* to be single? Ask yourself: Do I actually *want* to be married? Do I *want* marriage enough to seek it actively? To alter my life style to fit with marriage? To force myself to go out and look for a partner without letting up till I find the right one?'

If you answer 'No' to any one of those set of self-questions, the plain truth is that marriage is not one of your *'do wants'* at all. Or, at best, it's certainly not a strong enough objective for you to focus all your talents and energies towards achieving it. You're not focusing clearly enough on the goal but merely playing with the idea of being married.

The same basic rules apply to every conceivable variety of *'don't want'* situations. Winning means replacing present negatives with future-oriented positives right now.

To take our third question. If you don't want to be eternally short of money, you have to decide you *do want* to be richer by throwing yourself as wholeheartedly into the task as did Grant, Elvis and Caine. Agreed, all three had lived with spectre of poverty in childhood which provided them with a powerful goad. (Grant's father was a tailor's presser: Elvis's a barely literate labourer: Caine's humped fish crates round the London docks.) Yet millions of others were reared in similar depressing circumstances and did not haul themselves out.

Why again? A quote from Taurus-born Bing Crosby answers that neatly. He once described his climb to millionaire status and film fame by stating his actual talent was small but he had 'stretched it to the point of transparency!' In other words, he was stating he had recognized his singing ability early, focused his undivided attention on fostering it and timed each future move to display it without a moment's hesitation.

All of which goes to prove the point: *If you haven't got what You want out of life, you either don't know what it is or you don't want it enough to go all out after it.*

Turning Childhood Dreams into Adult Realities

When we're very young. . .in those earliest days before the daily drudge takes the gilt off our gingerbread. . .we all secretly believe we can do or be anything we fancy as soon as we're grown up. Further, since neither conditioning nor disappointments have then begun to narrow our expectations to any real extent, these early hopes and dreams are likely to be based on a surprisingly realistic assessment of our own natural talents.

So if you are now willing to admit to yourself that you, as an adult, aren't sure what you really want, you may have to look at far back as childhood in search of clues. For there's no doubt that people who gain their goals are those who have never forgotten their earliest dreams, never stopped focusing on them and hence have swiftly turned them into adult realities. If they want to become actors, artists, swimming instructors, they don't allow anyone—not parents, teachers, vocational guidance counsellors—to turn them into anything else.

As witness, the case of an Australian doctor who had achieved some of the most daring breakthroughs in modern surgery and who said in a film documentary of his work: 'As a youngster, I was told I had no aptitude for medicine. I'd never pass the exams. But I knew better. I knew the only thing I wanted to do was to be doctor in the research areas of medicine'.

In this type of story, you'll invariably find the natal chart shows outstanding skill in the chosen area which its 'owner' instinctively felt as soon as he/she was old enough to articulate the need.

One of my clients—a successful Australian playwright—is a further case in point. He told me he had composed his first original dialogue at the age of six and knew right then and there he was going to write plays for a living. (Once again, his natal chart supported such aspirations.)

At about the same age, I discovered I liked taking things apart to see what made them 'tick' and then putting them back together again. Toys, bits of old jewellery. I also noticed I enjoyed writing things down on paper. Little poems, fairy stories. Nothing spectacular about that although it did constitute early evidence of my marked Virgoan traits. The desire to analyse, the wish to communicate ideas through the written word.

At the same time, I sturdily resisted my Aquarian actress mother's attempts to interest me in her box of greasepaints. I liked neither the smell of them nor the thought of the footlights. (Far too many planets in Virgo to tackle anything as public or uncertain as show business!)

The purpose of quoting that brief scrap of ancient history is to emphasize how such little clues from the past can help you find and focus on *your* most deeply-felt, early desires and needs—perhaps unrecognized or forgotten in adult life—yet which point the way to fulfillment.

And in all honesty, I have to record I was nothing like as certain (as were some of the cases quoted earlier) of my own life direction, my own '*do wants*' in early adulthood. I made several detours into other professions and ideas along the way but finally I landed back where the basic 'Me' had always known it wanted to be. Taking things apart to see what makes them tick and then putting them back together again. (Charts and analyses nowadays.) *And* writing things down on paper. (Books and research this time.)

So don't despair if you also feel you've strayed off course. It's never too late to ring the changes in your own future. Indeed, you'll see when you *find* what your real needs are and *focus* on them that even painful past experiences—the ups and downs, false trails and set-backs—are never wasted. They've been lived through to be learnt from.

Assuredly, you can dodge many of those longer off-course detours once you thoroughly understand your natal chart since it provides a safe and sure short-cut to self-appraisal. Better still if you acquire this level of understanding when you're a young adult.

I was in my thirties, had qualified in three different professions, (psychology, law and journalism), had been twice married and become the mother of three daughters before I began to make a serious study of astrological science. (Hence quite a bit of water had flowed under my bridge!) What's more I still wasn't sure which of my three work options to follow till a set of Uranian transits back in the late 1960s literally thumped astrology down on my front doorstep. (More about this type of sudden, life-changing event in the chapter on the planet Uranus.)

By the time I had thoroughly grasped the significance of my chart patterns, my indecision vanished. I saw the path ahead clearly mapped out before me. Better still as I moved deeper into astrological research, it turned out my past 'detours' into law and journalism were not wasted efforts after all. Legal training ensured I would never accept any statement or theory unless it was supported by hard-fact evidence. My journalistic experience had happily taught me to write in a lucid, easily understood style. The psychology qualifications were not in any sense one of my 'detours'. In fact, I believe some training in this field is a 'must' for anyone who aspires to excel in astrological analysis. The two disciplines are natural partners as both aim to penetrate the secrets of human behaviour.

Your own chart can help you also to bring your past experiences into play, to reach the right conclusions about your own skills and, if necessary, to change your life direction. . .especially if you suspect you've been a square peg in a round hole for years. Use your chart now to begin working through your past to unearth your best abilities, your unused potentials. The next step then is to direct your mind to *focusing* clearly upon them so you can *time* your future moves to develop them to the utmost.

Which point brings me to a heartening thought for everyone. The transiting and progressing planets in their various forms and individual styles continually offer us the chances to make new starts, revive lost hopes, replace negative situations with positive ones and turn failure into success. All we have to do is be daring enough to rise to the occasion and reach for the sky!

However, since this introductory chapter is entitled 'What Future Forecasting Should and Shouldn't Be', we'll round it off with a short excursion into 'Tombstone Territory'. (My term for the makers of the sort of direful prophecies set out hereunder.)

Down Among the Doomies

Every top-rating textbook on astrology these days warns students of the enormous responsibility all practitioners bear when they advise clients. . .especially about the future.

In each one of the following list of 'Direful predictions' I've collected to serve as cautionary tales, you'll note the recurring and heavy emphasis on the word 'will'. This, of course, worsens the dangerously depressive effect of the 'prediction' because it gives the hearer the intentional impression that there is no way in the world of averting the oncoming disaster. If he/she is gullible or over-impressionable, behaviour at once becomes negative and fearful and that cannot fail to attract some sort of trouble. . .thereby 'proving' the prophet of doom to have been at least partially 'right'.

I should add that all these 'Direful Predictions' are actual cases and each time the maker of them claimed to be a qualified astrologer. *Not* a clairvoyant or fortune-teller. Thus the damage was magnified by pretending a totally false statement had scientific backing. Case 2 deserves added condemnation because the so-called astrologer had tried to use the science for motives of personal greed so that the client could be parted from a further $500 to 'cure' a mental disturbance which did not exist.

Direful Prediction 1

(Client at time was girl aged 18)

'You *will* marry several times and have three children. At the age of 10, one of them *will* die'.

By the age of 30, this client had been married twice and did in fact have three children. Actually they were triplets. As they were turning 10, she was flying to Europe with them to meet her second husband's family. Naturally, she was terrified. *And* had been worried to the point of despair for years as the earlier parts of the 'prophecy' had really happened.

The result? No tragedy of course. What had the 'prophecy' been based upon? From her chart, nothing more than Pluto transiting her fifth house!

Direful Prediction 2

(Client was mature woman with good IQ)

'This natal aspect means you *will* have a nervous breakdown in the next four months or become a schizophrenic', (pause) 'unless you begin a new course I'm starting shortly which will teach you how to avoid these conditions and will only cost you $500!'

The result? No mental disturbance whatsoever, helped by the fact that this woman was not gullible. What had the 'prophecy' been based upon? From her chart, nothing more than a discordant aspect between the Moon and Pluto!

Direful Predictions 3

(Client was young woman of 22 at the time)

'At the age of 51, you *will* very nearly succumb to a serious lung disease.'

Since the date of the disease's appearance was nearly 30 years in the future, the maker of this 'prophecy' was certainly safe from its being checked up on. Nevertheless, if this client had not seen a more responsible practitioner who reassured her, she could have begun a fear reaction that could have laid the groundwork for disease years later.

What had the 'prophecy' been based upon? Nothing more than a Gemini Ascendant!

Direful Prediction 4

(Extract from a magazine 'stars column')

This one was related to me by one of my own clients so I'll set it down as I heard it.

Client (on phone to me): 'I've just had a frantic call from a friend on holiday in Europe. She's terribly worried. She read in a women's magazine that all Taureans were going to have a bad car accident this week. She's taken it so seriously she's terrified of driving and rang me in Sydney to tell me where to find her will!'

Me: 'If that so-called 'prediction' were even remotely capable of coming true, one-twelfth of the entire population of the world would be having bad car accidents this week. And since it's rather difficult to have a car accident on your own, large sections of the other eleven-twelfths would be tangled up in the international mayhem too.'

'That sort of popular press, over-generalized 'prediction' is dangerous nonsense. Worse still, if readers of it are the impressionable type like your friend, it becomes a self-fulfilling prophecy.'

'In my view, serious astrology has never been a fatalistic science. It should never be stated that specific events *must* happen or even inferred that human free will is powerless to direct the future patterns of any life.'

Agreed, the Taurean lady of our story must have been very, very gullible and may have even exaggerated what the 'stars column' writer had 'predicted'. Nevertheless, the effect that 'prediction' had upon her verged on hysteria and so should remind everyone. . .practitioners as well as those who are simply studying the future-oriented areas of astrological science out of personal interest. . .that you actually *are* playing with fire.

Test the effect of what you propose to tell your client about the future by putting yourself into his/her shoes like this. Imagine, for instance, you visit some fortune-teller who tells *you* you're going to have a bad car accident next week. And who makes the pronoucement as portentously as if they'd got the bad news direct from a hot-line to the Great Beyond.

If you even half-believed the prediction, you'd be psychologically programming yourself into making serious driving errors every time you sat behind the wheel—out of a repressed but ever-present fear. If you were impressionable enough to believe it totally, you'd tangle yourself in a road smash-up before that week was out as surely as the green light changes to red. And doubtless, as the tow-trucks roared up to drag away the mess, you'd be shaking your aching head in wonder at the amazing 'accuracy' of your seer's prediction.

The Australian aborigines have the words for this technique. It's called 'Pointing the Bone'. And when the Bone is pointed at a tribal transgressor that individual dies. Quickly. And for no other reason than he was told he would. Don't think we who live in industralized societies are too sophisticated to respond like that. Everyone—no matter how tough or how intelligent—is impressionable to varying degrees.

And horrendously negative 'predictions' are still being made every day. Just recently, one of my clients reported she had driven up to a clairvoyant's door in her Jaguar and was nearly dropped in her tracks by this conversation. 'Is that car yours?'. . .'Yes'. . .'I see a man in the front seat with both his legs severed in the week before next Christmas!' This lady didn't wait to hear any more cheering news about her future but admitted she sold the car at once and scoured the papers that Christmas for reports of such a ghastly accident. There were none, of course.

It's difficult to assess the psychological motivation which prompts some individuals to specialize in prophecies of doom. Possibly it springs from their own negativity, bitterness or insecurity—all qualities which gain satisfaction from alarming others or simply 'putting them down'.

I'm stressing the very real dangers of making depressing or frightening statements about the future because newcomers to the field of astrological science rarely realize these risks at first.

On the other hand, I am not recommending that you suppress truth or gloss over future trouble-spots. But there are many positive, encouraging ways of phrasing comments. Blanket, hard-line statements about what '*will* happen' should be avoided like the plague to astrology they are.

At all times, (as we saw earlier) clients must be reminded of their own free will in handling future situations and the area of individual choice preserved. Anyone who disobeys these rules—that high-ranking astrologers have upheld for thousands of years—can wreak havoc in the lives of others. Sometimes with fatal consequences.

As witness a particularly terrifying tale of malpractice by a so-called astrologer related to me a couple of years ago. The client in this case was a woman who had just turned fifty. She had had a most unhappy love life and two broken marriages when she sought advice on her hopes of finding a new husband. Among other alarming predictions—

none of which could possibly have been based on the astrological chart—she was told: 'At your age you have no hope of re-marriage. There *will* be no more men in your life. Ever.'

Two days later she killed herself with an overdose of sleeping tablets. The chart was found beside her bed and a police enquiry followed. The 'astrologer', who also claimed to be a clairvoyant, left Australia fast and never returned.

Fortunately, irresponsible, ignorant and destructive soothsayers of the ilk we've just seen in action are the exception rather than the rule throughout the astrological field. But their very existence doubtless explains why some clients approach astrology in fear and trembling, accompanied often by plaintive cries of 'Don't tell me anything bad!' Plus the fact that negative and baseless 'prophecies' hand stacks of ammunition to the scoffers, bigots and knockers who love to denigrate the great science of astrology. In my view, everyone's analysis of his/her horoscope chart should be an illuminating, even exciting experience—not a ticket to a horror show.

Well, now that we've seen how to place future forecasting in its correct perspective—i.e. as the likely outcome of use or misuse of life potentials shown by the natal chart—we're ready to open the gates to tomorrow. To examine the planets which point the way ahead. To observe whether in their future movements they are placing emphasis on this life sector or that. Boosting this hope or baulking that ambition. And of course how and why they do it.

Quick Reference Check-Points for Chapter 1

Rub Out 'The Gypsy' In You

One of the surest ways of evoking criticism (at best) or ridicule (at worst) of your work is to use antiquated terms or make ill-defined statements, that sound more like Madame Zenobia at the village fair than a serious analyst. Phrases such as 'in evil aspect', 'ill-starred', 'malign', 'adverse' to list but a few. People who love to rubbish astrology will pounce on these to make fun of it *and* you.

While reading biographies of a famous actor and then an American senator, I ran across the following gems. Mentioning the actor's visit to 'renowned' astrologer, his biographer grabbed this chance to indulge in a spot of literary smirking: 'The raven-haired soothsayer declared he "was impractical in the most practical way", meaning???. . .'The crystal ball discovered "an ill-starred" Jupiter which was going to make him fat'.

In the second instance, the author stated several American politicians sought advice from fortune-tellers and added: 'It was remarkable how many sophisticated men were *superstitious*. . .The woman was one of a *tribe* of fortune-tellers and astrologers who had taken up *lucrative* residence in the capital of a nation. . .'Her *short* fingers tapped the upturned cards. . ."I'm working on your horoscope. . . I particularly like the look of your Sun. You have a good Moon, too". He paid her at the door, feeling as always that he was leaving a *whorehouse*'.

The *italics* in the above quotes are mine but it's barely necessary to show how this writer was dredging up every muddy epithet he could think of. At the same time he tried the usual trick of the habitual scoffer—lumping astrologers in with card-readers and fortune-tellers as well as implying all were frowsy charlatans.

In the above examples, archaic language and meaningless utterances gave these authors plenty more fuel for their flames. So do keep clear of either in your own work.

Bouncing Your Badgers

Everyone counselling on future-oriented event patterns has to learn to cope with badgers—the type who try to push, prod or goad you into exaggerating or overstating what the chart shows.

My very worst badger was a middle-aged businessman, who kept pounding the desk and shouting: 'Tell me I'm going to make a million by the end of next year! That's all I want to know!' The more I refused to say that or anything like it, the louder he shouted. In the end, I was forced to bounce him—hard!

Watch out for the types who try to badger you in like manner. If you allow them to coerce you into exaggeration or let them twist your words, they'll be down on you like the proverbial ton of bricks when their fantasies don't 'come true'.

'Dynamite—Handle With Care'

Whenever I lecture to students on chart forecasts, I also recommend they think of the future as if it were packed in a big, black box and labelled: 'DANGER. DYNAMITE. HANDLE WITH CARE'. For rash, wrong or ill-considered utterances about future events really do add up to 'dynamite' because of the indescribable damage they can cause to other people's lives.

Imagine the disastrous spin-offs that could follow from wrong advice on questions like: 'Ought I to leave my wife and children next June?'. . .'Should I invest $200,000 in Company X in October?'. . .'I'm supposed to have a major operation on 10 February. Tell me if I ought to have it or not?'

Note, too, that some clients phrase their questions in a manner that should ring warning bells in your head. Wording them in the style just quoted indicates the enquirer. . .consciously or unconsciously . . .is trying to transfer all liability for the decision on to you.

Do not accept it. The purpose of the chart is *not* to allow anyone to abdicate responsibility for his/her own life. As an advisor, your role is to indicate the pros and cons, the helpful or hampering planetary influences relevant to the matter in question. In the natal as well as the progressed chart, since different personalities respond differently to similar future event patterns. Never let clients or friends pass their buck to you.

Fatuous, Farcical or Just Plain Silly

Beginners in the field of astrological science are usually hesitant to make clear-cut definitive statements, which overall is commendable. Best to say nothing till you feel confident that you know what you're talking about. On the other hand, it's just as bad to take refuge in comments so vague or obscure they don't mean anything at all!

I've never forgotten one novice who rushed up to me one morning, crying excitedly: 'I've just discovered I *can* forecast the future. I told a man he'd be worried in May. *And he was!*'

Oh dear! Nobody gets through an entire month without worrying about *something*. This poor man must also have been most worried about what it was he was supposed to be worrying about!

That forecast was, of course, just plain silly. The following, which a client showed me from a typed horoscope he had obtained, verges on the farcical. 'Your soul inhabits a quiet garden, but your heart will float on a cloud of dreams in the year ahead.' That sort of stuff deserves a one-way trip to the rubbish dump. Always try to keep your statements clear, concise and easy to understand.

Check Off the Check-You-Outs

Many enquirers who write or phone about horoscopes have the totally false notion that all astrologers are clairvoyants. And further that your request for additional information—which will allow you to erect an accurate chart and answer their future-oriented questions in detail—is actually a cunning attempt to 'pump' them for facts. Facts which you plan to recycle later as part of your 'revelations' of their characters or projects.

Invariably, these types are also very suspicious about astrology, adopt a close-mouthed attitude and ask questions so purposely cryptic they might as well be written in code. For example: 'I have to make an important decision in the next three months. How will it turn out?'

Assuredly, if you're experienced in chart interpretation, you'll have some idea of what their decision concerns and where it may lead. But that can take a lot of time which would be better spent in examining the precise nature of the decision itself and then placing it in correct perspective.

Therefore, to such types, I always answer: 'I am not a clairvoyant. Clairvoyance has no place in astrology. The more clearly and completely you state your problem, the better I'll be able to deal with it. If you don't wish to do that, I suggest you look elsewhere for advice'.

Generally speaking, it's best to check this type of would-be client off your list. They are not genuinely seeking help but attempting to check you out and test your 'powers'. Sometimes, of course, this attitude originates from one or more bad experiences with fake clairvoyants.

One young university student who clammed up with me at first but changed her response later confirmed this. While waiting on the verandah for her interview with a self-proclaimed seer, she noticed a partition window had been left open and sat near it. From there, she overheard him cleverly quiz his client for details about her life which he later fed back as evidence of 'clairvoyance'.

Unfortunately, this man also claimed to be an astrologer which shows what reputable practitioners are up against in the public mind.

One Step Back—Two Strides Forward

Most questions about the future are asked by those who are pretty unhappy with the present. For example, an unsatisfactory work situation. . .a troublesome relationship problem. . .a worrying health condition.

Since (as discussed earlier) the causes of all kinds of present unhappiness and future discontent originate in our pasts—that's where we have to look first by means of the natal chart. Or, in other words, if you take one step back there in search of unfulfilled hopes, lost illusions, sad love stories, unhappy childhoods, you'll find you can take two strides forward in helping yourself or your clients towards a better future.

So tick off the following steps again to set them firmly in your mind. And remember—never, never discuss future planetary movements *without* relating each one to the natal chart.

I realize, of course, that some astrologers offer personal forecasts without taking the extra time and trouble to do this. In my view, that's tantamount to picking up an assorted pile of clothes off a rack and selling them to somebody without bothering to see if they fit.

Don't forget many people have similar future transits and progressions at a given time, but that doesn't say they will react to coming opportunities or set-backs in the same way. They'll handle either in accordance with their own unique birth patterns.

So when you begin your forecasting, work to this 1 – 2 – 3 – formula:

1. Focus your mind first on the natal chart, carefully noting what traits/potentials are working for or against the questions you're considering.
2. List the most positive qualities or talents that can be brought into play to achieve the desired changes.
3. Examine the future transits and progressions so as to ensure intended moves are timed to be made at the best possible moment.

CHAPTER TWO

Timing Your Life

'I'm waiting till the time is ripe'. . 'I knew it'd work. It was exactly the right moment!'. . 'Everything's going wrong. This isn't my day!'. . 'We've got to time this just right!'

Every day in every language in every corner of the globe, people make remarks like those without ever stopping to think why. In fact, such comments are so ordinary and so familiar, when their underlying meaning is questioned, the answer sounds faintly preposterous. But let's do some questioning, anyway.

Why are we so sure that *one* day or *one* moment is so much better or worse than any other? What inkling, hunch or presentiment tells us when to do this or not to do that? And where do these gut feelings—put into the words commonly used to express them in the above paragraph—spring from? The answer may startle you. They are atavistic. A contemporary oral demonstration of an ancient 'sense' which was already at work in the human psyche when our fur-clad forefathers ran across the prehistoric plains pursued by sabre-toothed tigers.

That strange 'sense' can be best described as an *instinctive awareness of the function of time*. And it is uniquely, exclusively human.

Archaeological digs have revealed that as far back as 11,000 years ago Man *alone* had begun to grasp the significance of time, was recording it and working with it to choose the right days, months, years for whatever he wanted to do.

Such evidence further infers that it was this constant awareness and management of time—coupled with a fast developing power of speech—that finally turned the evolutionary tables in favour of Man. He ceased living solely in the present, the 'endless now', as all other animals did and still do. He began to conceive the idea of 'tomorrow'.

Once he took the next step and looked skywards long enough to realize the sun, moon and planets all moved according to a predictable pattern—his daily, deadly battle for survival was over. Bar the roaring.

He could now do what even his biggest and most ferocious competitors in the animal kingdom could not. *He could use his new-found time 'sense' to order his life in such a way as to benefit from yesterday's mistakes and more importantly still, to plan ahead for tomorrow.*

Nothing epoch-making about that to twentieth century minds. Yet epoch-making it was! In the blink of an eye, evolution-wise, it transformed Man. Changing him irrevocably from the smallish, unprepossessing ape-like creature, who could easily have gone under in the savage world of prehistory, into the paragon of mammals. The master of all he surveyed.

Two evolutionary eye-blinks later, his talent with time had taken him over the top. It has made him the most terrifyingly destructive predator who ever walked on Planet Earth!

Strong words, maybe. Yet if this distinctively human time 'sense' had never evolved, civilization could not have developed. We should never have gone on to understand the laws of physics, smash the atom and land ourselves at last on the threshhold of nuclear destruction.

So our natural affinity with time and timing is no small thing. It has been an integral part of human thought, underlying our decisions, world-shaking or everyday, for aeons. And we're still trying to remain tuned in to it.

Less confidently than we once did. Our time 'sense' first developed from watching time in action—the movements of the sun and moon, the procession of the seasons. Today, our artificial, mechanized life styles have divorced us from nature. Thus we've lost confidence in the time 'sense', mistrusting it, ignoring it, even pretending it doesn't exist.

No citizen of the past would have made such a mistake. He hadn't the slightest doubt that there *was* a time for every purpose under heaven, because he saw the evidence all around him. Because he ordered his life according to the time set by nature and not by the clock. (Clocks were not invented till the tenth century and don't tell true solar time anyway. If you want to know what the time of day *actually* is—you must seek out a sundial.)

I've stressed the human time 'sense' and its ramifications at some length since the concept of time is the basis of all astrological doctrine. In its philosophical areas as well as its role in guiding the decision-making process. You *must* understand the function of time if you're going to work effectively in future forecasting.

Tuning into Your 'Time' Sense

So let's shut our eyes for a while on clocks, digital watches and computers and try to switch our mind back to the old ways of living in tune with time. We'll begin this step by considering the *Oxford English Dictionary*'s definition of 'time'. . .'moment or definite portion of time destined or suitable for a purpose'.

Interesting? Especially that word 'destined'. No-one could accuse such an august work of occultist leanings which confirms that the concept of time inexorably evokes the concept of destiny. Of handling time to direct the future.

So far, so good. Now, assuming we have a 'purpose', how do we find the time 'destined' to get it off the ground? Easily. We do what Man has always done. We look to the heavens. Nowadays, of course, we don't have to stand outside and search the night sky for planets and constellations. Neither do we have to rely on the simple recording devices of the past to plot their positions. That job's been done for us. All the information is clearly set out in the reference work which no astrologer can do without. . .the planetary ephemeris.

From this, we can delve back into past years to locate the origins of problems troubling us right now. This exercise is vital because tough decisions don't suddenly pop up like mushrooms in our path. Remember, a mushroom cannot emerge from the soil unless its spores were already there. The same goes for today's problems. We wouldn't be staring them in the face at this moment if the seeds had not been already sown. Sometimes in the recent past, sometimes as far back as childhood (as we saw in Chapter 1).

To illustrate: Let's say you're facing a momentous financial decision on the 7 April. You'd like to invest every penny you own in a scheme that could make a fortune for you *or* leave you destitute. *Before* you look at the planetary positions for that date and the months surrounding it, you must put your natal chart under the microscope. Does it show a profligate attitude to money? Does it imply you're easily conned?

What does it infer you want large sums of money for? Are you practical about money or a dreamer? What's your financial history been like since you became an adult—spending or saving? These are the sort of 'seed' questions you need to ask yourself and then to accept the impartial answers the chart offers.

Take the case of a young beautician who told me she was planning to open her first salon soon. The girl's natal chart fairly bristled with warnings against financial gullibility and impracticality in business affairs. The transits for the date and whole year in question were also ringing warning bells—loud and clear.

I said: 'Somebody's just offered to decorate your salon with genuine Louis IV furniture. There's no deposit and you only have to pay $10 per week.'

She gasped: 'How did you know?'

No, it wasn't clairvoyance. Just the sort of deceptive set-up you'd expect from this girl's natal and future patterns. Neptune (as we'll see in a later chapter) is usually the culprit when individuals lay themselves open to fraud, dishonesty or trickery.

Whatever your present or future decision, its results will largely depend on how and why the circumstances first arose—in the past.

I can't stress this point hard enough because you must never lose sight of it for a moment. None of the future planetary movements can extinguish your natal personality traits and attitudes. Very often they do the reverse. They ignite them—rather like putting a match to a haystack. If you can handle the ensuing conflagration, well and good. If you can't, you could find yourself running for your life.

But back to our general plan of action. Which planets are furthering our current purpose in the future and which are hindering it? In either their transits or progressions? Both of these are the technical terms used to investigate past, present or future planetary movements at relevant dates, but they are not synonymous and must never be confused. So, we'll set their basic definitions firmly in our mind before we start to look at them in action.

Like most astrological terminology, the terms derive from Latin words so when you understand this derivation you'll find their meanings easier to remember and more closely equated to common speech.

Transit

- The word comes from a Latin verb for 'going'.
- Hence when a planet is *transiting* any house of the horoscope, it is merely *going through* that house. (Just like when you say 'the goods are in transit by air', meaning they are going from their place of origin to a destination.)
- When a planet aspects another planet during a transit, it is simply *going over* the position of that planet. (Just like when an aircraft in transit passes over a certain spot on the map.)
- In a completed chart the letter 't' denotes a transiting planet and is placed before the planet's symbol. . .transiting Pluto in the fourth house square natal Pluto in the first house would be shown thus . . .t♇ ^{4}□♇ ^{1}

Progression

- The word comes from a Latin verb for 'moving onward'.
- Hence when a planet is progressing through any house of the horoscope chart, it has arrived there merely by moving onwards from its position in the birth chart. (Just like when you read 'The tour itinerary will begin in London and then progress through France to Spain', meaning there is a predetermined schedule for the trip.)
- When a planet aspects another planet by progression, it encounters the position of that planet simply by *moving towards* it along a predetermined path. (Just like a tour itinerary sheet shows you'll have progressed as far as Madrid by a certain date because the schedule requires you to take the route that leads to Madrid.)
- In a completed chart the letter 'p' denotes a progressing planet and is placed before the planet's symbol. . .progressed Sun in the eighth house opposition natal Moon in the second house would be shown thus. . .P.☉ ^{8}☍☽ ^{2}

In future chart interpretation, transits and progressions play quite different roles and supply different data.

I am seeking to explain these essential differences at some length early in this book because few texts seem to make them clear and easily comprehensible for beginners. Added to this, their calculation methods are different which can cause further confusion if they become mixed up in your thinking.

Broadly speaking, and as their definitions and names suggest, *Transits* show *external* situations—possible events, intervention of other people or outside influences on your life pattern. Circumstances that are of their own nature *transient*. *Progressions* reveal *internal* changes—altered mental, emotional, physical states within the self. Modifications which implement *progress* into new phases of being and feeling. These tend to give off a kind of 'vibe'—attracting others if a progression is boosting pleasing behaviour: rejecting if glum, uncooperative or dull responses are being stimulated.

In this inner-outer manner, they interact on each other. Obviously, if a more optimistic mental outlook, coupled with more friendly behaviour has been induced by a beneficial progression, tough transits aren't going to look like the end of the world. And, of course, vice versa. Even the most glittering array of transits won't start you sparking on all cylinders, if a gloom-laden progression has switched off the engine.

For beginners in astrological studies, the effect and calculation of transits is easier to comprehend on the one hand. On the other, there is no controversy among the experts on the methods to be used as there are with progressions.

So we'll look at transits first, commencing with a general discussion and then observing a set of them in action which affect everyone's life at given ages. However, first let's take a moment to observe two very interesting situations. (You'll note them appearing yourself if or when you've worked through sufficient charts to provide you with a personal yardstick.)

In some years of everyone's life, there is plenty of activity in both major progressions and transits. At other times, there are no major progressions and relatively few transits. The occurrence of a period of numerous planetary progressions and transits always indicates an important time in your life. . .often a turning-point which begins a completely new phase, such as marriage, for example. In years where there are few, or no planetary progressions and little transit activity, the inference is that in such years your life style will retain the existing status quo and no dramatic changes are likely.

Remember, of course, everybody has good and bad times in their lives so everybody has harmonious and inharmonious aspects through the years. The good times can be made better if you plan for them and use their potential to the utmost. The bad periods can be made easier by advance preparation, self-control *and* the determination to overcome and learn from mistakes and obstacles.

Bear in mind always, that troubles and disappointments are not designed to cause pain or depression. Their purpose is to spur you on to achieve. To develop yourself mentally, physically and spiritually. A life with a few problem aspects is invariably a very dull and unproductive existence!

Remember, too, the old proverb. . .'The stars impel. They do not compel'. This means the planetary aspects and positions steer you towards events and decisions. What *you* make of them ultimately, depends on your own free will. As you will note, you sometimes have harmonious and inharmonious aspects occurring almost simultaneously or close to the same period in your life. This often happens because life's important decisions always contain pro's and con's, events in favour, events against. The planetary movements reflect this.

What is more, I have regularly noted in my now very long experience with astro-analytical counselling, that current and future transits/progressions always reflect the *precise nature* of the problem/decision concerning yourself or a client. Exactly that. If the major question concentrates on marital difficulties, for example, the completed chart will show planetary link-ups through houses and aspects which not only stress marital affairs but have also forced them to the centre of the subject's attention. *Provided only*—and this is a most important proviso—that marital matters *are* the critical issue in the subject's life at *that* time.

What you fondly believe is your burning desire at any particular period in your life may in fact turn out to be no more than a side issue—a type of mental subterfuge, thrown up by the subconscious mind to divert your energies in the wrong direction. The sort of situation we examined in Chapter 1 with the man who was stubbornly setting his course for a petulant middle age because he insisted on pursuing marriage when he should have been advancing his professional career.

Tackling Transits

The use of planetary transits in Future Life Trend Forecasting has two purposes as we'll soon see. Thus it's useful to divide them into two groups—the fast-movers and the slow-movers. Sun, Moon, Mercury, Venus and Mars (the five personal planets) are classed as fast-moving. The remaining five, Jupiter, Saturn, Uranus, Neptune and Pluto are classed as slow-moving. The table below explains why and is set out in order of the planets' speeds. We say 'approximately' in the table heading because all the planets *except* the Sun and Moon (neither of which are planets in the astronomical sense) go *retrograde* from time to time. This means they backtrack, retracing their 'steps' over past positions before going *direct* again. A retrograding planet is shown in the ephemeris with the capital letter 'R'. When it resumes direct motion, the capital letter 'D' is shown. Due to the retrograde factor, all the planets except the Sun and Moon can spend much longer periods in some signs and houses than they do in others.

Approximate Times Taken by Planets to Transit all Twelve Zodiac Signs

FAST-MOVERS	
Moon	About 28 days
Mercury	Slightly less than 1 year
Sun	About 1 year
Venus	Slightly more than 1 year
Mars	Slightly less than 2 years
SLOW-MOVERS	
Jupiter	About 12 years
Saturn	About 29½ years
Uranus	About 84 years
Neptune	About 165 years
Pluto	About 248 years

NB

When analysing the specific effect of any transit, the planet's *sign, house position* and *aspects* must be calculated and considered.

As can be noted from the table at one glance, the transits of the fast-movers through any sign, house or in any aspect must be comparatively brief. Hence these are most useful for outlining events and circumstances on a particular day, week or month.

The slow-movers spend much longer in transiting any sign and house so their aspects too must be of much longer duration. Hence these are most useful for outlining the prevailing atmosphere, the chain of events affecting moves or decisions over several years.

Sun and Pluto Comparisons

For example, the Sun's aspect to another planet during a transit can move out of orb—i.e. out of range—in a day. Whereas Pluto, the slowest of all the known planets, can maintain an in-orb aspect intermittently for a couple of years. Consequently, Pluto transiting an aspect will have far more long-term effects on the overall life direction than a Sun transit aspect.

The movement of the heavy planets as they transit the houses (life sectors) of the chart cover large slices of time too. Pluto can spend as long as twenty years in a single house while the Sun can move in and out in less than a month. Thus Pluto will continue to instigate very far-reaching changes in the affairs of the house he is transiting over very long periods. Gradual but nonetheless inexorable and extreme changes.

Conversely, the Sun's impact on a house is comparatively brief and sharp. Added to that, the Sun transits each house once every year, whereas once Pluto has departed from any house he cannot ever return to it in the human lifetime. Therefore each sector of the life represented by each house will be influenced by a Sun transit every twelve months. Pluto transits influence the affairs of any house only once in every life and only a few houses at that. Because of his slowness, he can only move through less than half the twelve houses of the chart in any life.

To illustrate: Let's say you were born in 1923 with Pluto in Cancer in your seventh house. By the time you were age 67 in 1990 with Pluto then transiting the sign of Scorpio, the planet would only then have reached your twelfth house.

Later in this book we'll define and list individual interpretations for the transits and progressions of all the planets. But now, we'll round off this chapter with a general exercise in transit interpretation which, even those who are still feeling their way through astrological theory, will be able to join in.

Learn to Work with Your Planetary Switch-Points.

If you're feeling it's high time you took stock of your life. . .or turned it upside down and inside out. . .or looked high and low for its spiritual purpose. . .or just decided to accept the plain truth about it, you're simply responding to one of the major planetary 'switch-points' which change everyone's sense of direction at specific ages.

I've termed these highly significant planetary contacts 'switch-points' because their effect is much easier to understand if you think of your life as a long and winding railway track. You, yourself, are the driver of the train, which seems to be clattering uneventfully along when . . .clank! Something or someone seems to have suddenly switched the points on the railway track and equally suddenly you're careering off in a completely different direction! Who's the culprit? One of the heavy planets.

Now, let's take a close look at these planetary 'switch-points' so we can discover how to handle their consequences if some of them have already happened in your life. *And* prepare to work with them if they're still in the future. Naturally, you'll find their effects easier to specify if you have your own natal chart in front of you. Why? Because then you'll be able to see which houses (life sectors) are going to bear the brunt of a sudden switch to a new direction. Nevertheless, even without your own chart, you can check on the impact on your life of these planetary 'switch-points' by noting the approximate ages they occur for every human being.

There are, of course, many other important planetary link-ups in addition to those we'll discuss but it would take a small book rather than a short chapter to deal with them all so we'll stick to those which make the heaviest impact.

1. Saturnian 'Switch-Points'

Timing Age-Wise:

- Around 29 years (first)
- Around 58 – 60 years (second)

This pair of Saturnian aspects are generally known as 'the Saturn Return' or 'Saturn Conjunct Himself' in astrological terminology. They mean each time the planet has made a complete circuit of the natal chart as it takes him approximately 29½ years to complete the trip. (He is better known as the 'Great Taskmaster'.) Both times it happens it represents the end of a long cycle of demanding life experiences and the commencement of a completely new one.

Obviously, the first time Saturn throws the switches at around age 29 is the more significant because at that age you are at the peak of young adulthood with all the options of life direction laid out before you. This aspect is why nearly all of us at 29 feel itchy-footed, uncertain, freed from the restrictions of childhood finally but not sure which of the competing paths of choice we should take. And rightly so! Because Saturn drives a hard bargain and whatever you decide around age 29 will have to be lived through. . .for good or ill. . .till you begin to approach 60 years.

That 30 – year 'price tag' can't be dodged or ignored. So how does one make the right choice in Saturn's terms?

Basically, the right way to handle Saturn is to take the tougher choice. That is, to root up and throw out of your life all that is pointless and time-wasting, in favour of that which is worthwhile and developmental to your own personality. Saturn never favours those who look for the easy way out or the line of least resistance.

When you have an accurately-calculated chart in your hands, you can check (as noted earlier) where and what areas of your life will feel the Saturn choices most sharply. But the rules are the same!

When you come up to the second Saturn 'switch-point' as you approach 60, your choices are naturally more limited but you do have the benefit of a whole lot of living to help you decide where the next new path is going to lead you. (*And* in Saturn's terms the path is *not* into boring retirement!) Of course, if you make it to the ripe old age of nigh on 90, you'll have a third Saturn Return to handle!

Lastly, it is well worth noting that Saturn always forces us to take a mature view of life and its greatest decisions. Which is precisely why everyone under the age of 30 seems less 'old-headed', less set in their ways, more inclined to take things lightly. After 30, Saturn makes sure the time for 'playing it for laughs' is definitely over.

To help you get a firmer grip on what Saturn's about, here's a checklist of what famous English astrologer Margaret Hone called 'Saturnian Words'. They indicate how the planet's energy manifests positively or negatively in human personality. Favourable Manifestation in Personality equals: Aspiring, Cautious, Patient, Practical, Serious. Unfavourable Manifestation in Personality equals: Depressive, Dogmatic, Dull, Limited, Fearful.

Apply the unfavourable set of reactions, and you'll find you've tied yourself to a tiresome treadmill.

Apply the favourable set of reactions, and you'll find you're building the foundations of a secure but satisfying life style.

2. Uranian 'Switch-Points'

Timing Age-Wise:

- Around 28 years and 56 years
- Around 40 years.

At around 28 and again at around 56, Uranus makes favourable aspects to himself. . .technically termed trines. In both age groupings, these 'switch-points' work as eliminators, blasting people, things and situations out of your life because they have no further role or purpose in it. Both, too, you'll observe precede slightly the important Saturn Return points discussed above.

But Uranus is also known as the 'Great Disruptor', so the effects of these aspects may not feel all that comfortable at the time. Yet looked back upon, you'll observe they did progress you into a far more independent, more self-expressive life style.

The 28-year-old 'switch-point' is rather like blowing a whistle for freedom. . .from the past, from parental domination through adolescence and early adulthood.

The 56-year-old 'switch-point' forces you to ask what you expected of life, how much you learned and what the whole damned business has added up to. If the adding up is not up to much, this is the time when you shoot off in an often quite contrary direction.

However, neither of the foregoing has anything like the punch of the Uranian aspect which always pops up around the age of 40. This is often a genuine 'whammer' and is responsible for the old cry. . .'Life begins at 40!' Uranus slams home the fact that middle age is suddenly on your doorstep, that your life may be more than half over, and if you don't get up and go pretty smartly, you'll have had it. (Or to put it in the words of an American folk song, you'll find 'Your get-up-and-go has got up and went!')

Hence this is the time when cracks in shaky marriages/relationships suddenly look like yawning chasms. . .when you tell the boss what he can do with his crumby job. . .when your friends seem to have taken courses in 'How To Be Utterly Boring'.

It's a time, too, then when you have to keep a foot on the brake or Uranus will whiz you right off your railroad track and right down the embankment. Again, if you have your own chart you can check the area of your life which will feel the Uranian blast more forcefully.

To help you gain a clearer view of what Uranus is about, here's your checklist of 'Uranian Words'. Favourable Manifestation in Personality equals: Inventive, Original, Progressive, Magnetic, Reformative. Unfavourable Manifestation in Personality equals: Eccentric, Perverse, Rebellious, Wilful, Detached.

Apply the unfavourable set of reactions, and you'll find you've hurled yourself over a precipice.

Apply the favourable set of reactions, and you'll find you're bounding along at a cracking pace into a brave, new world.

3. Neptunian 'Switch-Points'

Timing Age-Wise:

- Around 42 years
- Around 55 years

At about age 42, Neptune gets into line behind Uranus and throws his weight as well into creating what is psychologically termed 'the Middle Life Crisis'. For, hard on the age 40 aspect discussed in (2), Neptune pulls up his age 42 aspect and sends us off in pursuit of impossible dreams and castles in the clouds. No wonder Neptune is often called the 'Great Illusionist!'

Looking at it from the standpoint of our train-driving analogy, this is where you suddenly find the track ahead is shrouded with fog and you can't see anything through it. The only answer to that is to reduce speed to slow and concentrate on keeping your wheels from slipping off the rails. Emotional confusion, undermining influences, escape into over-indulgences of all kinds permeate your thinking and the fantasy world becomes more real than the one you have to live in day to day. Thus if all those big, bright, shining dreams of youth have failed to come true, this is the 'switch-point' which can lure you into stopping in your tracks and making a desperate attempt to turn back into the past.

The second Neptunian aspect at around age 55 luckily does do a lot to rescue us from the muddles of its predecessor. By then, you have come to terms with the inescapable fact that you're not quite as young as you used to be and hence a sense of harmony and spiritual awareness begins to surface. Hand in hand with these responses come increased sympathy and compassion for others that will help to pilot you through the latter years of middle age.

To allow you to understand what Neptune is about, here's your checklist of 'Neptunian Words'. Favourable Manifestation in Personality equals: Inspirational, Sensitive, Imaginative, Subtle. Unfavourable Manifestation in Personality equals: Subversive, Unstable, Wandering, Deceptive, Hypersensitive.

Apply the unfavourable set of reactions, and you'll find yourself drowning in the depths of Neptunian disorientation.

Apply the favourable set of reactions, and you'll begin to see the spiritual light at the end of the long, dark tunnel.

4. Plutonic 'Switch-Point'

Timing Age-Wise:

Later 40's age grouping usually.

(Check your ephemeris each time for this 'switch-point'. For, due to Pluto's erratic orbit, it can occur around age 40 or past age 50.) As you'll have observed by now the time span between 40 and 50 is a fairly tough experience. . .with three of the major planets getting into the act. For as we approach the age of 50, Pluto pulls his switch too. And, to use the analogy of driving a train again, you suddenly find the track is blocked by a pile of obstacles. The only way then to move on is to clear away the debris so you can proceed with safety.

Hence, the Plutonic 'switch-point' forces you to review your whole life to date, cast off everything from the past that is slowing you down and turn your face towards a new kind of future. It adds up to a kind of spring-cleaning of the psyche. . .all those cobwebby repressions, hang-ups and self-doubts that have been gathering dust since as far back as childhood. Not for nothing is Pluto called the 'Great Transformer'.

In some ways, this is the toughest of the major planetary 'switch-points' because we all like to cling to the comfort of the familiar past and nobody likes to admit a large portion of it may have been a set of ongoing mistakes. But, remember, Pluto is *not* a character who takes 'no' for an answer. If you don't make the required changes yourself, he'll pull the whole scene apart before your very eyes.

To show you what Pluto is about, here's your checklist of 'Plutonic Words'. Favourable Manifestation in Personality equals: Eliminative, Regenerative, Revealing, Renewing, Transforming. Unfavourable Manifestation in Personality equals: Eruptive, Violent, Destructive, Cataclysmic, Extreme.

Apply the unfavourable set of reactions and you'll find yourself caught in a maelstrom of disintegration.

Apply the favourable set of reactions, and you'll find yourself cast in the role of a Phoenix, rising from the ashes of the past.

So there's a long-term view of all the major stops, starts, backtracking and diversion on to new lines as we drive along the railway track of life. Note carefully the times and ages when these planetary 'switch-points' occur in your own life and those close to you. This listing of the vital changes according to age is even more important if your spouse or life partner is considerably older or younger than you are yourself. Obviously, if you're older you'll have already experienced them and can thus help with advice and understanding. If you're much younger than your partner, you'll be able to appreciate what's happening and learn from it when the same 'switch-point' arrives in your own life.

Finally, a brief example of the planets in action. This will also help you if you're a beginner in astrological studies to plot the 'switch-points' whether they are in the past or the future. You'll need the ephemeris (Planetary Tables) and for quick reference Raphaels' *Geocentric Longitudes*. This last is a very small blue book which covers the positions of the heavy planets (except Pluto) from 1900 to 2001.

Now for our how-to-plot illustration. We'll take a male born on 6

October 1927. The ephemeris shows that at his birth, Saturn was at 3.50 degrees Sagittarius: Uranus at 1.02 degrees retrograde Aries: Neptune at 28.18 degrees Leo: Pluto at 17.05 degrees Cancer.

Saturn (1)

Feb – Nov 1956: Approaching and reaching age 29. Saturn moving to and fro over the point of the Saturn Return. Wife became pregnant, setting up a pattern of long-term responsibilities.

Dec 1985 - Sept 1986: Approaching age 59. (Second Saturn Return). Now retired and grandfather of two children by eldest daughter. Changes plans to leave vicinity of family. Took on part-time work to combat sense of purposelessness.

Uranus (2)

Sept 1955 – July 1956: Approaching and passing age 28, Uranus moving to and fro over the point of Uranus' trine to himself. Fairly recent marriage survived possible disruptive termination by a rival.

Oct 1968 – Aug 1969: Approaching and passing age 41. Uranus moving to and fro over the point of Uranus' opposition to himself. Moved house and attempted to set up more prestigious life style to rescue shaky family relationships.

Dec 1981 – Sept 1982: Approaching age 55. Uranus moving to and fro over the point of his second trine with himself. Finally accepted that marriage had never worked and could not be retrieved. Began to plan changes in profession requiring frequent travel.

Neptune (3)

Dec 1968 – Dec 1969: Approaching and passing age 42. Neptune moving to and fro over the point of Neptune's square to himself. New home had not solved the problems so opted out by distancing self from family group while still remaining in the marriage.

Jan 1983 – Oct 1984: Approaching and reaching age 57. Neptune moving to and fro over the point of Neptune's trine to himself. Began to plan early retirement in another part of Australia, far away from the family scene.

Pluto (4)

Nov 1978 – Sept 1979: Approaching and passing age 51. Pluto moving to and fro over the point of Pluto's square to himself. Separation from wife became permanent despite efforts to force resumption of cohabitation.

From the foregoing example you can judge how the planetary 'switch-points' affected the life and subject's reaction to them. Now set down your own 'switch-point' dates, understand their purpose and make your trip along your particular railway track a lot less bumpy!

How to Avoid Being 'Star-Struck'

One proverb I'm forever quoting to new students in astrological science is that well-known oldie: 'A little knowledge is a dangerous thing!' *And* it couldn't apply more to the beginner astrologer when interpreting future planetary transits and progressions. . .particularly if such knowledge has been picked up at random from textbooks and 'pop' forecasts.

'What on earth shall I do?' they'll cry, wringing their hands. 'I've got Neptune squaring Mercury in my chart all this year. I won't be able to think straight! Everything will go wrong, won't it?' Then they stand and virtually quake before you as if expecting some untold terrors to rain down upon them from the skies without pause. In my view, this reaction to any type of future trend is sadly mistaken. Even the more challenging aspects can bring beneficial results. . .if handled with common sense, stamina and a dash of positive thinking.

This is the same view taken by two of the greats in astrological analysis. . .Professor Carl Gustav Jung (also renowned as the 'father' of modern techniques in psychoanalysis) and Stephen Arroyo, (also a top psychologist and lecturer at US universities). Both agree anyone can avert drastic event patterns *if* a positive and *never* a negative approach is adopted.

Neither authority maintains tough transits or progressions should be reeled off like some kind of black litany of impending doom. The disaster bit seems to arise largely from earlier authors, writing in the first decades of the twentieth century, who tended to predict instant catastrophe from aspects as mild as Jupiter square Venus by transit!

I remember back in 1979 – 1980 when Saturn was conjunct several of my Virgo planets, a couple of astrologically-oriented friends phoning me and asking in sepulchral tones: 'Are you *all right*?'

'Of course,' said I jauntily. 'Why shouldn't I be?'

'But what about those Saturn conjunctions?'

'Yes. What about them?'

'Well, I've heard of people who've died, lost everything, fallen in a heap when Saturn makes conjunctions like that.'

'Have you really? Try reading Stephen Arroyo. He clearly states (*and* backs it up with loads of research) that any aspect is just what *you* make it.'

It is always vital when dealing with future periods to look at the entire chart. . .as a gestalt. Transits and progressions never operate as separate, isolated influences. As I often say to clients when consulting me: The map of the future the chart offers is a map of possibilities or probabilities, *never* certainties. It is like handling a canoe. You can row it on to the rocks or into the rapids. Or you can paddle it through calm water, grasping your opportunities as you go and taking steps to prevent a sudden wave from overturning your boat. The choice is always yours. Serious astrology has never claimed the chart will permit you to abdicate responsibility for your own life.

So next time you find yourself tangling with a team of dodgy-looking transits take the positive path *and* you'll never feel 'star struck' yourself.

Mapping Out the Future

Methods of future forecasting among professional astrologers vary greatly and—as I have said in my other books on astro-analysis—you should not blindly accept my approach or any other teacher's. Learn the techniques, then work with them, experimenting till you find the one that suits your own approach best.

Personally, I prefer as always to look for the clearest, broadest possible *outline* of future life trends. . .the peaks and troughs, the climaxes and the anticlimaxes—rather than daily, weekly or monthly patterns. Thus I invariably commence this part of the chart analysis by examining the transits of the heavy planets in the following order. . .(1) Saturn, (2) Pluto, (3) Neptune, (4) Uranus. . .working with both house positions and aspects. Between them, the four 'heavies' indicate significant events in the years under scrutiny, spotlighting the life sectors most affected. They also reveal the prevailing circumstances and the results of the intervention of other people in your affairs. Not briefly, but over lengthy periods.

We consider Saturn first when we look to the future as this planet sets up the overall pace of your life, according to the quadrant of your chart through which he is moving, as well as any aspects made. It takes Saturn between *5 and 10 years* to pass through each of the four quadrants. During that time, a strongly disciplining force is exerted on the affairs of the houses through which the planet is moving. Thus, to obtain the best results of any Saturn cycle, it's a matter of 'keeping your shoulder to the wheel and your nose to the grindstone', which is why he is often called 'the Great Taskmaster'.

However, while Saturn 'cracks the whip', so to speak, the other three heavy planets 'play the background music'.

The slowest and heaviest of these is Pluto. This planet rules the subconscious and thus brings about gradual, life-transforming and irreversible changes in your subconscious drives and most fundamental convictions. Pluto is hence often called the 'Great Transformer'.

The next of the heavy planets is Neptune. Also known as the 'Great Illusionist', this planet rules the spiritual and the non-material world and can therefore promote inspiration and idealism. . .but also circumstances in which you may become too easily impressed, gullible, deceiving yourself or being deceived by others.

The last of the heavy planets is Uranus. This planet is often called the 'Great Disruptor', because the predominant purpose is to break up the crystallized patterns of your life in the name of progress. Uranian changes are not extreme like Pluto's or subtle like Neptune's. They promote events which appear as suddenly as a flash of lightning. Thus it is important to 'keep your foot on the brake' when Uranus is affecting future patterns in your chart. Otherwise, the changes can come so fast that the sheer pace of them can be painful.

In calculating and interpreting planetary transits, a set of basic rules has been developed over the years and is now followed by all leading practitioners. These rules are not intended to force your thinking into a hide-bound groove. They are designed to keep you from straying off the track so it is best to observe them at all times.

Here they are.

Basic Rules for Planetary Transits

1. Orb of Effectiveness

When any transiting planet aspects the natal position of another planet the allowable orb is only *1 degree*, e.g. transiting Neptune at 0.38 Capricorn would be in an exact conjunction with a natal Moon at 0.38 Capricorn at the point of exactitude and also when one degree on either side of that point, i.e. while at 29 degrees of Sagittarius or at 1 degree of Capricorn. Once any transiting planet moves out of this orb, the effect of the transit dissipates.

2. Direct or Retrograde Motion

All planets except the Sun and Moon have periods of direct or retrograde motion, shown in the planetary ephemeris by the capital letters 'R' (Retrograde) and 'D' (Direct).

In practice, this means a transiting planet may pass out of the orb of aspect and then return to it later by the backtracking effect of retrograde motion.

This is particularly notable with the heavy planets, which may thus repeat an aspect as many as three times in a given period of months. In transit analysis, the dates the first aspect is reached usually indicate the commencement of an event pattern, which will be worked upon and developed by its repetition at later dates.

3. Hemisphere Emphasis (See diagram)

The horoscope 'wheel' is divided into four quarters or quadrants.

Northern Hemisphere	=	First, second, third, fourth, fifth and sixth houses
Southern Hemisphere	=	Seventh, eighth, ninth, tenth, eleventh and twelfth houses
Eastern Hemisphere	=	Tenth, eleventh, twelfth, first, second and third houses
Western Hemisphere	=	Fourth, fifth, sixth, seventh, eighth and ninth houses

Re-check basic house meanings from our diagrams and you'll see why:

- *Eastern Quadrants* planetary cycles create event patterns which display a 'go-it-alone' stamp—the need for the self to determine its own decisions as a single entity.
- *Western Quadrants* planetary cycles create event patterns which display a 'team-up-with-others' stamp—the need for the self to co-operate in order to achieve.

Hemisphere Emphasis in Transits

Southern Hemisphere Quadrants = Outer World Experiences
Northern Hemisphere Quadrants = Inner World Experiences
Eastern Hemisphere Quadrants = Individual Effort Experiences
Western Hemisphere Quadrants = Joint Effort Experiences.

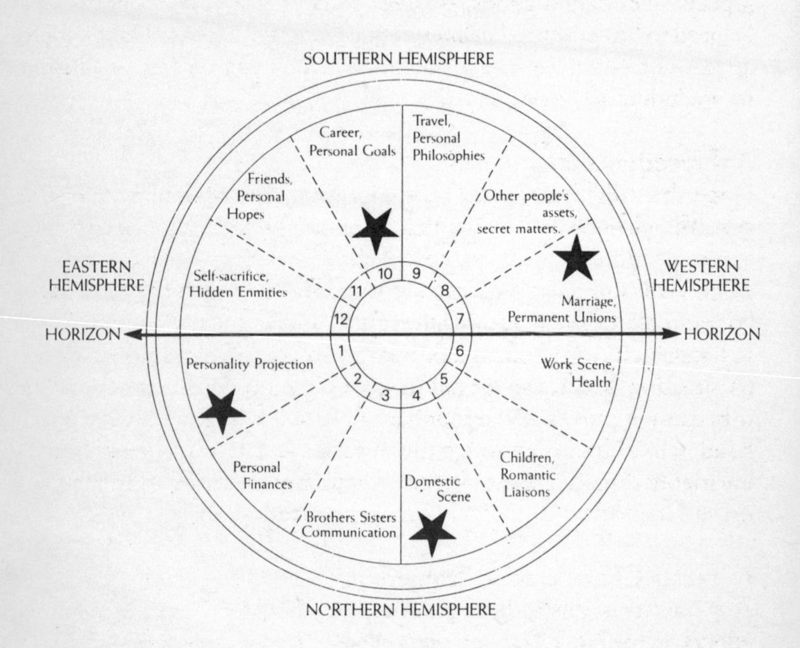

- *Northern Quadrants* planetary cycles create event patterns which display an 'away-from-the-world' stamp—the need for the self to withdraw into the most private sectors of life expression.
- *Southern Quadrants* planetary cycles create event patterns which display an 'up-and-at-it' stamp—the need for the self to step further out into the public arena.

Work with the cyclic divisions and you can watch the interplay upon each individual of private affairs (home, love, family, self-development) as against public affairs (work, occupation, personal career objectives) . . .decisions that involve co-operative effort as against those which require individual initiative.

4. Major versus Minor Aspects

Nowadays, most authoritative textbooks agree that only major aspects—i.e. conjunctions, sextiles, squares, trines and oppositions . . .need to be considered in interpreting planetary transits. These supply a clear-cut outline of event potentials which can be lost or blurred by including minor aspects.

5. Precedence of Houses

Since the Angular Houses—the first (self), the fourth (home), the seventh (relationships) and tenth (occupation)—add up to the corner-stones of human existence, any planets transiting these will make a more vivid impression on the life through the events they instigate. For example Uranus transiting the fourth usually rocks the family 'boat' to the point it's torn from its moorings and cast adrift in turbulent waters. (A situation which cannot fail to stir up the individual experiencing it because it strikes at the foundations of daily living.) On the other hand, while Uranus transiting the third (a much less significant house) invariably throws a bolt of lightning into mental interests, the impact on the individual is naturally far less shattering.

6. Natal Chart Transit Triggers

Any transiting planet, moving through any house will have perceptible effects on the life. However, such effect will generate more significant events if the transit triggers any major planetary configurations in the natal chart—such as T squares, stelliae, grand trines. When this occurs the entire pattern is activated, thus spreading its impact through several additional life areas. For example, assume a natal chart contains a grand trine in water, thereby linking three water sign planets in fourth, seventh and eleventh houses. A transiting planet aspecting any planet in the natal trine would produce an advantageous 'chain reaction', promising welcome changes in home scene, relationship matters and achievement of long-held wishes.

Transit Rules—At a Glance

- Allow 1 degree only for orb of effectiveness.
- Check for Direct and Retrograde Motion.
- Consider Hemisphere Emphasis.
- Use major aspects only.
- Allow greater effect for angular house transits.
- Look for triggering of natal chart configurations.
- Use slow-moving planets—Jupiter, Saturn, Uranus, Neptune, Pluto—to interpret long-term trends and changes. Use fast-moving planets—Sun, Moon, Mercury, Venus, Mars—for interpreting conditions around specific days, weeks.

Calculating Transits

I haven't mentioned this point earlier in this chapter because—in the true sense of the word—mathematical calculation is not required when dealing with transits.

Checking them is simply a matter of:

1. Listing the planetary positions from the ephemeris for the future period you're working on.
2. Setting down which of the houses in the natal chart each planet is transiting (or travelling through) during the specified period.
3. Noting if any transiting planet is within the one degree orb of any natal planet at any time in the specified period.

Two small and inexpensive paperback reference booklets are *indispensable* when examining long-term influences from the slow-moving planets. These are a kind of 'nutshell' version of the ephemeris and are titled *Pluto Tables* and *Geocentric Longitudes*. All astrology bookshops stock them. The current Pluto book lists the planet's positions on the first day of each month from the year 1851 through to 2000. The current *Geocentric Longitudes* book lists the positions on the first day of each month for Neptune, Uranus (shown by the older name of Herschel), Saturn, Jupiter and Mars from 1900 to 2001.

These little books give an at-a-glance view of the planets in each year of the future you wish to check. They're also handy if you want to look back at dates in the past when important decisions or changes occurred.

However, some new students tend to confuse transit listing with calculation of progressions. *And* since no textbooks I've read describe it in a step-by-step method, let's check a Pluto transit and aspects from a specimen natal chart. (See page 113.)

The specimen is of an actual person but, as always, the name has been changed to preserve confidentiality. We'll call her Clare Costumier.

Step 1

Turn to your Pluto Table and you'll see the planet moved by transit into the sign of Scorpio in December 1983 and continues to move through that sign until 1995, after retrograding briefly back into Libra in mid 1984.

Step 2

Look at the specimen chart (at end of Chapter 3) and you'll note it shows 3 degrees of Scorpio on the ninth house cusp and 6 degrees of Sagittarius on the tenth house cusp.

Turn back to the Pluto Table and observe Pluto reached 3 degrees 28 minutes of Scorpio in December 1984. Therefore on that date the planet began to move into the ninth house of our specimen chart.

The Pluto Table next shows that on 1 January 1998, Pluto will have reached 6 degrees 45 minutes of Sagittarius. On that date, the planet will begin to move into the tenth house of our specimen chart, thereby ending a 13-year (1985 – 1998) transit through the ninth.

Step 3

Compare the Pluto Table for the years 1984, 1985, 1986 and 1987 with the natal planetary positions in our specimen chart to check if any event-triggering major aspects occurred in these years.

Yes. Our chart shows Neptune posited in the ninth house at 5 degrees 16 minutes of Scorpio. Therefore a transiting Pluto/natal Neptune conjunction occurs between November – December 1985, then repeats itself between April – October 1986. (The repetition results from Pluto going retrograde as you can see in the table booklet.)

This is the strongest aspect in the years under consideration but our specimen chart also shows natal Pluto at 4 degrees of Virgo and natal Venus at 0.07 minutes of Virgo retrograde.

Another glance at the Pluto table thus shows transiting Pluto makes sextile aspects to Venus in July 1985—thus repeating the 1984 pattern. Plus another sextile aspect to natal Pluto from December 1984 – April 1985, repeating October – November of 1985 and again May – September 1986.

Here's how these Pluto patterns are recorded in your chart layout:

t♇ . . .ninth: 84 – 98:
t♇ * ♇ = Dec 84 – Apr 85: Oct – Nov 85: May – Sept 86
t♇ ☌ ♆ = Nov – Dec 85: Apr – Oct 86:
t♇ * ♀ = Jan – Nov 84: July 85

Step 4

What do we deduce from this Pluto transit and these transiting aspects for the subject of our specimen chart? Plenty of ninth house action for Clare Costumier. Final surfacing of a long-felt urge to travel, desire to expand experience through contact with foreigners, search for identity through breaking with the family ties of the past.

Did it happen like that? It surely did. Our specimen chart is that of a young Australian theatrical costume designer. Her previously vague intentions to go overseas slowly began to gel in December 1984 as Pluto entered her ninth house, and formed the sextile to the natal position. By February 1985 she stopped cogitating and started acting. By April 1985 she was on her way to Europe. Her natal ninth house planets had set the course for adventuring in foreign climes at the time of her birth. So when Pluto blew the whistle, it was 'all systems *go*!' She was off and running.

Of course, other transits and other natal indicators bear on the final outcome of her decision as we'll see in later chapters. Nevertheless, this is a good example of the Plutonic force at work on a life. There is always a kind of inexorability about the planet because decisions provoked by his transits stem from subconscious drives which are often slow in finding an outlet—our specimen chart subject was twenty-five years old at the time. Yet, when the outlet appears, the dormant drives erupt into action.

If you don't fully understand the foregoing transit instructions, go through them again and again till they're firmly set in your mind. All transits and transiting aspects are worked out in the same manner thus once you've got the hang of them you'll realize checking your transits is as easy as writing out a shopping list.

Putting the Future on Paper

Methods of recording planetary positions—prior to commencing interpretation of transits or progressions—vary markedly among practitioners. Some seem to do it all in their heads like mental arithmetic. Others make a few notes on the natal chart itself. Many say they never show the future calculations to clients. Personally, I prefer to set everything down on a prepared form which I always hand to clients as I believe they're entitled to see precisely what you have based your statements upon.

This practice demonstrates to everyone that no comment is conjured up out of the air—so to speak—but instead is based on mathematical calculation and scientific deduction. It is also has the added advantange of pointing out visibly the difference between fortune-telling and serious astrology.

Maybe, if you've already read my two companion books on astro-analysis—*How to Astro-Analyze Yourself and Others* and *Astro-Pick Your Perfect Partner*—you'll be thinking by now I have a mania for tables and data sheets.

I have. From observing students and even novice practitioners miss vital pointers, overstress certain patterns or completely forget highly significant planetary indicators, I long ago came to the conclusion such errors arose through failure to write out information in a clear and concise format.

The same applies to Future Life Trend Forecasting. That is why I designed (first for my own use and later for students) the all-in-one Natal Chart plus Transits/Progressions layout you see on the following two pages in blank. You'll note the future data is written on the right of the natal chart in each case. This practice ensures you never forget the dominant role of the natal patterns and makes it easy to link them up with transits and progressions. Further, if you need to refer back to your chart calculations even years later, you'll find them all clearly set out and as quick to read as when you first prepared them.

As a further aid to accurate record keeping, I have included a completed Transit Data Sheet for our example subject — Clare Costumier — showing the effect of Saturn transits on her actions and decisions.

NATAL CHART

Cardinal signs ....
Fixed signs ....
Mutable signs ....
Positive signs ....
Negative signs ....

Name: ....
....

Ascendant
10 9 8 7 6 5 4 3 2 1 12 11
Time:
Date:

FIRE signs ....
AIR signs ....
EARTH signs ....
WATER signs ....

B.T.Q.	PLANET	NATAL	ASPECTS
	♆ Neptune		
	♅ Uranus		
	♄ Saturn		
	♃ Jupiter		
	♂ Mars		
	☉ Sun		
	♀ Venus		
	☿ Mercury		
	☽ Moon		
	♇ Pluto		

PLANETARY PROGRESSIONS

19	19	19	
☉			
☽			
☿			
♀			
♂			

PLANETARY TRANSITS

Also included is a blank Transit Data Sheet for your own use. You will find similar blanks for the transits of Pluto, Neptune and Uranus in later chapters to help you record their effects for your own chart subjects.

Each Transit Blank Data Sheet contains:

- Reminder note on type of influence each planet exerts. (Printed.)
- Long-range effect on the house it is transiting. (To be written in by you.)
- Current effect of aspects formed during a transit. (To be written in by you.)
- Analyst's comment in brief so that statements made at time of interpretation remain on permanent record. (To be written in by you).

The last-named on the above list is of special value to both practitioners and students. Not only does it keep your original opinions fresh in your mind but helps combat the 'misquoting' problem.

Clients who are by nature somewhat depressive are often inclined to colour whatever comments you make with their own negativism. Thus they tend to exaggerate—twisting awkward future patterns from minor annoyances into cataclysmic disasters within their own minds. Some are even capable of turning your picture of their futures into a panorama of unrelieved gloom by ignoring the helpful indicators and concentrating on the tougher ones.

The opposite situation arises with the natural optimists. They tend to overdo the positive thinking routine until an advantageous future opportunity turns into a million-dollar deal. Some are even capable of insisting your picture of their future promised them a preview of paradise through remembering nothing *but* the helpful indicators and then blowing them up out of all proportion.

Neither result is good for the client *or* for your reputation. So your in-brief notes on each transit will ensure you can haul the depressives out of their abyss when necessary. *And* slip a bridle on the enthusiasms of the wilder-eyed optimists.

Lastly, remember future planetary aspects don't abruptly turn on and off like taps. There is always a tapering-off period as the transiting planet moves out of orb and—especially with the slow-moving planets—this can generate events beyond the stated dates. Sometimes beforehand too. As the old saying goes—'forthcoming events cast their shadows before them'. Thus life directional changes may begin even while a planet is approaching an important aspect.

Anyway, we've now wended our way through all the preliminaries in considering Future Life Trend Forecasting and our next step is to begin to put our technique into practice by working with Saturn in the next chapter. But before so doing, here are a couple of comforting thoughts which will come regularly to mind when you're fully familiar with transit and progression interpretation.

- These clear forewarnings of opportunities or set-backs ensure you shut the stable door *before* the horse is gone. . .instead of after!
- No matter how tooth-gnashing a transit may be, you can see it won't last forever. With its departure date down on paper before you, the time when happier days will be here again won't seem so far away.

Quick-Reference Check-Points for Chapter 2

Procrastinations and Transgressions

One of my Sagittarian clients (who always *tries* to look at life sunny side up) insists on calling the progressions and transits of the planets in his chart by the above-named titles for fun. He says it rather takes the sting out of their tails!

I found the idea amusing and also quite apt. For, if you 'procrastinate' too long with a favourable progression, you may well miss out on its benefical results. *And* if you do 'transgress' during an unfavourable transit, you're likely to find you've burnt your fingers rather more than somewhat!

Timing is precisely what the future trend patterns in a chart teach us. Flow with the planetary energies and you'll always make it. Pull against them and you're back to square one.

Neptune is, in my view, the sneakiest when transiting through a tough aspect because there's invariably a weird, 'submarine' quality as if all the events were taking place at full fathom five. For example, another client of mine had Neptune opposing her natal sun by transit all through one year. . .right at a time when the sale of a large property of which she was a co-owner with several others got under way. One prospective purchaser offered much more than a competing purchaser. Suddenly, the other co-owners all insisted on accepting the lower price. No reasons given. Letters went astray. Solicitors mysteriously lost vital documents. One even had a nervous breakdown. Negotiations became more bizarre by the moment. Emotional blackmail reared its ugly head. Neptune was giving out with the works!

My client was ready to throw in the towel. And probably would have, thereby losing a considerable sum, had I not stressed to her what the transit meant *and* that it would end. Instead, she kept calm, documented every fact, refused to be caught in the undercurrent and won out. Just as Neptune began to move away from the opposition! Which—as my Sagittarian client would put it—proves that if you don't procrastinate and never transgress, everything comes up roses in the end.

Religion and the Future

For thousands of years, astrology's role as a predictive medium has landed its practitioners in trouble with the 'powers that be'. Through earlier centuries, accusations of witchcraft, devilry, and dabbling in the black arts were hurled at it relentlessly, along with thundering denunciations from the pulpit. Today, you'd think such wild ideas would have deservedly died a natural death. But they have not. Even among well-educated laymen who certainly should know better. As witness the following note from my past files.

I had just begun taping the future section of a chart analysis when my client—a young technologist of 29—interrupted me with a gesture.

'Do you mind if I ask you a personal question?'

'No. Go ahead. What do you want to know?'

'Right then. Do you believe in God?'

I've been asked some very strange questions in my time, but this one threw me.

'Of course. Why do you ask?'

'Well, how can you do this sort of thing if you believe in God?

This time I nearly fell off my chair. I could not believe that intelligent people today could—even in their weirdest flights of fancy—imagine astro-analytical forecasting had something to do with black magic. But despite his tertiary education, this young man obviously suspected it did.

Tragic! Anyone who has made an in-depths study of astrological science cannot fail to see the hand of providence, God or whatever you wish to call the force which orders human life revealing itself in the horoscope chart. Offering a guiding light in times of inner darkness.

Still, the tale of the technologist was far from being an isolated incident and serves as a warning of the widespread ignorance and superstitions about astrology which continue to thrive in the public mind. Had astrologers restricted themselves to using the chart as the basis for guidance through personality analysis—its paramount purpose in my view—this sad state of affairs would never have occurred. (After all, no-one accuses psychiatrists or psychologists of devil worship!)

So, never forget that when you set out to forecast the future, you're moving into dangerous territory, where some people will be quick to scent a whiff of fire and brimstone in the air. To combat this, always maintain a professional atmosphere in your consulting room and in your own demeanour. . .if you intend to become a practitioner. Especially as you'll find there are always some 'astrologers' who actually seek to promote a sorcery-style image. Some go so far as using weird or outlandish pseudonyms instead of their own names, presumably to conceal their identity. Others demonstrate freakish behaviour such as the following which were related to me by stunned members of the public.

One was that of a middle-aged woman who apparently sees clients wearing a feather head-dress—like a witch-doctor!—and *also* uses a false, outlandish name! Another was that of an older man who does his consultations in the nude and asks clients to disrobe too. . .apparently 'to get the right vibes!' You can imagine the view of astrology clients would harbour after facing up to this pair.

First Not Last Resort

Every full-time practitioner is familiar with the distracted correspondent who begins something like this: 'I've tried everything. I must know what's going to happen. Astrology's my last hope!' Or the agitated voice on the phone which says something like this: 'I'm trying you as a last resort. I don't know what to do next!'

Whereas one cannot fail to feel sympathy for this sort of would-be client, they rarely want the type of help—through increased self-awareness and added self-control—the astrological chart can give them. They seem to think the astrologer has the keys to the golden heaven and can open all their doors for them. In a flash. Problems solved while you wait.

I always warn these types of enquirers—whatever their future-oriented questions—that, far from offering instant answers, serious astrological forecasting seeks to locate the origins of current troubles in the past. Thus they'll need to start looking at themselves through the magnifying glass of the chart and work on the personality traits that have created the present distress. That means, of course, making a genuine effort as well as changing their viewpoint. In my experience, little is gained by those who come to astrologers 'as their last hope'.

As mentioned earlier in this chapter, that amounts to shutting the stable door after the horse is gone. Much better results ensue if you look to the chart as your first resort rather than the last. Steering your way clear of whirlpools instead of sinking into them.

Testing your Timing Sense

Apropos of our earlier discussion on the sense of timing which is uniquely human, I have run across several intriguing cases where individuals actually 'knew' their birth time—*without* documentation or information from family members. One especially comes to mind.

Few countries note birth times on birth certificates. Australia has never done so. This client was a 36-year-old woman, the maternity hospital had lost her records, her parents contradicted each other as to her time of birth. Father said 8.00 p.m. Mother said 8.00 a.m.

'They're both wrong', said the lady. 'It was about 11.30 a.m.'

After I had obtained all the details from her to rectify and locate her birth time, checking both father and mother's suggestions, I found with a slight shock she was right. The only time that fitted her life history and personality type *was* the 11.30 a.m. time. Two months later she rang me back in great excitement. The hospital had finally found the lost records of her birth. . .at 11.30 a.m.! That case happened ten years ago and I've encountered several similar ones since.

Without making too much out of it, these cases do suggest that perhaps even prior to and during the birth process our 'timing sense' is already working. Think about it for yourself. If your birth time has been accurately recorded officially in hospital records, see if that time 'feels' right. It should. If you have no way of knowing your birth time—a common problem with adopted children or those born during wars—concentrate hard and see if a time suggests itself. This may be a very helpful clue to yourself or an astrologer while rectifying your chart.

Chapter Three

Planets That Point the Way Ahead

Saturn—The 'Great Taskmaster' in Transit

If you're used to thinking of planets in their usual order of significance—Sun, Moon, Mercury, Venus, Mars, Jupiter, Saturn, Uranus, Neptune and Pluto—you're probably wondering why I've placed Saturn first here. Once you thoroughly understand how this planet works, the reason becomes obvious.

In future forecasting, Saturn must take pride of place because that is his right. It belongs to him since through his transits, he sets the overriding pace and style of each life during whatever years are under investigation. That's how he earned the title of the 'Great Taskmaster'.

Incidentally, new readers may also be wondering why Saturn and the other planets are personified in most texts with the pronouns 'he/she' instead of referring to each one as 'it'. This is done partially because they were all named after gods and goddesses in the ancient world. Partially too because their energies manifest in human life patterns in a masculine or feminine manner—directly and forcefully or subtly and emotionally.

Saturn's energy is incontrovertibly masculine. There's nothing soft or yielding about him. So let's take the personification one step further and for now visualize him as a circus ringmaster. This mental picture will help place his influence during his transits in a more vivid perspective and makes it easier to think of him directing us all around the ring of life. Standing sombrely but formally garbed in black and white evening dress among all the circus noise and glitter. Loudly cracking his whip to order the next act out onto the sawdust. Cracking it louder still if anyone or anything circling around him moves out of line.

Without the central figure of the ringmaster to command system and sequence, the circus programme would disintegrate into chaos and confusion. So also with the programme of each life. The whip is a warning that nothing but the best of efforts will pass muster. No slacking off or slouching through your performance will get by. The testing and trying goes on and on, sometimes whipping an ambition we yearn to achieve right out of our hands. Sometimes cracking down so hard we doubt our ability ever to measure up.

But to discourage is neither Saturn's intention nor his purpose. It is to discipline us and make us accept the truth of the old maxim—'If you don't succeed at first—try, try again!' Perhaps for the same goal in a different way. Perhaps for a different goal in the same way.

To apply our circus analogy again. If you see yourself swinging through life on the flying trapeze but your true talents are those of a lion-tamer—grappling with problems that snarl and claw at your slightest flinch—Saturn won't let you take to the air. You might manage a few steps up the ropes but before you know it you'll be down amongst the big cats again. Not because Saturn seeks to wreck your hopes. Only because he insists you do what you're cut out to do.

Clues as to Saturn's view of your life purpose must be first looked for in the natal chart before considering his transits. I have already discussed these Saturnian patterns in my two companion books but if you wish to look at him in still greater detail, read Dr Liz Greene's excellent work—*Saturn: A New Look At An Old Devil*. The entire 196-page book is devoted to explaining Saturn's significance in the natal chart from the standpoint of a psychologist. Clear evidence of the important Dr Greene ascribes to this planet.

Later, Dr Greene published a further book—'*The Dreamer of the Vine*' which recounts the life of Nostradamus in the form of a novel and which describes numerous instances of Saturn in action. Throughout this book, Nostradamus speaks of Saturn as 'The Lord of the World', adding further that 'he requires payment for each human being's journey through life in his own coin: patience, forbearance, tact, reflection, steadfastness'. A somewhat grim set of attributes but one must agree with the maestro. If you have powerful Saturnian influences at work in your natal chart, you can forget about looking at life as a laugh-a-minute romp or relationships as beds of roses. The more so when transits activate these natal patterns. Nostradamus copped a lot from Saturn during his own lifetime and I sympathized with his views. Having started off with some fairly tough Saturnian aspects myself. . .*and* being very impatient, unforbearing, often tactless, non-reflective and hardly steadfast at the outset. . .I have watched with a kind of awful fascination over the years as Saturn forced his precepts upon me. The hard way, *of course*! But that's the way we all have to learn from Saturn. He gives nothing to those who play about. He gives only to those who work—shoulder to the wheel and nose to the grindstone.

So having braced our shoulders and noses for Saturn-style effort, let's follow him through first his cycles and then his transits of the twelve houses—reminding ourselves at all times, he's working to help us help ourselves.

The Saturn Cycles—Circles in Time

The Zodiac itself is a circle. So is the individual horoscope chart. And circles have neither beginnings nor ends. Think of what happens when you decide to keep walking in a wide circle. You come back eventually to where you started. You begin walking round it again and then again. Each time the terrain becomes more familiar, you notice more landmarks, more detail as to where the path gets slippery or stony or where it's smooth and easy to traverse. That's the scenario for the Saturn cycles. The planets leads your life round the circle of the horoscope chart, obliging you to look and learn, to change and develop.

The chart circle is divided into hemispheres (as shown diagrammatically in Chapter 2). Now we subdivide it again into quarter-spheres or quadrants to find the Saturn cycles. Astrological authors have given them various names which all add up to the same idea. I term them as set out hereunder and have tagged them as in our diagram on the adjoining page. Their names make Saturn Cycle interpretations fairly clear but in any case we'll define them in greater detail later in this chapter.

1. The Withdrawal Cycle : (Saturn moving from first to fourth house cusp)
2. The Development Cycle : (Saturn moving from fourth to seventh house cusp)
3. The Achievement Cycle : (Saturn moving from seventh to tenth house cusp)
4. The Stabilization Cycle : (Saturn moving from tenth to first house cusp)

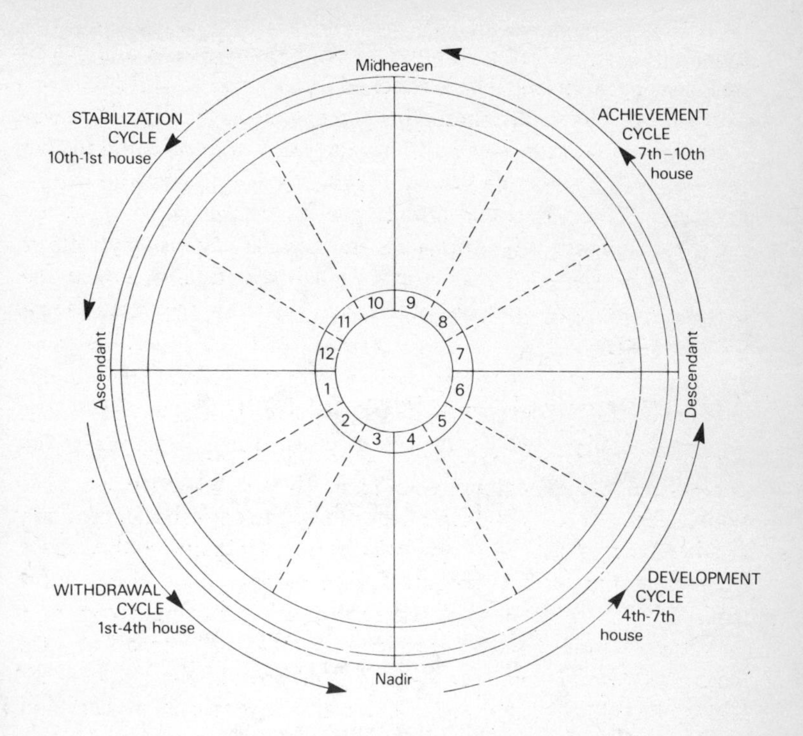

Saturn Cycles Through the Quadrants

Glance again at our diagram. You'll see that Cycles (2) and (3) are *Ascending Cycles*. . .(1) and (4) are *Descending Cycles.*

There's meaning to be gleaned from these pointers, too. As Saturn ascends or rises from the bottom of the chart (called the Nadir) towards the peak (called the midheaven), passing over the Descendant on his way, he's on the up-grade, thus manifesting as a boosting energy. As Saturn descends or sinks from the midheaven peak back down towards the Nadir low-point, passing over the Ascendant on his way, he's on the down-grade, thus manifesting as a restraining energy. Hence it follows that you will find it easier to push your plans through to a positive outcome while Saturn is on the up-grade—more difficult (but not impossible) when he's sinking down.

Since Saturn is the fastest of the four heaviest planets, he is the only one of them capable of making full circuits of the horoscope chart in the average human lifetime. This fact alone makes his cyclic position at any stage in any life of primary importance.

It takes him 29½ years to travel right round the chart which gives a rough average of 2½ years' sojourn in each of the twelve houses plus another rough average of 7½ years in each cycle or quadrant. But never use these rough averages in practice. Interception of signs in the individual chart and other factors may lengthen his stay in a particular cycle to as much as ten years or shorten it to as little as five. You must always check the commencement dates of each Saturn cycle by noting the degrees on the cusps of the angular houses—first, fourth, seventh and tenth —in each chart you do. Keep in mind too that between birth and age approximately 60, Saturn will have completed two full circuuits of each chart. If you make it to 90, he will of course have done the rounds three times. Thus except in cases where people die during the younger age groupings, you'll be looking at Saturn passing through the same cycle twice or even thrice.

Here's how the Saturn Cycle pattern manifests in the life of the male, born 6 October 1927, we discussed in our 'Planetary Switch-Points' section in Chapter 2. If you don't follow at once how the dates were chosen, get out your *Geocentric Longitudes* booklet to find Saturn's sign and degree in the years when our subject reached the listed ages. At the same time, looking at your own chart, write down in list format (as shown) the precise dates and the age you had reached when Saturn commenced each one of his four cycles. Then work out a similar list for future dates and ages.

If you are in the younger age groupings, this simple form of pre-planning will enable you to prepare for the onset of forthcoming Saturn cycles. If you are in the older age groupings such as our test subject, you'll be able to observe the outline of your past life with greater clarity and put past lessons to better effect in the future.

SATURN CYCLES—DATE PATTERN EXAMPLE—SUBJECT BORN 6 - 10 - 27

Years checked: 1927 (Birth Year) through to 2001.

Birth Chart
Indicators: first house cusp .... 29 degrees Scorpio
fourth house cusp .... 9 degrees Aquarius
seventh house cusp .... 28 degrees Taurus
tenth house cusp .... 9 degrees Leo

Birth Position of Saturn. . .3 degrees 50 minutes Sagittarius in first house

Withdrawal Cycle Occurs: Thrice in lifetime

1. Birth to age 6 (1927 – 1933)
2. Again 29 to age 35 (1956 – 1962)
3. Again 58 to age 65 (1985 – 1992)

Life Effect:

1. Product of 'shotgun' marriage in small country town—unhappy parents—emotionally and financially deprived childhood. (First time in cycle.)
2. Unstable marriage—responsibilities for two children—slow progress at work. (Second time in cycle.)
3. Broken marriage—no affection from adult children—some ill health—early retirement. (Third time in cycle.)

Development Cycle Occurs: Thrice in lifetime

1. 6 to age 14 (1933 – 1941/1942)
2. Again 35 to age 44 (1962 – 1971)
3. Again 65 to age 74 (1992 – 2000/2001)

Life Effect:

1. Sent to live away from home with relatives—better atmostphere domestically—improved school results and sporting successes—shown to have high IQ. (First time in cycle.)

2. Rise from employee to executive status—impressive work record—name becoming well recognized in profession. (Second time in cycle).
3. Not completed at time of writing—further isolation and alienation from adult children and grandchildren likely—new interests and easier adjustment possible. (Third time in cycle.)

Achievement Cycle Occurs: Twice in lifetime

1. Age 14 to 20 (1941/1942 – 1946/1947)
2. Again 44 to age 50 (1971—1976/1977)

Life Effect:

1. Worked hard at school and tertiary education to achieve professional status—left family home permanently—obtained sought after job in foreign country. (First time in cycle.)
2. Rose to top executive status with international reputation—travelled widely through profession. (Second time in cycle.)

Stablization Cycle Occurs: Twice in Lifetime

1. Age 20 to age 29 (1946/1947 – 1956)
2. Again 50 to age 58 (1976/1977 – 1985)

Life Effect:

1. Obtained important professional job in Europe—married professional woman and returned to Australia—became a father. (First time in cycle.)
2. Respected figure in specialist field—marital situation deteriorated to point where wife and children left family home—accepted this easily. (Second time in cycle.)

Now, test the long-term effect of the Saturn Cycles on your own life story in the same concise style. As you can see it's quick to prepare, requires no mathematical calculations but is extremely illuminating. Note what events occurred in your own life against the dates and ages of the cycles (as shown in the example). If you can't remember much, spend some time in quiet introspection. You may well be unconsciously repressing memories that are perhaps painful but nevertheless highly indicative of present and future behaviour. (It requires only a few moments' thought to realize our test subject's unhappy and deprived childhood constituted behavioural patterns which led finally to career successes at the expense of marital and family happiness.)

Hence, this valuable exercise will not only help you recall your past and long ago changes in life direction but also reveals how even childhood conditions affect your actions and attitudes. . .both today *and* tomorrow. For each time Saturn repeats a previous cycle, the results emanating from it will be better or worse than before—depending on how well you reacted the first time you experienced it. There are always echoes of past events/situations when Saturn re-enters a cycle. Thus, once again, reviewing earlier advances or mistakes allows us to handle the future more effectively. I know I learned a lot more about my own early days—what made me into the person I am, where I went wrong and what I did right—simply by working through old Saturn Cycles. Their ability to indicate the ebbs and flows, the high points and the low in every life endows them, in my experiences, with overriding significance. . .especially in planning your future. Therefore, we'll define and go over them at rather greater length than some of the other future planetary movements.

1. The Withdrawal Cycle (Definition)

This cycle covers the transits by Saturn of houses one, two and three and concludes at fourth house cusp. Some individuals experience this cycle in childhood, thereby inferring a tougher start to life. (Difficult birth. Unwanted child. Unhappily married parents, etc.) Others have to face up to it much later.

The dates and ages at which the Withdrawal Cycle begins and ends depend on where Saturn was positioned in the natal chart at the time of birth. (This, of course, applies to the other three cycles as well.) To use an old-fashioned phrase, the Withdrawal Cycle usually signifies your enrolment in the University of Hard Knocks. Taken in the negative sense, it is a cycle of set-backs, disappointments, trials. Taken in the positive sense, it is a cycle of slow reassessment of the self, of rethinking objectives and accepting new responsibilities. If you buck against the disciplinary pressure of Saturn, you'll feel it as the former. If you willingly pick up the heavier bags you're being told to carry, you'll feel it as the latter.

Although it is far from being the most comfortable part of the chart for Saturn to transit, you'll realize at the end of it, your agonizings were not in vain or piled on to you capriciously. You'll have learned life's not quite the bowl of cherries you may have thought it was and along with this discovery should come the determination to march forward with a more purposeful tread and on a surer footing.

To gain an in-depth understanding of how Withdrawal Cycles affected your life story and the stories of those you care about, delve into your memory and set out the events in flashback style like the glimpses of my Saturnian experiences from age 6 to mature adult. The first flashbacks give an impression of the kinds of events which can be expected as Saturn moves between the first and fourth houses of every chart. Of course, some individuals get off more lightly than I did—others find the cycle much tougher.

Illustration from Life: First Saturn Withdrawal Cycle

Schedule of Events

Age 6: Saturn entering and transiting my first house. Started at small preparatory school. This was not a tear-jerking switch. I liked learning and being an only child was looking for playmates. Up till that time, my best friends had been cats. (They still are!)

Tonsils soon began giving trouble so was forced to have them removed. Haemorrhaged badly. Neck gland abscess followed. Severe cold sores on lips also caused heavy bleeding. I found these two trips to hospital very frightening as I was terrified of anaesthetics and doctors.

Age 10: Saturn transiting my third house (communication/educational skills)—sent to new, larger school. This was something of an upheaval.

Four months later my father dropped dead in the seat of a car—young and without warning. This began a black period in the home and out of it, with mother collapsing into fits of hysterical weeping whenever father's name was mentioned or I disobeyed her.

Teachers and other pupils treated me differently. Being a Federal politician who had represented Australia in overseas delegations, my father was public figure so everyone knew about him and his death. As a sort of half-orphan, I felt something of an oddity and kept to myself as much as possible. (With many planets in Virgo, that wasn't difficult!) I wanted to do what I could to help mother but wasn't sure how. My school results declined noticeably.

Age 12: Saturn approaching my fourth house. Mother abruptly changed my school again. I felt slightly disoriented at first but at least nobody kept asking about my dead father anymore. Slowly I began to realize my troubles were over.

Later, as Saturn started to ascend through his Development Cycle, I felt better able to handle the idea of being a one-parent child. My exam results improved dramatically. At the same time, I came to what was then a rather scary conclusion. Mother clearly expected me to pick up the torch my father had dropped. She expected me too to become a 'VIP'. (With many planets in Virgo, that *would* be difficult!)

Now, those events seem as long ago as the Fall of the Roman Empire, yet working out your own flashbacks serves to depict more vividly the repercussions of each cycle. Even looking back through these ancient dates revived memories I'd half forgotten yet which had played their part in setting my feet on the path I chose.

I only wish I had understood the Saturn impact when he re-entered the Withdrawal Cycle as I approached age 35 for the story began to unwind like a remake of an old film. Different people were playing the leading roles, the situations were updated but the 'plot' was the same heavy mixture as before.

However, this time around rescue was at hand. Before this second time in the cycle ended, Saturn (with a little help from Uranus) had dropped astrology—like a bolt from the blue—into my life!

2. The Development Cycle

Saturn crossing fourth house cusp and moving through fifth and sixth houses up to seventh house cusp.

As its name implies, this commences a period when the difficulties and set-backs which plagued you during the preceding cycle slowly recede into the past to make way for new projects, new ideas, new outlets for energy. Gates that seemed permanently stuck gradually swing open. Red lights change to green and successes (at long last!) look like happening to you instead of everybody else *but* you.

This is very much a time to drive steadily and undeviatingly ahead to pursue your goals, to apply your hard-earned knowledge and if necessary, gather added skills. Just how far and how swiftly you progress depends on how well you've digested the hard lessons Saturn taught you in his previous cycle.

Overall, this period represents a new boost to your life direction as Saturn's pressure changes from a restricting force to an expanding one. Don't waste it. By the time this cycle repeats itself you'll be nearly 30 years older! Again, if you've already experienced Saturn's Development Cycle once, list those past dates and events in your life in consecutive order to gauge how you used it and what resulted from it.

This short exercise will ensure you don't miss opportunities the second time around and provides added insight into the life history of yourself or those you care about.

Illustration from Life: First Saturn Development Cycle

Schedule of Events

Here are a few further in-brief glimpses of how Saturn's first Development Cycle affected me.

Age 12 to 20: Saturn moving from fourth house to seventh house cusp. In these years, I completed secondary school without too many hassles and did pretty well in the only school subject which really turned me on—English.

Age 15 to 17: With Saturn passing on into my fifth house (love affairs among other things), I found myself entangled in a rather heavy relationship with a Geminian—8 years older than myself. That hung on intermittently until Saturn was well into my sixth house when I suddenly felt trapped and broke it off.

Life swung along relatively easily from then on. I obtained my BA degree with a major in psychology and without having to work like a fiend to pass the exams.

Mother had never remarried but by now had accepted widowhood and we'd arrived at as good an understanding of each other as is possible with one strongly Aquarian parent and one strongly Virgoan daughter.

There was no pressing financial need for me to start earning. Thus as Saturn approached my seventh house cusp, I decided to add to my qualifications by following father's footsteps and studying law. (He had begun to practise as a barrister a few years before his death.) Mother approved, saying it was 'always wise to have another string to your bow'. In fact, this turned out to be one of the most fateful decisions I ever made.

Although I did not realize in those days that Saturn's Development Cycle even existed, it had nevertheless opened the doors to what promised to be a busy and interesting adult life.

The Achievement Cycle

Saturn crossing the seventh house cusp and moving through eighth and ninth houses up to tenth house cusp.

Again, as its name implies, this begins a time when results come more easily. Provided only you've spent the preceding cycle getting your act together, Saturn now rings up the curtain on your performance. In many ways, this cycle offers the culmination of projects and ideas commenced during its predecessor, offering genuine success and satisfaction if you have disciplined yourself to these ends.

But—and there are always 'buts' with Saturn—if you're involved in marriage or any other type of close partnership, Saturn's movement through the seventh house puts heavy pressure on it and increasing demands on you. If such involvement was not developmental to your life purpose in the long-term, it often terminates during this period or soon after. Perhaps, the best way of describing the Saturn's

Achievement Cycle is to say it's the time when the chickens come home to roost. That's why you need to do all you can to ensure you've been raising the right kind of chickens!

Illustration From Life: First Saturn Achievement Cycle

Schedule of Events

Now for a few further flashbacks into what was happening to me during this cycle.

Age 20 to 26: Saturn moving from seventh house to tenth house cusp. As Saturn entered the seventh, I began legal studies, met and married a fellow student—all in the same year. By the middle of the next, I was the mother of a Geminian baby girl. Before the middle of the year after that, my young Cancer-born husband was dead at only 24.

These dramatically life-changing events happened with staggering swiftness in less than 22 months. (They were not, of course, solely the handiwork of Saturn. Several other planets were involved as I discovered long afterwards.)

Even looking back at them now through the blur of so many years, I still remember the shock, the bewilderment, the pain. Why had it happened? What could I do? Nothing. Just pick up the broken threads and go on with my life.

So I did. I finished my Law degree as Saturn began to approach the tenth house cusp and my daughter turned four and a half. I realized then that I did not really wish to practise as a lawyer and was casting about in my mind for the right career choices. When Saturn crossed the tenth, the opportunity to achieve a long-held wish came up—through nothing more than what seemed a chance conversation with another student.

Not a cheering story, you might think, for one of Saturn's most helpful cycles. And certainly not the usual one. However, as ever with Saturn, you must look for the underlying purpose beneath each sequence of events. In my case, they were designed to goad me into trying to achieve—not through a happy marriage—but on my own. That was what I (years later) understood my chart demanded so that's what Saturn set in train.

The Stabilization Cycle

Saturn crossing the tenth house cusp and moving through eleventh and twelfth houses up to first house cusp.

Once more, the name of this cycle gives the clue to its effect. As Saturn passes over the highest point in the chart—the tenth house cusp (or midheaven)—the time is one of culmination. Of gaining whatever hopes and ambitions we've been working towards, consciously or unconsciously, during the preceding 15 years.

Nevertheless, as we saw earlier, Saturn is a hard taskmaster, so he hands us exactly what we deserve. Hence the tenth house cusp crossing can be one of great satisfaction. Or equally great dissatisfaction. (What we believe we want is not always what we need.) From that point on, Saturn begins to descend slowly but surely so this period becomes more of a time to build on past effort and consolidate your gains. And less of a time to strike out in new directions.

In a sense, the Stabilization Cycle resembles climbing down the side of a mountain. The descent is easier and usually less dangerous than the upward climb—provided you watch your step, don't let go of the ropes and fall, clattering down to the bottom.

Nevertheless, it is important during this cycle to observe the days of wine and roses are drawing to a temporary close. The Withdrawal Cycle is looming on the horizon so—in order to wend your way more comfortably through that—do all you can now to place your life, your goals and your intentions on a solid, stable foundation as Saturn moves through the tenth, eleventh and twelfth houses. Decide what is possible and what is not within the range of your particular skills and abilities. The Stabilization Cycle is a time when you're best advised to keep your feet on the ground and leave shooting for the stars till much later.

Illustration From Life: First Saturn Stabilization Cycle

Schedule of Events

Herewith the last set of flashbacks into my initial experience with this cycle.

Age 26 to 35: Saturn moving from tenth house to first house cusp. As Saturn entered the tenth, I was suddenly handed the chance to realize an ambition I'd first felt in childhood. . .to become some kind of a writer. Through that 'chance' conversation—but of course, it wasn't 'chance'—I was offered a job as a journalist with a metropolitan daily. I couldn't believe my good fortune and took to journalism like the proverbial duck to water.

Three years later, I was working at it in England with Saturn (unbeknownst to me then) moving through my eleventh. Right on cue I met and married my second husband—a Libran and Australian like myself—shortly before returning home.

All went well enough for starters but as Saturn arrived in my twelfth house, troubles and personality clashes were brewing up between us. I wanted to remain a career woman: he wanted a homebody. I finally gave in and by the time Saturn was again approaching my first, my mother became ill and died. (Saturn was once more in the same position and very close to the same degree he had been occupying when my grandmother—who had virtually reared me from infancy to age four—had also died nearly 30 years before.)

Without mother, there was no-one left outside the home I could turn to. My husband's increasingly bitter jealousy of his predecessor who had been dead for more than 11 years—was venting itself on his young step-daughter, despite the fact we now had an Aries baby girl of our own. Anger and resentment were boiling over on all sides.

The stage was perfectly set for another stint of learning, readjusting and starting again. Looking back at it now, I think I was coming dangerously close to the point of despair as Saturn's second time in the Withdrawal Cycle (still as yet unbeknownst to me) got under way again.

Yet, as mentioned earlier, just when that gloomful period was dragging to its close some six years later, astrology suddenly appeared like a flash of light in my life. Even in my earliest studies of the science, I gradually began to realize there really *was* a glimmer of brightness at the end of what till then had seemed like a never-ending tunnel. That these years of emotional turmoil had *had* a purpose. And, best of all, that they would *not* drag on forever.

Once I had checked over with the aid of my chart the events of that first time in the Withdrawal Cycle in childhood, I knew without doubt my life would soon take an upward swing again—just as it had in those long-gone days of yore. And, of course, it did. Right on schedule. That is why I have described these flashbacks into parts of my own tussles with Saturn. To show you how understanding his cycles—past, present and future—allow us to:

- Work more effectively with these mysterious circles in time.
- Appreciate that neither great days nor grim last forever.
- Plan ahead confidently by learning from past errors instead of bewailing or regretting them.
- Appreciate there is an unfolding purpose at every staging-post in the journey through life.
- Be ready to recognize the landmarks as we come eventually back to the same point in the circle we travelled through so many years before.

Saturn House Transits—Pressure Points in Time

Wherever Saturn is in the natal chart or by transit, there is invariably a sense of being *pressured*—of being obliged to make changes in expectations and desires whether we like it or not! The manner in which we handle these pressures determines whether the outcome will be agreeable or disagreeable, developmental or obstructive. If you know anything about the oriental martial arts of Kung Fu or Judo, you'll understand that you never meet force with force in a contest. You yield to the pressure thus ensuring the impact is lessened or even deflected altogether. That technique exemplifies the right response to any Saturn contest too. Don't fight it head-on. Step back. Give way. Consider how you can counter attack the problem by moving in a different direction.

With all house transits, you need to have the meanings of each one of the twelve at your fingertips. If you're unsure of them, a condensed note on house meanings appears in the heading of each transit but it's also advisable to read up their complete descriptions in my companion book—'*How to Astro-Analyze Yourself and Others*'. Each house pinpoints a specific life sector. Any planet transiting a house pulls a switch—to put it metaphorically—which lights up the affairs of that house.

Naturally, transits of any one of the four angular houses. . .first, fourth, seventh, tenth. . .must create a greater impact on anybody's life because events are being promoted which affect fundamentals. . .the presentation of the self, the conditions in the home, the quality of relationships, the direction of occupations. However, that does not mean the succeedent houses. . .second, fifth, eighth, eleventh. . .or the cadent houses. . .third, sixth, ninth, twelfth. . .should be ignored or discounted. Transits through them are always less drastic in provoking portentous life changes yet still make significant contributions in altering existing circumstances.

But before we get down to Saturn house transit definitions, wipe your mental slate clean of the fear-generating ideas (which some old-style books still promote) that Saturn transits inevitably bring gloom, doom, losses, ailments and assorted miseries in their train. The result is quite the reverse if you appreciate the psychological significance of Saturnian pressures and respond to them constructively.

When lecturing to students, I often liken Saturn's transits to a 'spring-cleaning' of whatever house he's working in at any given time. All the useless items we've been hoarding for years have to be ruthlessly pulled out, sorted over and thrown away. Misdirected ambitions, pointless relationships, ill-founded hopes, cobwebby dreams, self-imposed responsibilities. Just like old clothes or unused furniture, which once fitted and suited us well but now merely clutter up our space, they have to go. Naturally, we're reluctant to throw them away. Human nature is like that. We hang on to the past because it is familiar. A known quantity. Yet we cannot live there. The present is where we belong. The future is what we must look towards. If we dig our heels in—even for the most apparently high-minded motives—and refuse to tackle Saturn's 'spring-cleaning' wholeheartedly, he does not hesitate to force the task upon us. Then the events can become very disagreeable indeed.

As witness the case of a young Capricorn man who could not bring himself to see eye to eye with Saturn and because of that lost one. Literally! Like nearly all those born under the sign of the Goat, he had a very strongly-developed sense of responsibility, family duty and respect for age. He had been living with and looking after an eighty-year-old great-aunt since his late teens, whose demands upon his time had gradually gone beyond all reason and become outrageous. Other chart factors encouraged him to accept uncomplainingly the impositions the old woman heaped upon him but deep within, his Aries Moon was seething with repressed fury.

As Saturn began to transit his first house, thereby also activating several ominous planetary configurations in his natal chart, his great-aunt intensified her demands on his time even more. One evening, she insisted he change the locks on all the doors that very night. The awful events, which erupted from that annoying but commonplace chore, must not be construed solely as the work of Saturn. But the moment of truth had come. The gauntlet was thrown down at this young Capricorn's feet. Do something about this preposterous situation—*or else!*

The young man did not. Instead he dutifully took up hammer and chisel, began work on the first lock, struck hard to loosen the wood but hit off centre. The chisel flew up and pierced his left eye. Months in hospital followed as doctors struggled to save the eye but without success. By the time he was fit again, he was wearing a glass eye but the aunt problem was solved. She had gone into a nursing home.

When he came to see me, all these events were far in the past. He was happily married with a young family. Nevertheless, once he understood why this disabling 'accident' had happened, he was better able to ensure he would never again allow himself to be dominated like that. To be kind and caring is one thing. To permit another human being to take control of your life is quite another. Had he resisted the old woman's cantankerous demands, he could have freed himself from a wretched situation much less painfully. Since he could not bring himself to confront her, the Saturn transit forced his hand. Again literally.

As many researchers in both psychoanalysis and astrological theory have shown accidents do *not* happen accidentally. Behind each one lies a turmoil of repressed feelings which causes the fatal mistake in judgement which in turn causes the 'accident'. Our young Capricorn wanted desperately to escape from his miserable life style but could not desert what his conscious mind *wrongly* conceived as his bounden duty. So, as the Saturn transit applied maximum pressure, his subconcious mind arranged his escape for him. By the simple process of causing mounting stress to make him mishandle the chisel.

This reasoning as to what causes accidents may seem hard to grasp at first if you have not considered the underlying psychological background to them. Yet it is patently true and here serves as an example of handling a Saturn transit the hard way. If our man had dealt with his problem by tackling it, he could have saved himself a great deal of unnecessary pain. That goes for all of us. The choice remains always and exclusively ours.

Saturn House Transits—Definitions

When assessing the potential positive or negative effect of any transit on the person experiencing it, always take into consideration:

1. Anticipated individual response to the life changes the transit inaugurates. (Personality traits as shown by natal chart.)
2. When natal planetary patterns or major configurations are activated by the transit. (E.g. grand trines, t-squares.)
3. What aspects to other planets occur during the currency of any transit. (This blends conflicting or compatible energies.)
4. What houses are linked by a transiting planet in aspect with a natal planet. (This intermingles the affairs of differing life sections—again in a conflicting or compatible manner.)

As in my companion books, I'll keep listed interpretations concise. Firstly, to encourage you to think for yourself about them. Merely copying out my ideas or any other author's extends neither your confidence nor your expertise. Secondly, clear, concise listing permits quicker reference and easier assimilation.

As you read through the following interpretations of Saturn's transits through each of the twelve houses, remember your mental image of Saturn as the 'Taskmaster'. This will help to convince you that successful handling of events promoted by each Saturn house transit requires serious, responsible and sustained effort. Accept the disciplining force and the transit will offer wisdom and advantageous changes: buck against it and the effect will be one of irksome restriction and detrimental changes.

FIRST HOUSE SATURN TRANSIT EVENTS . . .
substantially alter self image and personal environment.

Positive Responses Promote	• Accomplishment through steady application. • New opportunities for self-reliance. • Better capacity for discipline. • Benefits through more stable, conservative attitude.
Negative Responses Invite	• Stagnation of ambitions. • Loss of confidence in self. • Obsession with health fears. • Bouts of severe depression.

SECOND HOUSE SATURN TRANSIT EVENTS . . .
substantially alter earning power and use of own moneys.

Positive Responses Promote	• More systematic management of money. • Improved financial foresight. • Monetary rewards from hard work. • Prudent handling of expenditures.
Negative Responses Invite	• Irksome limitations on earning power. • Heavy, unplanned-for expenditure. • Constant worry over money. • Financial set-backs.

THIRD HOUSE SATURN TRANSIT EVENTS . . .
substantially alter mental attitudes and educational skills.

Positive Responses Promote	• Benefits from further studies. • Successes in work using

	communicative skills. Systematic handling of agreements and contracts. • Supportive assistance from siblings or close associates.
Negative Responses Invite	• Delays and set-backs relating to documentation. • Narrow, depressive interpretation of ideas, projects. • Loss of faith in intellectual abilities. • Confrontations with siblings or close associates.

FOURTH HOUSE SATURN TRANSIT EVENTS . . . ***substantially alter domestic circumstances and home atmosphere.***

Positive Responses Promote	• Benefits from willing acceptance of home responsibilities. • Successful business activities within the home. • Opportunities to gain security in domestic affairs. • Assistance from older individuals connected with home, family.
Negative Responses Invite	• Burdensome demands from those sharing home. • Loneliness and isolation within the home. • Problems with aged or ailing relatives. • Emotional disturbances through domestic disputes.

FIFTH HOUSE SATURN TRANSIT EVENTS . . .
substantially alter romantic liaisons, concern with children, creative talents.

Positive Responses Promote	• More enduring romantic ties. • Attraction to mature, influential individuals. • Application in use of creative/artistic abilities. • Willing acceptance of needs of children.
Negative Responses Invite	• Breaks and disappointments in love affairs. • Severe problems with own children or those close to self. • Misdirected use of talents. • Losses through unwise speculation.

SIXTH HOUSE SATURN TRANSIT EVENTS . . .
substantially alter working environment, health concerns.

Positive Responses Promote	• Benefits from concentration on work skills and proficiency. • Opportunities for slow but steady advancement in job. • Realistic attitude to overall health. • Responsibilities shared with co-workers.
Negative Responses Invite	• Uncongenial working conditions or unemployment. • Distancing of self from colleagues. • Workaholic behaviour and overstrain. • Chronic poor health through poor daily regimen or overwork.

SEVENTH HOUSE SATURN TRANSIT EVENTS . . .
substantially alter marital affairs, partnerships in love or business.

Positive Responses Promote	• Improved relationships through sensible co-operation. • Realistic foundation for any long-term partnership. • Willingness to share responsibilities fairly. • Benefits through links with older partners.
Negative Responses Invite	• Irksome situations in marriage/unions. • Refusal to accept shared duties/obligations. • Break-up of relationships through inability to develop them. • Selfish, demanding attitudes.

EIGHTH HOUSE SATURN TRANSIT EVENTS . . .
substantially alter joint/shared financial liabilities and handling of deceased estate assets.

Positive Responses Promote	• Gain through legacies, inheritance, monetary gifts. • Ability to administer shared assets wisely. • Work opportunities related to financial matters. • Benefits through skills of partners.
Negative Responses Invite	• Resentment and arguments over joint/shared moneys. • Delays and hindrances in obtaining moneys due. • Refusal to accept expert advice on financial decisions.

- Morbid fear of death through loss of older relative/associate.

NINTH HOUSE SATURN TRANSIT EVENTS . . .
substantially alter involvements with foreigners, travel decisions.

Positive Responses Promote

- Work opportunities encompassing travel and foreign contacts.
- Benefits through tertiary education.
- Development of new interests through exposure to foreign cultures.
- Successful business overseas trips.

Negative Responses Invite

- Impediments/obstructions in dealings with foreigners.
- Unexpected blocks to travel and lessened educational benefits therefrom.
- Worry and doubts relating to overseas transactions.
- Misunderstandings in handling cultural/religious differences.

TENTH HOUSE SATURN TRANSIT EVENTS . . .
substantially alter career aims and personal status.

Positive Responses Promote

- Opportunities to achieve career ambitions.
- Assistance from influential individuals.
- Promotion/advancement through acceptance of responsibility.
- Respect from superiors.

Negative Responses Invite

- Loss of status and employment
- Misuse of authority through self-seeking attitudes.

- Disapproval from employers or professional associates.
- Frustration of major ambitions.

ELEVENTH HOUSE SATURN TRANSIT EVENTS . . .

substantially alter friendships and involvement in group activities.

Positive Responses Promote

- Support from valuable friends and organizations.
- Profitable social contacts.
- Satisfaction of private wishes.
- Humanitarian interests with like-minded groups.

Negative Responses Invite

- Involvement with self-centred, narrow-minded individuals.
- Pretence of friendship to gain backing.
- Joining of groups for ulterior motives.
- Lack of satisfying social life.

TWELFTH HOUSE SATURN TRANSIT EVENTS . . .

substantially alter spiritual viewpoint and capacity for self-sacrifice.

Positive Responses Promote

- Deepened self-awareness and understanding of own motivations.
- Benefits from introspection and reflection on past experience.
- Willingness to sacrifice own aims to aid others.
- Psychological insight into problems of self and intimates.

Negative Responses Invite

- Deliberate isolation of the self and bleakness of spirit.
- Psychosomatic illnesses and chronic depression.

- Acts of disguised emnity from supposed friends/intimates.
- Real or imagined punishment for past wrongdoing.

So much for Saturn's twelve house transits and the somewhat heavy scenes, event-wise, they generate. Very little sparkle about any one of them but then that's definitely *not* Saturn's style. The event pressure is always towards establishment of order, tried and true methods, tireless persistence in the face of adversity, the long, slow, steady haul onwards and upwards. These sober responses get you solid results. The flashy dashes do not.

When interpreting Saturn house transits, keep in mind the *present age* of yourself and your subjects. Obviously, for example, a third house transit with its pressure on study and educating the mind will create markedly different mental interests in the case of a schoolchild or teenager than it will in the case of an elderly or old person. The young subject, if he/she reacts positively, will work far harder and more consistently towards acquiring skills required for the chosen future occupation. The elderly subject, again if the reaction is positive, will seek out new mental interests as a hobby or as part of a self-development project.

As noted earlier, dealing with Saturn is far from a fun thing. But don't despair if the thought of years of having 'to keep on keeping on' plunge you into the 'Slough of Despond' temporarily. That's only natural! Learning in such a hard school is sometimes painful but it surely guarantees we never forget the lessons!

Now, we're ready to watch what happens when transiting Saturn comes close enough to natal planets to link his energy with theirs.

Saturn Transit Aspects—Encounters in Time

When transiting Saturn approaches any one of the natal planets, compare the encounter to running into a friend or enemy as you're walking down a long road. If it's a friend you see, the meeting will be pleasant, even profitable. You might hear good news or be offered welcome help. If it's an enemy, the meeting is likely to be very unpleasant. You'll need to keep your wits about you to get past without trouble.

That, in metaphorical phrasing, is precisely what happens when transiting Saturn makes aspects to each one of the natal planets as he journeys round the wheel of the horoscope chart. When his energy combines comfortably with that of the planet encountered, the events stimulated thereby will appear friendly to your present purpose. If the two planetary energies clash, the events stimulated will appear hostile to your objectives at that point in time.

So look at your own charts now, recording on your transit sheets which Saturn cycle is in progress, which house he is travelling through and what major aspects he is making to natal planets during the periods under consideration.

Major transiting aspects to be considered are:

- Conjunctions, trines, sextiles.
- Squares, oppositions.

Conjunctions usually produce a particularly powerful effect in shaping events since they mean the transiting planet is literally 'hovering' directly above the natal planet. The two energies are thus closely intermingled. Results will be helpful if these energies blend harmoniously, disconcerting if they don't.

To allow for this either-way influence, we'll list conjunctions separately in our Saturn Aspect Interpretation Tables.

Trines, Sextiles usually produce a harmonious effect in shaping events since the energies of the transiting planet and the natal planet blend comfortably. Tensions ease, projects affected go more smoothly.

However, when interpreting bear in mind the sextile is a comparatively mild aspect and so less likely to bring notable changes.

Squares, Oppositions usually produce a distinctly discomforting effect in shaping events as their energies conflict sharply. Problems erupt, demand resolution.

Of the two, the opposition is considerably easier to handle. The planets concerned bring together opposing but not necessarily hostile energies. Self-awareness will increase from the struggle.

Squares are almost always problem-makers. The transiting and the natal planet have nothing in common, their energies contradict each other. Obstacles seem to appear out of nowhere, perplexity flourishes.

Please note I've used the *sequence* listing format for all Transit Interpretation Tables rather than the *group* type, favoured by some authors.

Sequence listing sets out each transiting aspect like this:

> Transiting Saturn conjunct Sun: transiting Saturn trine or sextile Sun: transiting Saturn square or opposition Sun, and so on.

Group listing puts all the same aspects together: E.g.,

> Transiting Saturn conjunct Sun: transiting Saturn conjunct Moon: transiting Saturn conjunct Mercury, etc.

I prefer sequence listing for two reasons in teaching students. Firstly, it makes for faster, easier reference when working on future planetary movements. Secondly, it aids comprehension of the sometimes subtle yet significant distinctions between differing transiting aspects to the same natal planets.

To illustrate: Saturn is always a disciplining force. This shows up sharply when he is the directing planet in a series of events during transit aspects. Hence each description of the Saturn impact strikes such a uniformly heavy note, they may sound similar, even repetitive, at first readings.

They are not the same, of course. Yet you can't get away from using and re-using weighty words like—obligation. . .concentration . . .determination. . .practicality. . .caution. . realism. . .restraint. . . responsibility. Each one of them evidences a distinctively Saturnian maxim—'Slow but sure wins the race'. If that's a maxim you can accept without cries of dismay or groans of anguish, you'll survive the toughest of them unscathed. If not, you'll need to change your ways or Saturn will do it for you. And none too gently.

Orbs of Effectiveness

When assessing the impact of any aspect, remember it is only operative when it is within the orb of 1 degree.

Let's illustrate from the ephemeris with Saturn's positions for the year 1987.

1 January 1987 = Saturn at 15 degrees 26 minutes of Sagittarius
14 October 1987 = Saturn at 16 degrees 58 minutes of Sagittarius

Why has he moved apparently only 1 degree in more than 9 months? A glance at the ephemeris shows he retrograded from 31 March 1987 and through to 19 August 1987.

Now, let's say our example natal chart shows the Sun at 16 degrees 20 minutes of Virgo. The transiting Saturn/natal Sun aspect made is a square. Troublesome. How long in 1987 will the aspect remain effective? Another glance at the ephemeris shows it is in orb for most of January 1987, out of orb until early June 1987, then back in orb until end of July 1987, out of orb again till mid-September 1987, then back in orb until it finally ends in late October 1987.

At first reading, new readers may think that sounds complicated. Once you look at the Saturn columns in the ephemeris for 1987, you'll see that recording when a transiting planet is in or out of orb with a natal planet couldn't be simpler.

Some authors maintain that aspects only generate events when wholly within the 1 degree orb. I believe in instances such as our example where the transiting planet is almost continually moving to and fro (rather like a car backing and filling) over an aspect, its influence extends throughout the entire period. Stronger when in orb but not inoperative during the out-of-orb periods. Why? Because planetary influences do not turn on and off with the abruptness of a bathroom tap. Neither do events. Once started, they don't stop in mid-flow just because the event-instigating planet is briefly out-of-orb.

Therefore, in our example, it would be reasonable to infer the transiting Saturn square natal Sun aspect would effect the future of the individual experiencing it for almost an entire year.

So note the full term of each transiting aspect on your transit sheets as well as the dates when it is within the 1 degree orb.

Saturn Transit Aspects—Interpretation Table

Transiting Saturn Aspecting Natal Sun:
Energy Blend: Discipline/Personal Goals.

Saturn/Sun Conjunction *Event Prognosis: Restrictive, Demanding*
t ♄☌☉:
This is a time when past efforts climax in satisfaction or disappointment.

Energy is inhibited, vitality lowered. Best to concentrate on existing plans rather than take off in new directions. Conflict with authority figures, usually males, is likely. Physical strain from heavier responsibilities can weaken determination. Long-standing problems come up for resolution.

⋆ Where chart subject's training or circumstances are appropriate, this transiting aspect generates:
- Heavier professional obligations
- Disciplinary confrontations with children
- Increased personal status and recognition of merit

Saturn/Sun Trine or Sextile *Event Prognosis: Hopeful, Reassuring*
t♄△☉: t♄∗☉

This is a time when rewards for work well done can be expected. Favourable recognition from social or professional superiors is easier to gain. Demonstrated ability to cope with heavier work burdens brings advancement. Generally a good reception for carefully-considered plans and presentation of original, but well-documented ideas.

⋆ Where chart subject's training or circumstances are appropriate, this transiting aspect generates:
- Opportunities for satisfying educational pursuits.
- Rewards for efficiency at executive level
- Profitable new friendships and group activities

Saturn/Sun Square or Opposition *Event Prognosis: Dubious, Stressful*
t♄□☉: t♄☍☉:

This is a time when ambitions and aims run up against a brick wall. Blocks and set-backs proliferate if egotistical aspirations overcome common sense. Patience and steady application are required in face of disappointments. Rigidity in attitude or dictatorial demands bring censure and disapproval. Maintaining a sensible health regimen will avert health problems caused by overwork.

⋆ Where chart subject's training or circumstances are appropriate, this transiting aspect generates:
- Mistakes in financial speculation
- Disillusionment or serious conflict in partnerships
- Lack of satisfying social activities

Transiting Saturn Aspecting Natal Moon

Energy Blend: Discipline/Emotional Concerns.

Saturn/Moon Conjunction Event Prognosis: Restrictive, Demanding

t♄☌☽:

This is a time when self-pity arising out of emotionally frustrating circumstances can cause continuing depression. Lack of support or empathy with female intimates/associates adds further sense of isolation. Worry over domestic expenditure will be eased by necessary economies. Diverting attention to stimulating mental interests relieves emotional pressures.

⋆ Where chart subject's training or circumstances are appropriate, this transiting aspect generates:
- Slow-down in ability to earn
- Poor result from public relations efforts
- Estrangements through insensitivity to others

Saturn/Moon Trine or Sextile Event Prognosis: Hopeful, Reassuring

t♄△☽: t♄⚹☽:

This is a time when emotional equilibrium is more easily maintained and hence private affairs are looked upon more realistically, run more smoothly. Improved rapport and valuable assistance is likely through female intimates/associates in balancing domestic responsibilities with interests outside the home. Results are further improved by a more objective emotional outlook and willing acceptance of wise advice.

⋆ Where chart subject's training or circumstances are appropriate, this transiting aspect generates:
- Good results from home improvements
- Better rapport with parents/older relatives
- Settlement of financial dealings

Saturn/Moon Square or Opposition Event Prognosis: Dubious, Stressful

t♄□☽: t♄☍☽:

This is a time when the temptation to isolate the self emotionally and reject help from those cared about insidiously develops. Inevitably, family or love relations become strained and clashes can also occur in the work place through repressed feelings of loneliness and deprivation. A sustained effort to balance the conflicting demands of duty and emotional need will prevent self-pity and much unhappiness.

* Where chart subject's training or circumstances are appropriate, this transiting aspect generates:
  - Losses through unwise handling of money/possessions
  - Delays in business transactions
  - Hampering obligations in family affairs

Transiting Saturn Aspecting Natal Mercury

Energy Blend: Discipline/Mental Interests

Satury/Mercury Conjunction *Event Prognosis: Restrictive, Demanding*

t♄☌☿:

This is a time when mental attitudes turn down towards pessimism. Infuriating delays and tangles bedevil just about everything which involves communication—letters, business contacts, interchange of ideas. Thinking is set into a narrower, more conservative mould, cutting back on enthusiasm but promising profitable, single-minded attention to a major project.

Awaiting with calm and patience the outcome of ideas reduces anxiety and mental strain.

* Where chart subject's training or circumstances are appropriate, this transiting aspect generates:
  - Professional work in field of communications
  - Liabilities concerning siblings/friends/groups
  - Involvement in legal matters

Saturn/Mercury Trine or Sextile *Event Prognosis: Hopeful, Reassuring*

t♄△☿: t♄✶☿

This is a time when all forms of pre-planning of mental work bring optimum results. Precise, practical thinking leads to well-presented ideas, backs up study or educational programmes, promises added satisfaction from intellectual pursuits—provided tendency towards mental inflexibility is kept under control. Promotion or career advancement is possible through impressively boosted powers of disciplined thought.

* Where chart subject's training or circumstances are appropriate, this transiting aspect generates:
  - Helpful instruction from older, well-educated individuals
  - Opportunity to apply improved work methodology
  - Job possibilities related to science or technology

Saturn/Mercury Square or Opposition *Event Prognosis: Dubious, Stressful*
t♄□☿: t♄☍☿:
This is a time when the ability to see eye-to-eye with others becomes close to nil. Tendency to appear autocratic in pushing own ideas must be controlled and chip-on-the-shoulder mental attitudes resisted. Severed business and personal relationships can occur from conflict of opinions, hopes of mental compatibility can be shattered. Challenges to long-held views appear on all sides. Disciplining the self towards greater mental flexibility will avert break-ups and business defeats.

* Where chart subject's training or circumstances are appropriate, this transiting aspect generates:
  - Delays in finalizing contracts, legal documents
  - Hindrances from love or business associates in joint projects
  - Rejection by others of innovative plans

Transiting Saturn Aspecting Natal Venus

Energy Blend: Discipline/Reciprocation of feelings

Saturn/Venus Conjunction *Event Prognosis: Restrictive, Demanding*
t♄☌♀:
This is a time when capacity to respond to displays of love, affection or friendship becomes noticeably more discriminating. Light, shallow or trivial liaisons rarely survive the test. Relationships based on genuine caring and concern are strengthened. Overriding desire is for harmony based on sincere not pretended regard. Tendency to spend extravagantly or indulge the self in pursuit of pleasure or love affairs needs to be resisted.

* Where chart subject's training or circumstances arc appropriate, this transiting aspect generates:
  - Benefits from entertainment or social activities
  - Occupational opportunities in artistic/creative fields
  - Attractions to considerably older lovers/partners

Saturn/Venus Trine or Sextile Event Prognosis: Hopeful, Reassuring
t♄△♀: t♄✶♀:
This is a time when friends, lovers, partners show themselves in realistic colours and the rosy spectacles of fantasizing drop from the eyes. This process ensures that only those involvements that are worthwhile, based on calm assessment and unfeigned compatibility of interest retain significance in the life. Business associations also profit from a more realistic appreciation of common aims.

* Where chart subject's training or circumstances are appropriate, this transiting aspect generates:
  - Useful recommendations from friends in creative/artistic work
  - Pleasing contact with past partners/intimates
  - Helpful steps up social ladder

Saturn/Venus Square or Opposition Event Prognosis: Dubious, Stressful
t♄□♀: t♄☍♀:
This is a time when the rocks along the road to love or friendship assume the proportions of mountains. Not infrequently the result is an avalanche of broken links, separations and disillusionment. Anger, bitterness or recrimination won't help. Honest reappraisal—of how and for what purpose the relationship began in the first place—can ease the situation. If the bond was based on delusion, false hopes or grasping at security, this pressure can break it irrevocably.
* Where chart subject's training or circumstances are appropriate, this transiting aspect generates:
  - Involvements with unreliable, demanding individuals
  - False offers or promises in love or business affairs
  - Deliberate provocation or derogatory comments from close associates

Transiting Saturn Aspecting Natal Mars
Energy Blend: Discipline/Physical Drives

Saturn/Mars Conjunction *Event Prognosis: Restrictive, Demanding*
t♄☌♂:
This is a time when any inclination to live by the 'might is right' philosophy leads to disaster. Sexual, physical or mental energy can be misdirected or even misinterpreted as some form of duress or coercion. Opponents—actual or imagined—seem to obstruct ambitions, thereby fuelling barely-disguised feelings of anger, bitterness or resentment. Vigilant control of behaviour smacking of egotism or aggression is the best way around this one. Avoid decisions emanating from irritable or rebellious attitudes.

⋆ Where chart subject's training or circumstances are appropriate, this transiting aspect generates:
- Impulsive, foolhardy commitments in work or private life
- Health disturbances through severe nervous tension
- Loss of opportunities through uncompromising, tough attitudes

Saturn/Mars Trine or Sextile *Event Prognosis: Hopeful, Reassuring*
t♄△♂: t♄✶♂:
This is a time when restraint and vitality work well together. Sensible planning, carried out with vigour and flair, impresses others and wins worthwhile support. Patience in reaching desired goals comes more easily: overblown expectations settle into more realistic directions. Hard work coupled with good judgement in all important issues adds up to accomplishment as long as the push for success is not pursued too uncompromisingly.

⋆ Where chart subject's training or circumstances are appropriate, this transiting aspect generates:
- Successes through use of physical strength and endurance
- Wise application of initiative to achieve faster results
- Accelerated effort in significant, personal activities

Saturn/Mars Square or Opposition *Event Prognosis: Dubious, Stressful*
t♄□♂: t♄☍♂:
This is a time when antagonism flourishes and can far too easily create unwise decisions, provocative actions. The underlying cause is anger in its many forms—from annoyance, pique, indignation through to violent rage. This must find an outlet but not in shouting down or fighting pitched battles with others. Divert all the bottled-up force into less dangerous physical activity such as energetic work programmes or demanding sporting activities. Avoid confrontations with naturally quarrelsome individuals.

* When chart subject's training or circumstances are appropriate, this transiting aspect generates:
  - Risk situations involving machinery, firearms, police
  - Mistakes in plans through rashness, haste
  - Wasted energies on futile propositons

Transiting Saturn Aspecting Natal Jupiter
Energy Blend: Discipline/Enthusiasms

Saturn/Jupiter Conjunction *Event Prognosis: Restrictive, Demanding*
t♄☌♃:
This is a time when caution and optimism combine to create either highly successful utilization of opportunities or a feeling of being forced to look before leaping, which can produce impatience and irresolute behaviour. 'Those who travel slowly invariably arrive' is the best slogan for this one. Abiding by it promises financial betterment and steady gains—usually through the good offices of influential individuals.

* Where chart subject's training or circumstances are appropriate, this transiting aspect generates:
  - Introductions to individuals who bring new opportunites
  - Good results from matters relating to law or governmental authorities, business or professional advancement
  - Benefits through public relations programmes or good publicity

Saturn/Jupiter Trine or Sextile   Event Prognosis: Hopeful, Reassuring
t♄△♃: t♄*♃:
This is a time when opportunities can be equated with 'the little acorns that into great oaks grow'. Even the smallest advantage, chance, lucky break (whatever term fits best) can, if carefully nourished and tended, shoot up into something big and impressive. Not overnight, of course. Neither Rome nor oaks were built in a day. The same applies to translating new openings for advancement into solid, viable achievement. Constructive optimism not unbridled opportunism is the best course.

* Where chart subject's training or circumstances are appropriate, this transiting aspect generates:
  - Fruition of long-term aims/objectives
  - Interest or successes in political sphere
  - Improved co-operation with superiors or elders

Saturn/Jupiter Square or Opposition   Event Prognosis: Dubious, Stressful
t♄□♃: t♄☍♃:
This is a time when the high road to success disconcertingly narrows into small, dark street. The message is to tread more warily rather than rush heedlessly onwards. Often this represents a period when past excesses of enthusiasm (or even outright opportunism) can lead to greater errors of judgement if allowed to continue unchecked. Reliance on luck, 'smart-operator' tactics, or indolence bring crashing let-downs.

* Where chart subject's training or circumstances are appropriate, this transiting aspect generates:
  - Cut-backs of activities and plans for expansion
  - Absence of 'lucky breaks' or favours from others
  - Foolish neglect of important duties

Transiting Saturn Aspecting Natal Saturn
Energy Blend: Discipline/Self-Appraisal

Saturn/Saturn Conjunction   Event Prognosis: Restrictive, demanding
t♄☌♄:
This is a time when the self is obliged to take a long, critical look at

its own scoreboard of failures or successes, attainments or deficiences . . .twice in the average lifetime, (see Chapter 2) at around age 29 and again as age 60 approaches. If the private scoreboard looks uninspiring, the effect on self-esteem is deflating but that should never be taken as a signal to down tools and mope. Honest appraisal of either 30 or 60 years of living promises new beginnings and more stable conditions plus willingness to discard ideas/ambitions which have led nowhere.

* Where chart subject's training or circumstances are appropriate, this transiting aspect generates:
  - Mistakes from choosing easy, materialistic solutions
  - Testing decisions affecting whole way of life
  - Wrong moves based on fear of future responsibilities

Saturn/Saturn Trine or Sextile *Event Prognosis: Hopeful, Reassuring*
t♄△♄: t♄*♄:
This is a time when balancing alternatives and approaching decisions in a level-headed manner comes naturally. The result is that personal aims are achieved without hassles as well as being based on calm, mature assessment. Reputation and status move up-scale, usually through the loyalty of associates or stated approval of influential, older individuals. Progress in well-considered, well-founded projects is steady and long-range planning can be entered into with confidence.

* Where chart subject's training or circumstances are appropriate, this transiting aspect generates:
  - Elimination of long-standing obstacles to self-improvement
  - Business associations based on mutual respect and compatibility
  - Rewards for help given in past years

Saturn/Saturn Square or Opposition *Event Prognosis: Dubious, Stressful*
t♄□♄: t♄☍♄:
This is a time when a nagging sense of insecurity can undermine all steps in the decision-making process. This shakiness seeps into private relationships as well as occupational affairs like muddy ooze in a previously clear pool. Fearful, withdrawn or stress-generated behaviour serves only to cloud issues even more—particularly in dealings with

superiors or authority figures. Stimulates as well a feeling of being disliked/unpopular socially or in the work-place. Look for hidden reasons why others take on the role of obstacle-makers.

★ Where chart subject's training or circumstances are appropriate, this transiting aspect generates:
- Intolerable demands from old relatives or parents
- Nervous disorders through stress and anxieties
- Financial set-backs and opposition from superiors

Transiting Saturn Aspecting Natal Uranus

Energy Blend: Discipline/Revelation

Saturn/Uranus Conjunction *Event Prognosis: Restrictive, Demanding*
t♄☌♅:
This is a time when the sensation is one of trying to ride on a whirlwind with a sackful of rocks. The desire to fly high, to flee the daily slog into new and more exciting avenues of expression is held down to earth so that tensions mount up into erratic, apparently inexplicable stops and starts. Long-established life styles are often overturned, leading to breaks away from burdensome bonds and into new occupational areas. Changes from gut level upwards have to be made and adjusted to.

★ Where chart subject's training or circumstances are appropriate, this transiting aspect generates:
- Unexpected work developments involving scientific skill
- Slow removal of handicaps to ambitions
- Complete change of occupation or employment

Saturn/Uranus Trine or Sextile *Event Prognosis: Hopeful Reassuring*
t♄△♅ : t♄✱♅:
This is a time when the old and the new elements of each life blend more comfortably, so that even dramatic changes can be made with calmness and confidence. Personal creativity is boosted yet without the tendency to push original ideas brashly. Best results stem from blending progressive thinking, inventive solutions with well-tested procedures in work or home scene, thus merging the new order smoothly with the old.

* Where chart subject's training or circumstances are appropriate, this transiting aspect generates:
  - Opportunity to settle finally long-standing problems
  - Rewards for ingenuity in scientific work
  - New projects utilizing past experience effectively

Saturn/Uranus Square or Opposition Event Prognosis: Dubious, Stressful
t♄□♅: t♄☍♅:
This is a time when the thing most to be feared is fear itself. Fear of change, fear of breaking out of well-cushioned but narrow ruts or of any situations in the life that are tedious and inflexible. Separations, quarrels and tension-based behaviour are common and prevent workable compromises unless great self-control is exercised. The struggle here is between old duties and the desire for new freedom. The answer is again—patience coupled with awareness of the rights of others.

* Where chart subject's training or circumstances are appropriate, this transiting aspect generates:
  - Blocks to inventiveness by reactionary individuals
  - Sudden loss of status through rebellious attitudes
  - Stubborn adherence to erratic, biased views.

Transiting Saturn Aspecting Natal Neptune
Energy Blend: Discipline/Illumination

Saturn/Neptune Conjunction Event Prognosis: Restrictive, Demanding
t♄☌♆
This is a time when imaginary problems take precedence over real ones so that much mental energy is wasted in worrying about things that should be forgotten or are never likely to happen. Niggling anxieties, constant apprehension about private or business affairs are typical and have to be fought against by clear-headed instead of foggy thinking. Hidden enmities sometimes surface in intrigues and behind-the-scenes plotting. Best to avoid becoming embroiled and concentrate on the task in hand.

- ⋆ Where chart subject's training or circumstances are appropriate, this transiting aspect generates:
  - Interest in meditation, religious matters, mysticism
  - Activity concerning hospitals, social work
  - Attraction to dangerous dabbling in psychic or occult fields

Saturn/Neptune Trine or Sextile Event Prognosis: Hopeful, Reussuring
t♄△♆ : t♄∗♆:

This is a time when inspiration and intuition light the path ahead so that attempts to lift the mind beyond the purely material level meet with greater success. Often, too, the search for purpose in life leads to studies of subjects that have a spiritual connotation. Overall, the increased ability to achieve inner harmony and overcome selfish motivations promotes a sense of calm stability which benefits health in both mind and spirit. Egotism is not rewarded. Understanding and self-abnegation are.

- ⋆ Where chart subject's training or circumstances are appropriate, this transiting aspect generates:
  - Ability to tune in to political or cultural changes
  - Benefits through kindness and charitable behaviour
  - New links with spiritually advanced individuals

Saturn/Neptune Square or Opposition Event Prognosis: Dubious, Stressful
t♄□♆: t♄☍♆:

This is a time when escape from responsibility through imaginary ailments or psychosomatically-inspired illnesses becomes a serious danger. Withdrawal from the real world, encouraged by fear of inadequacy or incompetence, can create manifestations of negativism at all points. Reliance on medical or 'pleasure' drugs, alcoholic indulgence, or physical flight from daily duties often complicate conditions even further. The answer is self-acceptance, balancing good and bad characteristics without self-condemnation, reducing fears and desires to escape reality.

- ⋆ Where chart subject's training or circumstances are appropriate, this transiting aspect generates:
  - Serious alcohol or drug abuse problems

- Mental disorientation requiring treatment
- Exposure of past wrong doing

Transiting Saturn Aspecting Pluto
Energy Blend: Discipline

Saturn/Pluto Conjunction   Event Prognosis: Restrictive, Demanding
t♄☌♇:
This is a time when the sensation is like witnessing a volcanic eruption as previously repressed subconscious drives burst out into potentially destructive action. Intensification is the key word—of feelings, of personal force, of the will to eliminate anything standing in the immediate path. As a result, plotting and secret dealings emerge in overt power struggles. Former behavioural patterns are discredited, new ones forcibly established. Success or reputation diminish rapidly if built on manipulation or exploitation of others. Respond with fortitude and forbearance. Decisions have very long-range consequences.

⋆ Where chart subject's training or circumstances are appropriate, this transiting aspect generates:
- Problems with legislation and officials
- Entanglements in matters relating to deceased estates or corporate moneys
- Coercive tactics in business or private life

Saturn/Pluto Trine or Sextile   Event Prognosis: Hopeful, Reassuring
t♄△♇: t♄⚹♇:
This is a time when strongly-stimulated farsightedness works towards personal and financial security. Accurate recall of past decisions produces solutions to current uncertainties. Demonstration of just, fair-minded thinking disarms those capable of enmity and undermining actions. Purposeful, resourceful actions, boosted by obvious will power, evoke rewarding activity in work requiring disciplined thinking.

⋆ Where chart subject's training or circumstances are appropriate, this transiting aspect generates:
- Satisfactory outcome in matters concerning speculation or undercover investigations

- Successes in introducing reformative measures in public or personal affairs
- Advancement in technical work

Saturn/Pluto Square or Opposition *Event Prognosis: Dubious, Stressful*
t♄□♇ : t♄☍♇ :
This is a time when danger appears from concealed sources, threatening possible intimidation by unscrupulous or downright dishonest individuals. Problems proliferate if moves involving borrowing or lending money are carried out. Peculiar fears and premonitions create continuing anxiety, extending even into sexual life. Family battles can develop in use or distribution of shared or jointly-held assets and crystallize into harsh, unkind behaviour. Best to clear the mind of irrational doubts and base actions on upright, equitable attitudes.

⋆ Where chart subject's training or circumstances are appropriate, this transiting aspect generates:
- Risks of serious losses of prestige in career
- Attempts at emotional blackmail from opponents
- Sexual frustration and reduced physical powers

Now, we've looked at Saturn in his three categories of transit action—by Cycle: by house: by aspect—take your own chart and complete the Saturn Transit Sheet blank in this chapter for the future period you wish to examine in the same style as example. But don't draw any final conclusions yet. Saturn's transits are simply our first consideration—the basis of the framework in Future Life Trend Forecasting.

The next move is to tackle Pluto. Also known as the 'Great Transformer', we'll see why he gained that title and how his transit patterns add further depths and perspective to coming events—in the next chapter.

Quick Reference Check-Points for Chapter 3

Prophecy by Personality

Rasputin, the sinister peasant-prophet of pre-revolutionary Russia, whose clairvoyant powers raised him from an obscure Siberian villager to personal counsellor to the last of the Tsars was *not*—according to his latest biographer—a clairvoyant at all. His supposedly supernatural faculties derived from no more than an unerring skill in reading character by which he deduced the future actions of others.

Since this approach accords exactly with my own view of forecasting and the techniques set out in this book, Rasputin's successes serve to prove my point. It is not known if he studied astrology. Probably not as he was barely literate. He apparently relied on highly-developed natural powers of observation and perception. You can achieve the same accuracy. In character reading and future forecasting by means of the horoscope chart.

Once you thoroughly understand the character of your chart subjects through meticulous study of their natal patterns, you don't need to be a clairvoyant to 'see' their futures. You *know* whether they'll be capable of grasping an opportunity, rising to an occasion or even stooping to underhand means to achieve their ends. You *know* what their ambitions/goals are or are not. You *know*—when transiting planets promise gains or warn against errors—how they'll handle the situations triggered.

Transits—like happiness—mean different things to different people. Some welcome chances to pit their strengths against unpleasant, perhaps dangerous events. Others crumble at the first sign of thwarting. Their natal charts will tell you who is who.

Dialogue with a Self-Deceiver

The low, nervous voice on the other end of the phone quickly identified itself as that of a very jittery young man who had once buttonholed me—chart in hand—after one of my lectures.

'I want to put an ad in the paper that I'm a professional astrologer but I don't want to go to gaol!' the voice blurted out.

'What's going to goal got to do with practising as an astrologer?' I asked, astonished.

'Well, I don't want to get caught for breaking the law. I'm not a trained astrologer and I haven't got any experience. I'm just sick of my job. It's boring and I'm too good for it. I've read a few astrology books . . .—naming some works by leading authors—. . .but they're all pretty stupid. I can do it better.'

'If you've no training and no experience, why do you think you know better than authors who've been practising astrology for years?'

'I just do!'

Regrettably, this young man represents one type of individual who wants to become an astrologer for all the wrong reasons. And I'm sure he had no idea of how much damning information he was giving away about himself by saying what he did. I've run across many like him. Often visibly neurotic, they deliberately or unwittingly deceive themselves as to their own motivations which (as the above dialogue shows) are a sticky mix of ego-tripping, misplaced intellectual arrogance and dreams of what they fondly believe is 'easy money'.

One of their identifying features is their attempt to discredit established authorities. Perhaps, to disguise their own ignorance or big-note themselves. The first author this young man called 'stupid' has been a world figure in the field of astrological science for more than twenty years. Another hallmark is their overwhelming, even aggressive, negativism, which they invariably project into their dealings with clients, vehemently prophesying disasters and calamities by the score. Added to that, they are self-absorbed and so invariably lack objectivity in analysis. They deceive themselves and thus it follows—as night the day—they cannot help deluding others.

Watch out for these types if you plan to seek the services of an astrologer yourself. Don't hesitate to ask for particulars of qualifications and experience. If your questions are dodged, look elsewhere. Australia, and I believe many other countries, have organizations which regularly hold examinations in astrology and will not allow membership until students have acquired the necessary qualifications.

These organizations do all they can to police the activities of outright charlatans as well as untrained 'practitioners' who make fraudulent claims or behave unethically. However, at present there are no legal bars to unqualified individuals falsely claiming to be professional astrologers—in Australia and presumably elsewhere—so astrological organizations have little power to enforce their regulations.

Hopefully this will change. In the meantime, the damage done to other people's lives and the science itself by the either incompetent or unscrupulous types goes on and adds up to a never-ending battle for all skilled, responsible practitioners. Not only must we fight ceaselessly against the prejudice and ignorance of those sections of the populace who wouldn't know one end of the horoscope chart from the other, yet take it on themselves to loudly denounce astrology. (These are 'the enemy outside the gates'—so to speak. And happily, as public awareness increases their number is dropping dramatically.) But we must also struggle to defeat the lowering of work standards caused by the insidious undermining of a small, ever-growing army of fakes, fools and ego-trippers—'the enemy within'.

The Saturnine Look

As a teenager, I devoured piles of rather bad romantic novels in which the strong, silent hero was usually described as looking 'dark and saturnine'. Then, I wasn't quite sure what 'saturnine' meant. Later, of course, I realized it was just one more example of how the planets have given their names to everyday terms describing temperament or appearance. For example: 'sunny' disposition (solar traits strong): 'mooning about' (moon traits strong): 'mercurial' nature (Mercury traits strong): 'jovial' manner (Jupiter traits strong—Jove being another name for the god after which the planet was named).

The *Oxford English Dictionary* defines 'saturnine' as 'of gloomy temperament or looks'. Many people born under the sign of Capricorn, which Saturn rules, certainly fit this description as do those where Saturn is powerfully positioned in their natal charts.

Gloom, too, is undoubtedly the common mood of anyone experiencing pressure from a heavy Saturn transit. Life does take on a darker hue in those periods but we can lighten the picture immeasurably if we remind ourselves that we're merely being forced to face facts. Often unpalatable but always instructive!

Tailoring to Measure

As you can see from reading the Saturn transit interpretations in this chapter, the variety of events which can stem from them is close to multitudinous. But in accurate forecasting, you must learn to be *selective*—to move from the general to the particular—choosing from the transit lists the type of events which are *possible* in the life of your chart subject.

For example, any transit pattern which promises successes in technological work is not going to produce that result if your chart subject is a professional dancer. Such a person would have neither the skills nor the interest. Or, a transit pattern which threatens set-backs in political affairs will offer a useful warning for someone aspiring to become a member of parliament but be quite meaningless for an average housewife.

Thus it is always of paramount importance to consider occupation, age, standard of education, ambitions, and the capacities shown by the natal chart before making any future-oriented statement. When talking to students, I often liken the process to making a hand-tailored suit. If you examine such a suit, you'll observe that not only has an enormous amount of preparatory measurement and detailed work gone into the tailoring, but also that is made to fit *only* the person who ordered it. The same goes for transit interpretations. They must be 'hand-tailored' to fit!

A Shoulder to Cry On

As the world moves into the Age of Aquarius, all the ancient Piscean Age values are being ripped open, turned upside down and starkly discredited. Family life, economic systems, time-honoured political dogma are all being hurled into the dust as Uranus races us to the brink of what Aldous Huxley once labelled the 'Brave New World'.

The result? Chaos in the human psyche because nobody knows where they are going anymore or who (if anybody) cares about them. But, despite the ever-deepening gloom, astrology can offer us all a strong shoulder to cry on and remind us there *is* always a beacon on the top of the darkest mountain. Hence, I feel, that astrology's role as a counselling science will become constantly more emphasized. Especially since a sympathetic practitioner is always prepared to consider attentively a client's problems, thereafter offering practical and realistic ways of dealing with each one.

Further, Future Life Trend Forecasting when handled positively will renegerate hope and motivation by demonstrating that nothing bad lasts forever, although it often feels like that at the time. Not even the most horrendous problem, not even the grimmest state of affairs. *And, what's more, the actual dates when the dark days will be over can be clearly and confidently stated.*

Chart Key:
* 't' at right—'transiting'
* Circled figures (1)=reference on Transit Sheet
* Small uncircled figures=house position.

Saturn Cycles and Aspects

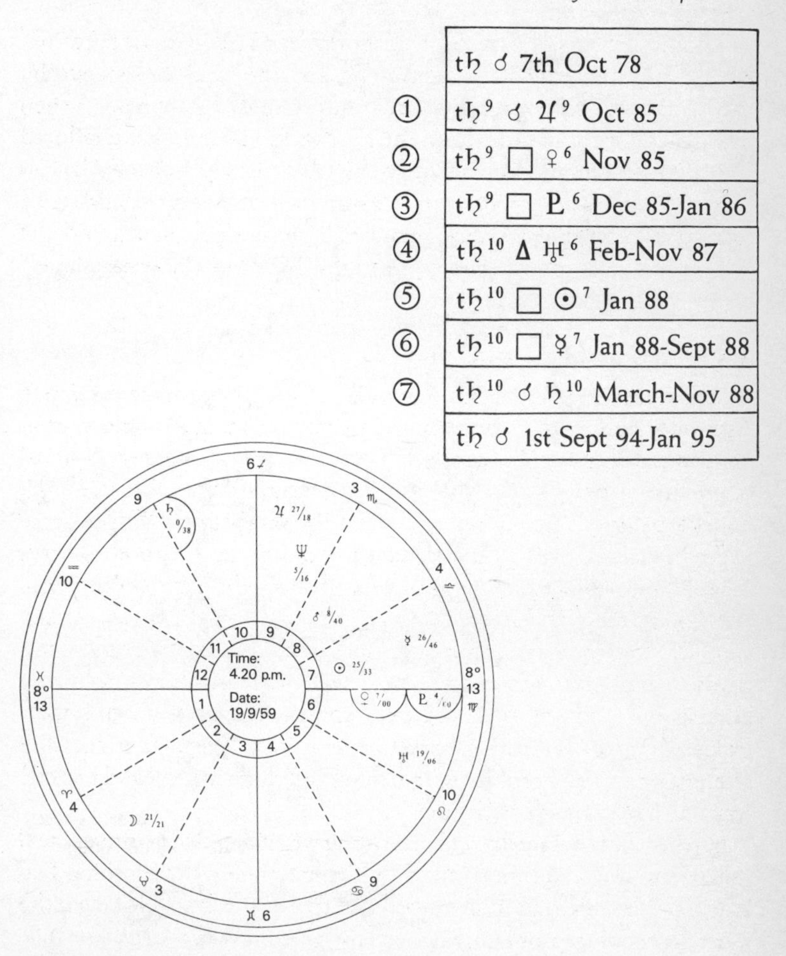

	t♄ ☌ 7th Oct 78
①	t♄^{9} ☌ ♃^{9} Oct 85
②	t♄^{9} □ ♀^{6} Nov 85
③	t♄^{9} □ ♇^{6} Dec 85-Jan 86
④	t♄^{10} △ ♅^{6} Feb-Nov 87
⑤	t♄^{10} □ ☉^{7} Jan 88
⑥	t♄^{10} □ ☿^{7} Jan 88-Sept 88
⑦	t♄^{10} ☌ ♄^{10} March-Nov 88
	t♄ ☌ 1st Sept 94-Jan 95

Name: Claire Costumier
Born: 4.20 p.m. 19/9/59

Saturn Example Transit Sheet — Chart of Clare Costumier

FUTURE LIFE TRENDS: Years examined–1985 to 1988

SATURN TRANSIT SHEET:
(*Reminder Note:* The planet Saturn always promotes events which *consistently* require you to apply serious, responsible and concentrated effort to gain best results. It is a strongly disciplining influence with regard to the attainment of your goals and objectives.)

Long-Range Saturn Effect:

Time Spans Involved in Current Cycle: Achievement Cycle–1978 to 1986.

Effect of Cycle: Good results from applied effort. Career boosts.

Time Spans Involved in Current House Position: 9th–83 to 86: 10th–86 to 89.

Effect of House Transit: Developmental for this chart subject. Had obtained career qualifications to age 20 in 1979 so was able to use Achievement Cycle to best advantage. Type of career in film/theatre costuming benefits from travel. Had saved money well to utilize travel opportunity.

Comments in Brief: From Saturn standpoint, both career and overall life experience should both benefit. Some caution necessary in late 85 and during 88 due to Saturn aspects. Should experience satisfying sense of achievement–Jan-Oct 86. Commencement of stabilization cycle in 86 and continuing to Jan 95.

Current Saturn Effect:

Time Spans Involved for Each Transit Aspect: ① Oct 85: ② Nov 85: ③ Dec 85-Jan 86: ④ Feb-Nov 87: ⑤ Jan 88: ⑥ Jan-Sept 88: ⑦ Mar-Nov 88.

Effect of Major Operative Aspects: Some pros and cons here. May expect too-easy results though opportunities arise (1&2). Work-related trouble likely by contact with unreliable persons (3). Better handling of career and boosted creativity (4). Clash between career and males (possible love/marriage partners) indicated (5). Needs to watch egotistical thinking in all partnerships (6). Onset of full maturity with decision as to opposing life choices necessary.

Comments in Brief: Interesting pattern for young, attractive female. Transit effects overall suggest close relationships with foreigners, possibly marriage or its equivalent. Natal chart shows contrary mix of naivety, perfectionism and push for own way. (Pisces Asc./Virgo Sun./Aries Moon.) Events will test these attitudes.

Saturn Example Transit Sheet

FUTURE LIFE TRENDS:

SATURN TRANSIT SHEET:

(*Reminder Note:* The planet Saturn always promotes events which consistently require you to apply serious, responsible and concentrated effort to gain best results. It is a strongly disciplining influence with regard to the attainment of your goals and objectives.)

Long-Range Saturn Effect:

Time Spans Involved in Current Cycle:

Effect of Cycle:

Time Spans Involved in Current Position:

Effect of House Transit:

Comments in Brief:...

....

....

....

Current Saturn Effect:

Time Spans Involved for Each Transit Aspect:

Effect of Major Operative Aspects:

Comments in Brief:...

....

....

....

Such knowledge alone is a great comfort to someone caught in a problem patch (and this happens to all of us), bringing a feeling of reassurance and new beginnings. 'Comfort' and 'reassurance' are words that should be written on every counsellor's heart in letters of fire. I don't mean false comfort or sugary reassurance, of course. No use patting the client on the head and telling them not to worry when a love affair's fallen heart-rendingly apart, the house has burned to the ground or a retrenchment notice has turned up in the pay packet. The counsellor's task is to show that there is a way out of every problem, to direct the client towards the right solution and explain how the future planetary movements will light the way to better days.

Chapter Four

The Super-Slow-Moving Planets— Their Role in Long-Range Life Changes

Having watched Saturn directing the *visible* pattern of events, our next move is to delve deep beneath the surface to unearth the *concealed* reasons why crucial changes happen in every life. This exercise requires digging down into subconscious motivations. . .the dark, uncharted territory of Pluto. Then searching for the spirit which moves each human being to act. . .the shadowy, incorporeal realm of Neptune. For no single transiting planet is ever responsible for the births, deaths or marriages of our most important hopes, desires and ambitions. These occur in each life story from a complex interplay of forces which not only deliver the opportunity but also the inclination to make this move or that.

After all, if you look behind a dramatic event, you'll perceive you don't suddenly decide to wed or throw over one way of life for a radically different one *just* because somebody offers you the chance to do so. There's a very long story behind every decisive action that sweeps your feet off the old, well-worn path onto the new. And an equally long list of consequences that flow from such action.

Although this seldom registers in the conscious mind, each momentous, life-transforming decision has a background or preparation which begins at the subconscious level and extends far back in time. Such decisions may seem to emerge without warning—fully-fledged before your eyes—but you can be sure their embryos have been hatching quietly inside your mind for years. A growing, niggling dissatisfaction with your job. . .a gradually intensifying sense of loneliness and losing out on life. . .a developing fear of getting older but getting nowhere much. . .these feelings form the hidden components behind apparently sudden, sometimes drastic decisions.

But why do these big decisions abruptly materialize at one particular date or in one particular year and at one particular stage of your life instead of earlier or later? Simply because the time for a show-down has come. And because you're now ready to confront it.

Pluto—The 'Great Transformer' in Transit

Show-downs in their most literal sense are Pluto's specialty. They result from his transits activating important natal patterns, so we'll observe him in action first. . .through his transiting house positions and transiting aspects.

Not surprisingly when you get to know him, Pluto's show-down style verges on the cataclysmic. Hence the consequences and spin-offs in other life sectors are far from mild. Pluto is out to *transform* your life. Inexorably. Visibly. Sometimes even violently. Which fact, of course, explains how he earned his title. Old ways, old concepts, old desires—if these have been leading you down the wrong path—are ruthlessly uprooted to make room for the new. Pluto announces the times for final endings and fresh beginnings. For destruction followed by regeneration.

However, in Pluto's case we don't have to consider his cycles as we did with Saturn because the planet moves far too slowly. Check the chart of Clare Costumier in Chapter 3 against the ephemeris and you'll observe that Pluto crossed her seventh house cusp in 1960 (when she was aged only 1) and will not cross her tenth house cusp until 1998 (when she will be aged 39). . .which means it will take 38 years for Pluto to travel through her seventh, eighth and ninth houses. More than half the average lifetime! By comparison, Saturn covered the same distance in less than 8 years.

From these comparisons of planetary speeds alone, we can understand immediately why Saturn's average 2½ year sojourn in any house adds up to a shorter, sharper impact—not unlike a rap on the knuckles. Pluto, on the other hand, has all the time in the world to create whatever 'renovations' deemed necessary in the house he is transiting. Anywhere between 10 and 20 years. So his impact gathers force slowly until it erupts into radical, extreme changes in life direction—best likened to the rumblings that go on for years before a volcano finally blows its core.

Although Saturn never spares the rod in enforcing discipline in every life, Pluto doesn't bother with anything so rudimentary. He's concerned with bringing far-reaching changes at the gut level. In our most deeply-felt convictions and concepts as to what living is all about. And he doesn't take 'no' for an answer. Pick up your own chart right now and see for yourself. Note the date when Pluto entered a particular house and when he left it so you can do a 'before-and-after' check.

To illustrate: Let's say Pluto entered the tenth house (career/objectives) in 1959 and left it in 1975 as the planet did in one of my chart subjects. During those 16 years, this woman changed her personal aims radically and the actual profession in which she was working no less than three times. The final career choice was so far removed from and so wildly at odds with her 1959 ideas, she admitted that if she'd been told her final professional destination in the late fifties, she would have refused to believe it.

Certainly, the above is a particularly vivid example of Pluto at work but it is far from unique. Think carefully about your own Pluto house transits by dating them and documenting their events. You'll see how totally and fundamentally they changed your beliefs and concepts within the life sector the planet was affecting.

New Frontiers of Perception. . .Or. . .New Maps of Hell

That heading may sound a little heavy-handed at first glance but Pluto *is* heavy-handed in the 'either/or' events he presents. The scene is invariably out of the all-or-nothing genre. You *either* throw yourself into making and accepting the required changes, which undoubtedly demand a greatly heightened and far less materialistic perception of your life purpose. *Or* you'll find all hell let loose around you *until* you do.

To understand why Pluto-generated changes have such a climactic effect, we need to remember that they derive from the subconscious mind. That deep gut of being wherein lie all our long-lost memories, unrealized hopes, irrational fears and more fevered imaginings.

Astrologically speaking, the subconscious is the domain of Pluto. Mythologically speaking, Pluto was the ancient Greco-Roman god of Hades—the gloomy abode of the dead. (A pre-Christian version of Hell.) This dark, subterranean underworld was a place into which the light of day never penetrated and from which no-one ever returned.

In many ways, the above equates pretty well to the psychological definition of the subconscious mind and serves to remind us that—as with the twelve signs of the Zodiac—none of the planets was named at random. Remember the basic mythology surrounding the gods or goddesses from whom the planets take their names and you're well on the way to understanding the kind of influence they exercise over past and future events.

In the case of Pluto, the naming was notably apt. For in the dark 'underworld' of the subconscious, we try to bury everything about ourselves which the conscious mind rejects. Sins (real or imagined), sexual hang-ups, ugly or frightening desires—all those parts of our personalities we'd rather not know about or even admit—are buried deeply there in the hope that they'll never return to the light of day either.

They don't stay buried, of course. . .as any practising psychiatrist can tell you. They come back to haunt us in the guise of disturbing dreams, strange fears in the night, even odd or peculiar habits. Think of Shakespeare's Lady Macbeth and her obsessive washing of her hands. Her conscious mind could see they were clean but her subconscious, fermenting with guilt, continually re-stained them with the blood of the murdered king.

In far less grisly ways, something akin to that happens to all of us when we try to repress the truth about ourselves. That is why we have to force ourselves to peer down into that dark subterranean region and face what we find there.

Pluto, in his transits and aspects, instigates events which oblige us to do just that—look at gut-level truths. And when he is pressing for this result, it's no use saying to yourself: 'I don't want to think about that! I won't talk about that! I'll pretend that never happened!' Especially if 'that' refers to some wrong you believe you have done to yourself or to others.

As a psychiatrist colleague of mine once put it. 'We must go down into the depths, meet the monsters of the subconscious mind without fear, pat them on their heads and say 'Hi, Kids'. Do that and they have no further power to hurt or destroy us.' A somewhat unconventional style of stating it but nevertheless true. (I might add that this doctor told me he had studied astrological science and found it an invaluable tool in diagnosing psychiatric disorders.)

Pluto's transits and aspects generate events which help you to break through the subconscious barriers into new frontiers of perception. New ways of looking at your role in life. New views of your past and future. Often this greatly heightened perception will reveal that some past misdeed (for which you may have been subconsciously punishing yourself for years) did not deserve the heavy load of guilt it invoked. Perhaps, you did no wrong at all. Or, if you did, you'll perceive how you can right it and thus make peace with yourself.

Conversely, those who stubbornly refuse to cross the new frontiers of perception Pluto offers find themselves staring at new and more frightening maps of hell. Their own private hells, of course, where they burn themselves up with repressed anger, guilt and self-recrimination. Tormenting themselves by blaming fate or other people for their own miseries. A grim and gloomy scene. Just an unpleasant as if they'd actually landed in the dark underworld of the ancient myths.

This was the sort of inner abyss a successful, 30-year-old business woman condemned herself to when—following a sudden marriage—she suffered miscarriage after miscarriage. The best specialists agreed there was nothing wrong with her reproductive organs. The problem was inside her head. She did want a child but she did *not* want to abandon her thriving business, although she would not consciously admit this to herself or her husband.

Subconsciously, she saw a child as an ongoing burden. A never-ending responsibility which would put paid to her career. A discontented, very negative woman friend had added fuel to these doubts by endlessly complaining her own life had been ruined since she had a baby. There was no acceptable way my client could justify to herself her wish to continue working since her husband was even richer than she was. Yet with many planets in Gemini, the thought of becoming what she called a 'stay-at-home-Mum' was intolerable.

As usual—with Pluto transiting her fifth house (children/conditions after marriage)—the subconscious had taken control. It allowed her 'to do the right thing' by her marriage vows by becoming pregnant, then promptly got rid of the babies through repeated miscarriages.

Her endless trips to hospital, plummeting sexual desire and mental anguish were tearing her apart. The answer was ridiculously simple. Even when I put it to her, I was amazed that her guilt, fear and mental confusion had multiplied to the point she had not thought of such an obvious solution herself. 'Tell your husband frankly about your fears of motherhood. Train an assistant now and let her run the business under your supervision for a while before and after the baby is born. Later, employ a live-in nurse to help you care for your child.' Within ten months, she was the mother of a healthy young son and had had no sign of trouble throughout the pregnancy.

I've set out this story in some detail to stress the power of the subconscious over the physical body as well as the mind. And further, the significance of Pluto's transits in compelling us to dig deeper and deeper until we unearth the true story beneath the problem situations we've embroiled ourselves in.

Pluto House Transits—Lights in the Dark

Wherever Pluto is situated in the natal chart, there is a continuing sense of being *compelled*—of being forced into dealing head-on with the affairs of that life sector. Along with this comes a feeling of stumbling in the dark. As if you are being dragged towards something you cannot see and probably don't want to meet anyway. Yet you cannot resist the force that's taken hold of you.

During his transits, Pluto throws shafts of light into this darkness—*if* you're prepared to apply the highest degree of self-honesty as to your own motivations and expectations. Indeed, your willingness to accept the stark truth about yourself determines how easily or uneasily you run the obstacle race of Plutonic experiences.

Maybe, your natal chart shows the type of work you've trained yourself to do isn't right for you. A particular Pluto transit will focus a spot-light on your discontent, creating events that force the necessary changes.

Maybe your natal chart shows you've been avoiding marriage or permanent union because you're secretly afraid of failure. Again a particular Pluto transit will initiate relationships that force you to admit this and alter your attitude. You can try to refuse the challenges but you won't get away with it. Pluto-style events will merely pile on the tension till you've *got* to act! He's not concerned with small modifications in life direction. He's pushing for sweeping, right-off-the board changes.

When dating Pluto transits, you'll need to use the little book of *Pluto*

Tables mentioned in Chapter 3. Stick to the interpretation rules set out in that chapter too. This habit will ensure you never make the fatal mistake of isolating Pluto-generated events from the natal chart and other current planetary patterns.

As you work your way through the following concise descriptions of the effect of Pluto's transits through each of the twelve houses, remember your mental image of the planet as the 'Great Transformer'. This will help to set in your mind that optimum results from each Pluto house transit flow from digging deep into the gut of being, accepting what you find there and redirecting your life on the strength of that knowledge. Look for the shaft of light in the darkness and the transit will profoundly develop your faith in yourself: turn your eyes away from it and the enveloping darkness will grow blacker still.

For an illustration of Pluto Transits at work on an actual life history, check the 'Pluto Example Transit Sheet' for our chart subject—Clare Costumier—at the end of this section. With it is also a blank you can use for your own Pluto transit summaries.

FIRST HOUSE PLUTO TRANSIT EVENTS . . .
radically alter self image and personal environment.

Positive Responses Promote	• Increased sense of independence. • Opportunities to express individuality. • Marked improvement in self-presentation. • Resourcefulness in exchanging old life styles for new.
Negative Responses Invite	• Irrational, obsessive behaviour. • Attempts to dominate associates. • Egotistical demand for personal freedom without regard for others. • Wrong actions emanating from subconscious compulsions.

SECOND HOUSE PLUTO TRANSIT EVENTS . . .
radically alter earning power and use of own moneys.

Positive Responses Promote	• Profitable changes in source of income. • Added capacity to acquire money and possessions. • Radical alteration in financial expectations. • Wise business decisions leading to greater independence.
Negative Responses Invite	• Upheavals in business partnerships. • Break-ups caused by dictatorial demands involving money. • Lowered living standards due to financial failure. • Severe reversals through over-acquisitive pursuit of money.

THIRD HOUSE PLUTO TRANSIT EVENTS . . .
radically alter mental attitudes and educational skills.

Positive Responses Promote	• Deep-rooted changes in all forms of intellectual activity. • Profitable interest in further education. • New directions in personal relationships through sweeping changes in thinking. • Regenerated mental perspective from increased awareness.
Negative Responses Invite	• Crises and clashes between old and newly-forming concepts. • Serious disturbances if superficial values are retained.

- Disorienting confrontations with siblings or associates through faulty communication.
- Defeats through stubborn or reactionary attitudes.

FOURTH HOUSE PLUTO TRANSIT EVENTS . . .
radically alter domestic circumstances and home atmosphere

Positive Responses Promote	• Release from unhappy or hampering home situations. • Enlightened recognition of effect of childhood conditioning. • Beneficial changes in domestic scene or place of residence. • Strenghtened position of authority within the home.
Negative Responses Invite	• Clashes with intimates through misguided attempts to reform them. • Regressive behaviour from inability to free the self from inappropriate childhood conditioning. • Hostile home atmosphere emanating from autocratic behaviour. • Loss or alienation of important relatives.

FIFTH HOUSE PLUTO TRANSIT EVENTS . . .
radically alter romantic liaisons, concern with children, creative talents.

Positive Responses Promote	• Fervent romantic or sexual liaisons. • Revised, more co-operative conduct with children. • Burgeoning of creative talent with gaïnful results.

	• Renewed interest in satisfying pleasures or speculative ventures.
Negative Responses Invite	• Flare-ups with children or romantic partners through attempts to over-control. • Pursuit of personal pleasures to point of folly. • Trickery or underhand scheming by intimates. • Attractions to unsuitable or manipulative individuals.

SIXTH HOUSE PLUTO TRANSIT EVENTS . . .
radically alter working environment, health concerns.

Positive Responses Promote	• Profound changes in attitude to work. • Revitalized physical strengths and adoption of good health regimen. • Insight into work procedures and expectations of colleagues. • Beneficial changes in working environment.
Negative Responses Invite	• Tensions and health problems through uncongenial working conditions. • Unwise changes in career direction caused by irrational dissatisfaction. • Formation of dangerous or destructive habits affecting health. • Involvement in work-related plotting and behind-the-scenes conspiracies.

EIGHTH HOUSE PLUTO TRANSIT EVENTS . . .
radically alter joint/shared financial liabilities and handling of deceased estate assets.

Positive Responses Promote

- Financial benefits through inheritance or division of assets.
- Increased insight into handling joint/shared moneys.
- Wise investment in business projects of inherited moneys or family gifts.
- Intensified awareness of meaning of life through deaths of associates.

Negative Responses Invite

- Financial disasters through unwise borrowing.
- Involvement in dangerous occult or psychic practices.
- Exploitation or emotional blackmail by creditors.
- Feuds over shared moneys caused by autocratic demands.

NINTH HOUSE PLUTO TRANSIT EVENTS . . .
radically alter involvements with foreigners, travel decisions.

Positive Responses Promote

- Advantageous changes in personal philosophy through exposure to foreigners/foreign cultures.
- Life-changing experiences through travel and furthering education.
- Revived interest in religions and ideologies.
- Replacement of old intellectual concerns with new values.

Negative Responses Invite

- Dangerous or difficult confrontations with foreign invididuals/foreign ideas.
- Rejections by others through refusal to integrate in new environments.

	• Losses or disappointments during long-distance travels. • Attraction to strange religious activities and false prophets.

TENTH HOUSE PLUTO TRANSIT EVENTS . . .
radically alter career aims and personal status.

Positive Responses Promote	• Complete, possibly several, changes in career directions through radical reassessment of aims. • Added status in community from boosted personal skills. • Aids to advancement from superiors or authority figures. • Application of intelligence and willpower to achieve lasting recognition.
Negative Responses Invite	• Ruthless pursuit of own ends at expense of others. • Emergence of compulsive power-seeking attitudes, leading to own downfall. • Use of unethical means to gain control over business associates. • Reversals from refusal to accept wise advice.

ELEVENTH HOUSE PLUTO TRANSIT EVENTS . . .
radically alter friendships and involvement in group activities.

Positive Responses Promote	• Aid from influential, forward-looking friends and wider range of friendships. • Achievement of deeply-felt hopes and long-held wishes. • Mentally regenerating involvement in

worthwhile group activities.
- Assistance for own projects from governmental sources.

Negative Responses Invite
- Association with undesirable or false friends.
- Severance of links with discerning, informed individuals in favour of good-time seekers.
- Attraction to secret societies and subversive movements.
- Disappointments in gaining desired goal through undue influence or bad advice from intimates.

TWELFTH HOUSE PLUTO TRANSIT EVENTS . . .
radically alter spiritual viewpoint and capacity for self-sacrifice.

Positive Responses Promote
- Graphic recall of past life through dreams and mental flashes to release repressed memories.
- Eradication of outworn or inappropriate self-image.
- Increased awareness of own subconscious motivations with ability to monitor them.
- Gradual emergence of new personal environment after dissolution of old.

Negative Responses Invite
- Appearance of secret enemies or revelations of own past misdeeds.
- Isolation and loneliness through previous alienation of friends/intimates.
- Peculiar illnesses or ailments of psychosomatic origin.
- Addiction to health-endangering habits or degenerate life styles.

That takes care of Pluto's twelve house transits and the relentless probing of the dark terrain of the subconscious mind their events bring about. In many ways, they do amount to a descent into the gloomy underworld of being but always hand us torches to light our way.

There is, of course, nothing hurried about the life-transforming changes they press towards. Like the Mills of God, they grind slowly but they also grind exceeding small. It is vital to remember, however, that no human being—as noted earlier in this chapter—can experience all twelve of Pluto's house transits. You have to belong to the centenarian-plus set to live through even half of them as it takes the planet the best part of 300 years to travel through all the signs of the Zodiac.

Thus—even more carefully than with the Saturn house transits—it is important to take into consideration the *present* age of yourself and your chart subjects. Then you'll be able to assess the number of houses Pluto has already traversed in past years as well as those he is likely to reach in the normal lifetime.

Clearly, if a very young person or child experiences—say, Pluto's transit of the seventh house—well before the age when marriage or permanent partnerships are possible, that person will emerge into maturity with a vastly changed view of what union demands.

Compare our specimen chart of Clare Costumier in Chapter 3. Pluto began to move into her seventh when she was only 14 months old. He did not leave it until she had passed through puberty and was 15 years old. What effect did this have on her adult attitude to marriage or its equivalent? Tremendous! The marriage of her parents was not a happy one: her Pisces Ascendant made her acutely aware of this even in earliest childhood: as a very young adult, she consciously welcomed suitors while subconsciously rejecting them. Pluto had made an indelible mark. Through the events he presented in the shape of her parents' slowly disintegrating partnership, he ensured she would never enter into marriage lightly or repeat their mistakes.

Now, check your own charts and note down your conclusions as to the effect of past Pluto house transits. Observe the slow yet radical and extreme changes in thinking and expectations these have engendered. You'll find this exercise highly illuminating.

Our next step is, of course, to examine the aspects Pluto makes to other planets during his lengthy transits. Remember, in years when no transiting aspects appear Pluto's house position by transit will continue to promote events appropriate to the affairs of that house. However, when he does make transiting aspects, the event picture sharpens in focus. The need for decisions becomes more urgent.

As we saw the Saturn in Chapter 3, the effect of transit aspects depends on whether the planet Pluto encounters is friendly or hostile towards him.

Follow the same procedure as in Chapter 3 also.

- Look for conjunctions, trines, sextiles, squares and oppositions.
- Check the orb or effectiveness.
- Fill out your Pluto Transit Sheets.
- Observe Pluto's transiting aspects operate for much longer periods than Saturn's.
- Note that Pluto can never repeat the same aspect to the same natal planet more than once in the human life-span in any chart—except during retrograde motion.

This last point is of special significance and shows up vividly when you contrast the occurrence of Saturn's transiting aspects with those of Pluto in the following manner.

Since Saturn moves through all the signs of the Zodiac in about 29½ years, everyone who lives past the age of 30 will have experienced each one of the Saturn transit aspects once. Those who reach and pass age 60 will experience them all twice and possibly three times as they move towards their nineties. With the increasing average life-spans of the late twentieth century, it is likely that an even larger slice of the population will face Saturn transit aspects for the third time around.

Thus it is advisable to examine each Saturn aspect in detail. Especially in the case of older chart subjects so their responses to a repeated transit many years later in their lives can be compared to their original reaction to it. Have they learned from the first one? Or are they going to make the same old mistakes?

This repetition of transiting aspects does not occur with the three heaviest planets—Pluto, Neptune and Uranus. They move far too slowly. For example, Saturn can reach a conjunction with his own natal position up to three times in very long-lived individuals. Neither Pluto (who requires approximately 248 years to return to his natal position) nor Neptune (who requires approximately 165 years to do the same) could even remotely approach it during the human life-span. Even Uranus rarely manages it. A person would have to be around age 84 for this to happen. Therefore the sort of response comparisons we make with repeating Saturn transiting aspects (as in Chapter 3) cannot be applied to Pluto, Neptune or Uranus.

Indeed, it is not possible for transiting Pluto ever to make conjunction aspects to some natal planets in certain charts for example. Let's say you were born with Sun/Mercury in Gemini and Pluto in Leo. Pluto could never reach a transiting Pluto/natal Sun or transiting Pluto/natal Mercury conjunction even in the longest lifetime.

Interpretation Format for Slower-Moving Planets

Due to the factors just discussed, the Transiting Aspect Interpretation Tables for the slow-movers will be set out in a more compact format than those we've seen for Saturn. This format has been devised to bypass as much as possible the noticeably repetitious statements employed to describe the various transits in many textbooks.

Some writings tend to use virtually identical phrases or very similar wording in interpretations of all major aspects made by the transits of the slow-movers to each natal planet. This practice, though hard to avoid, makes for monotonous reading. To save endless repetition, I've grouped all major transiting Pluto aspects into ten short sections . . .one for each of the ten natal planets.

Always remember that an apparently helpful transit does not automatically bring happy results, any more than an apparently difficult transit automatically brings disasters. Much depends on how the individual experiencing it handles the events implied thereby.

Remember too, (as we saw with Saturn) to be *selective* in choosing interpretations from the Event Projection Tables. Allow always for your chart subject's natal patterns and personal circumstances in deciding which type of projected events are possible and which could not—at any stretch of the imagination—apply to him/her.

To cover the full range of possible events in the endless variety of human lives, transit interpretations have to be couched in fairly general terms. The skilled analyst's task is to *particularize* them to suit the chart subject's needs and life direction.

To help you make the best use of the ten sections in each set of Transit Interpretation Tables, I've added a short reminder note on the combined influences of the transiting planet and natal planet in every case. This ensures you understand *the precise type of energies* being blended by the transit every time you check your tables. Recognition of the effect of these energies can easily be missed by new students, especially as many textbooks do not include reminder notes. Yet failure to understand the nature of the planets contacting each other during transits leads to serious errors in event interpretation.

Aspect Checklist. . .All Major Planetary Transits

1. *CONJUNCTIONS* between a *transiting planet and any natal planet* infer events—within the range described in Interpretation Tables—which are designed to introduce change and challenge in their *most intense forms.*

   The conjunction is the most direct contact possible between two planets. Both are in the same sign and in the immediate vicinity of each other.
2. *TRINES or SEXTILES* between a *transiting planet and any natal planet* present change and challenge within the same event range but encourage *easier adjustment* thereto.

   The trine or sextile demonstrate comfortable combining of the two planetary energies. Both are in compatible signs.
3. *SQUARES or OPPOSITIONS* between a *transiting planet and any natal planet* promise the same type of events but provide *constant conflict* as forcibly changing inner needs collide with the thrust of the ego.

   The square or opposition are the most awkward kinds of contact between the two planetary energies. Both are in incompatible signs.

Note: Clearly the tougher Transiting Planetary Aspects (such as squares and oppositions) are more likely to promote the more unpleasant events listed in the Event Projection Tables, but even the easier aspects (such as trines, sextiles and some conjunctions) can bring trouble if the natal chart suggests resistance to the thrust for change.

Pluto Transit Aspects—Interpretation Table

Transiting Pluto Aspecting Natal Sun

Energy Blend: Transformation/Personal Goals

Reminder Note: the *natal Sun* in every chart reveals the basic ego thrust . . .the true, unalterable self. . .the workings of the conscious mind.

Pluto in every chart points to the gut feelings. . .the unrecognized urges and desires. . .the workings of the subconscious mind.

Thus all contacts between transiting Pluto and the natal Sun—whether by conjunction, trine, sextile, square or opposition—create varying degrees of change and/or conflict between what *the ego* wants for itself and what *the subconscious mind* is striving to express through it.

The purpose of these transits is to search out and destroy self-made blocks to character development. Bent on change, even to the point of shattering the very foundations of the self and its image, Pluto can wreak havoc of earthquake proportions through events if the ego resists such changes.

Pluto/Sun Event Projection

Anyone experiencing these transits faces incidents and situations designed to:

- Uproot outdated ambitions, established concepts, outgrown life styles.
- Destroy notably egotistical objectives and self-centred planning.
- Induce power struggles with authority figures or power-seeking intimates/associates.
- Create opportunities to demonstrate leadership skills if not based on egotistical aims.
- Expose latent tendencies to dominate or coerce others.

Pluto/Sun Transit Management

Anyone experiencing these transits is strongly advised to:

- Apply firm restraint on self-seeking or desire for self-aggrandisement.
- Respond readily to newly-emerging inner needs rather than attempting to force issues.

- Tackle resolutely unexpected challenges to personal status or life objectives.
- Avoid attempts to intimidate or pressurize others, especially in the work-place.

Transiting Pluto Aspecting Natal Moon

Energy Blend: Transformation/Emotional Needs

Reminder Note: The *natal Moon* in every chart reveals the basic emotional make-up. . .the secret self. . .the imprinted response patterns.

Pluto in every chart points to the gut feelings. . .the unrecognized urges and desires. . .the workings of the subconscious mind.

Thus all contacts between transiting Pluto and the natal Moon—whether by conjunction, trine, sextile, square or opposition—create varying degrees of change and/or conflict between how *the emotions* manifest themselves and what the subconscious mind is striving to express through them.

The purpose of these transits is to lay bare inhibitions and repressions in emotional life, thereby freeing the response mechanisms. As ever, Pluto's demand for change is peremptory, uncompromising. If it is consciously resisted in any close relationship, events may burn out the ties irretrievably.

Pluto/Moon Event Projection

Anyone experiencing these transits faces incidents and situations designed to:

- Force total revision of past or current emotional involvements.
- Reconstruct relationships with females in friendships or family affairs.
- Loosen constricting ties with spouse, love partners or children.
- Induce physical distress/illness if emotions become overreactive.
- Create domestic strife arising out of attempts to force obedience from intimates.

Pluto/Moon Transit Management

Anyone experiencing these transits is strongly adviced to:

- Practise forbearance in all types of emotional duels.

- Seek out origins of own emotional expectations by concentrating on recall of childhood memories.
- Avoid provocative or antagonistic actions in domestic scene, especially if linked with jealousy or possessiveness.
- Base all changes in home or family matters on honest, realistic appraisal of needs of all persons directly concerned.

Transiting Pluto Aspecting Natal Mercury

Energy Blend: Transformation/Mental Interests

Reminder Note: Natal Mercury in every chart reveals the basic mental inclinations. . .type and grade of intellect. . .powers of communication.

Pluto in every chart points to the gut feelings. . .the unrecognized urges and desires. . .the workings of the subconscious mind.

Thus all contacts between transiting Pluto and natal Mercury—whether by conjunction, trine, sextile, square or opposition—create varying degrees of change and/or conflict between how the thought processes operate and what the subconscious mind is striving to express through them.

The purpose of these transits is to revolutionize thinking habits and mental attitudes, thereby opening the mind to new interests, concepts and objectives. Once again, Pluto's thrust for change cannot be ignored. If the thinking mind refuses to move out of its accustomed grooves, events literally jolt it without mercy into broadening its vistas.

Pluto/Mercury Event Projection

Anyone experiencing these transits faces incidents and situations designed to:

- Revolutionize mental attitudes, creating new intellectual interests.
- Promote determination to unearth secrets and root issues underlying major decisions.
- Increase understanding of own mental capacities, entrenched beliefs and personal philosophy.
- Cause fanatical adherence to own opinions and refusal to accept wise advice.
- Induce mental strain by driving the self too hard.

Pluto/Mercury Transit Management
Anyone experiencing these transits is strongly advised to:

- Open the mind to new avenues of thought and education.
- Resist urge to thrust own ideas on others by force.
- Accept realization that former mental attitudes are no longer appropriate.
- Use extreme caution in investigating matters relating to the occult or supernatural phenomena.

Transiting Pluto Aspecting Natal Venus

Energy Blend: Transformation/Affectional Affairs

Reminder Note: Natal Venus in every chart reveals the basic capacities to give and receive affection. . .choice of and attraction to pleasures . . .desire for harmony.

Pluto in every chart points to the gut feelings. . .the unrecognized urges and desires. . .the workings of the subconscious mind.

Thus all contacts between transiting Pluto and natal Venus—whether by conjunction, trine, sextile, square or opposition—create varying degrees of change and/or conflict between how the affections operate and what the subconscious mind is striving to express through them.

The purpose of these transits is to probe down to the deep centres of affectional responses, thereby releasing fears and inhibitions. As before, Pluto's insistence on change is urgent, undeviating. If consciously resisted in any area of love or friendship, events may intensify sense of isolation from anyone close.

Pluto/Venus Event Projection
Anyone experiencing these transits faces incidents and situations designed to:

- Redefine type and depths of relationships sought or encountered.
- Promote intensity of response to point of obsession with a lover or intimate friend.
- Heighten ability to gain pleasure and satisfaction in love, friendships or pastimes.

- Alter existing liaisons through new sensitivity to needs of intimates.
- Cause fanatical or compulsive pursuit of love.

Pluto/Venus Transit Management
Anyone experiencing these transits is strongly advised to:

- Resist tendencies towards overreaction or over-demand in love/friendship.
- Counteract desire to seek pleasure and physical gratification at any cost.
- Examine potential compatibility with care before rushing recklessly into love affairs/friendships.
- Develop latent creative/artistic skills through determined effort.

Transiting Pluto Aspecting Natal Mars

Energy Blend: Transformation/Physical Desires

Reminder Note: *Natal Mars* in every chart reveals the basic physical strengths. . .force and direction of sexual drives. . .degree of natural vitality.

Pluto in every chart points to the gut feelings. . .the unrecognized urges and desires. . .the workings of the subconscious mind.

Thus all contacts between transiting Pluto and natal Mars—whether by conjunction, trine, sextile, square or opposition—create varying degrees of change and/or conflict between how the physical drives operate and what the subconscious mind is striving to express through them.

The purpose of these transits is to force into the open hidden doubts and fears, thereby permitting deepened understanding of sexual appetites and vital energies. Pluto's drive towards change, revelation and transformation is particularly forceful in this most physical life sector. Attempts to mis-channel it inevitably bring events that culminate in private anguish and self-recrimination.

Pluto/Mars Event Projection
Anyone experiencing these transits faces incidents and situations designed to:

- Reconstruct sexual life and use of physical energies through increased vigour.
- Break down deep-rooted repressions emanating from childhood conditioning and disturbing adult sexual behaviour.
- Force confrontations with enemies/rivals over egotistical actions or sexual jealousy.
- Attract undesirable love/sex involvements leading to dangerous or even violent conflicts.
- Undermine personal or work progress through tactics of secret rivals or treacherous opponents.

Pluto/Mars Transit Management
Anyone experiencing these transits is strongly advised to:

- Avoid risk-taking caused by sexual tension, frustration or unexpressed anger.
- Apply powerfully boosted energies to positive self-development rather than provocation of crises.
- Abstain from indulging in underhand schemes or links with undesirables.
- Restrain possessiveness or sexually-based suspicions at all times.

Transiting Pluto Aspecting Natal Jupiter

Energy Blend: Transformation/Personal Expansion

Reminder Note: Natal Jupiter in every chart reveals the basic ability to use opportunities. . .behave with optimism. . .broaden personal horizons.

Pluto in every chart points to the gut feelings. . .the unrecognized urges and desires. . .the workings of the subconscious mind.

Thus all contacts between transiting Pluto and natal Jupiter—whether by conjunction, trine, sextile, square or opposition—create varying degrees of change and/or conflict between innate capacity to use opportunities and how the subconscious mind is striving to direct it.

The purpose of these transits is to release blocks to self-confidence and advancement, thereby encouraging assurance in making use of valuable chances without wilful opportunism. Pluto pushes hard for progressive self-development but never at the expense of others or by means of exploitation. Refusal to break out of confining ruts results in events leading to lost chances and hopes denied.

Pluto/Jupiter Event Projection

Anyone experiencing these transits faces incidents and situations designed to:

- Stimulate confidence and optimism through valuable opportunities.
- Attract offers for advancement in occupational/professional affairs.
- Restrain rashly expansive ambitions, leading to overexertion or pursuit of personal aggrandizement.
- Warn against too forceful assertion of own authority or contempt for cautionary advice.
- Induce changes in use of personal authority or reconstitute religious beliefs.

Pluto/Jupiter Transit Management

Anyone experiencing these transits is strongly advised to:

- Stop, look and listen before leaping into new enterprises or financial transactions.
- Resist desires to pressure others into accepting own beliefs or religious views.
- Respect the rights of intimates/associates to disagree with or question new decisions.
- Assist those in need of help without expecting reward or gratitude.

Transiting Pluto Aspecting Natal Saturn

To avoid repetition, for all aspects between transiting Pluto and natal Saturn, please turn back to Chapter 3 for interpretation of 'transiting Saturn aspecting natal Pluto'.

Conditions, events and responses evident at such times are virtually the same. A difference in emphasis arises from the fact that Pluto/Saturn aspects during transits last far longer and thereby extend their pressure for change over much longer periods in any life.

Further, when Pluto is the directing force, events produce much deeper, more radical changes in both long-held concepts and overall life direction. At these times the cataclysmic, convulsive, uprooting energies of Pluto shake the rock-hard, unyielding disciplinarian forces of Saturn.

Transiting Pluto Aspecting Natal Uranus

Energy Blend: Transformation/Revelation

Reminder Note: *Natal Uranus* in every chart reveals the basic capacity to make or adapt to drastic changes. . .exhibit independence and originality . . .free the self from restrictions.

Pluto in every chart points to the gut feelings. . .the unrecognized urges and desires. . .the workings of the subconscious mind.

Thus all contacts between transiting Pluto and natal Uranus—whether by conjunction, trine, sextile, square or opposition—create varying degrees of change and/or conflict between innate sense of freedom and how the subconscious mind is striving to direct it.

The purpose of these transits is to blow away—with the combined blast of an earthquake and a whirlwind—anyone or anything hampering personal progress, thereby exposing new and startling territories to explore.

Both Pluto and Uranus are energies of enormously constructive *or* destructive power. Attempts to ignore the demand to break with the past or cling to the old ways let loose events of devastating effect.

Pluto/Uranus Event Projection

Anyone experiencing these transits faces incidents and situations designed to:

- Compel integration of own behaviour with current social standards in morals and ethics.
- Provoke rebellion against existing conditions and attempts to overthrow authority.
- Instigate search for new and more progressive methods in problem-solving and creative endeavours.
- Eliminate hindrances through severing of restrictive ties or work associations.

- Force substitution of new, freer life style through total relinquishment of the old.

Pluto/Uranus Transit Management
Anyone experiencing these transits is strongly advised to:

- Control irritation or violent reactions to events which limit personal independence.
- Apply both caution and deliberation before openly opposing others.
- Divert attention into newly-developing interests to reduce resentment towards authority figures or superiors.
- Sustain effort rather than seeking instant solutions or easy roads to success.

Transiting Pluto Aspecting Natal Neptune

Energy Blend: Transformation/Illumination

Reminder Note: Natal Neptune in every chart reveals the basic ability to seek spiritual advancement. . .use intuitive knowledge and imagination . . .pursue non-material goals and aspirations.

Pluto in every chart points up the gut feelings. . .the unrecognized urges and desires. . .the workings of the subconscious mind.

Thus all contacts between transiting Pluto and natal Neptune—whether by conjunction, trine, sextile, square or opposition—create varying degrees of change and/or conflict between individual spirituality and how the subconscious mind is striving to direct it.

The purpose of these transits is to widen perception of inner needs and spiritual values, thereby deflecting effort away from materialistic ends or ambitions.

Pluto opens the flood-gates to awareness so that the waters of Neptunian inspiration can pour out. Attempts to dam back the flood create events that can sweep misdirected hopes and illusions to destruction.

Important Note: the *opposition aspect* between transiting Pluto and natal Neptune cannot occur in the charts of any person now living or born this century.

The *sextile aspect* between transiting Pluto and natal Neptune does not occur in charts until their subjects are well into middle age.

The *square aspect* between transiting Pluto and natal Neptune does not occur in charts until their subjects have reached the late sixties age groupings.

Pluto/Neptune Event Projection
Anyone experiencing these transits faces incidents and situations designed to:

- Deepen understanding of individual search for faith and purpose of living.
- Stimulate imagination and increase personal vision.
- Create foolish fantasizing and attraction to impractical schemes/ideas.
- Introduce gullible thinking, either through deceiving the self as to own motivation or by duplicity of others.
- Reveal well-kept secrets as a result of confiding in untrustworthy associates or giving in to pressure.

Pluto/Neptune Transit Management
Anyone experiencing these transits is strongly advised to:

- Maintain personal ideals and behaviour at the highest possible standards.
- Refuse to be drawn into intrigues or behind-the-scenes plotting through subtle coercion from others.
- State ideas/plans plainly and practically to avoid misconceptions or accusations of secrecy.
- Obtain expert, impartial advice in settling any matter relating to financial affairs.

Transiting Pluto Aspecting Natal Pluto

Energy Blend: Transformation/Regeneration

Reminder Note: When any transiting planet makes any major aspect to that planet's natal position, the effect is one of outright confrontation. To use an analogy, it can be compared to finding a very old photograph of yourself and staring at it as you look in a mirror. The face you see is the same yet it is different. The past 'you' confronts the present 'you'. The effect is startling, even disturbing.

So it is when identical energies are forced into 'face-to-face' contact. They are obliged to combine but not necessarily comfortably. The affairs of the house being transited may not happily merge with the affairs of the planet's natal house.

Pluto/Pluto aspects during transit demonstrate this confrontation effect with events typical of this planet's pull towards change through compulsion and regeneration.

The purpose of all Pluto/Pluto transits is to direct searchlights into the darkest recesses of the subconscious mind, thereby illuminating the deeply-embedded repressions, inhibitions, compulsions and obsessions which the ego strives to ignore.

Nevertheless, as Pluto's harsh beams cut through the concealing camouflage to the centre of being, the truth is thrown up in startling relief and with this planet's characteristic inexorability. Attempts to hide from the light create events which can destroy or throw into chaos the long-established foundations of daily existence.

Important Note: The *conjunction or opposition aspect* between transiting Pluto and natal Pluto cannot occur at all in the normal human life-span.

The *trine aspect* between transiting Pluto and natal Pluto does not occur in charts until their subjects have attained the latter years of life.

The *square aspect* between transiting Pluto and natal Pluto occurs in charts where their subjects have reached their forties.

Pluto/Pluto Event Projection

Anyone experiencing these transits faces incidents and situations designed to:

- Release energy to eradicate fears and inhibitions which slow down regeneration of the self caused by holding on to past involvements.
- Terminate long-standing disputes or misconceptions through improved powers of observation and self-appraisal.
- Force caution in all types of financial dealings, especially those where heavy borrowing or lending are likely.
- Develop resourceful handling of personal crises in business or private affairs.

- Cause ongoing upheavals in life direction if useless or outlived associations/concerns are not discarded.

Pluto/Pluto Transit Management
Anyone experiencing these transits is strongly advised to:

- Avoid becoming embroiled in dangerous psychic practices or occult dabbling.
- Seek the hidden meaning of sudden flashes of memory or significant dream experiences through deliberate concentration.
- Accept willingly difficult changes in life direction without regrets.
- Break with conditions or individuals that encourage reverting to past life styles.

Pluto Example Transit Sheet — Chart of Clare Costumier

FUTURE LIFE TRENDS: Years examined—1984 to 1998.

(*Reminder Note:* The planet Pluto always promotes events which *slowly* produce deep-rooted, irreversible changes in your subconscious drives and most fundamental convictions. It is a powerfully transforming influence and creates new directions in your life.)

Long-Range Pluto Effect:

Time Spans Involved in Current House Position: Ninth—1984 to 1998.

Effect of House Transit: Chart subject responsive to Pluto's pressure to explore ninth house experiences. Natal Jupiter and Neptune in natal ninth promised opportunities and spiritual development through exposure to foreign cultures so groundwork had been laid at birth for this transit to activate after maturity.

Comments in Brief: Since Pluto's entry into ninth followed swiftly on Saturn's, some doubts and fears as to outcome of travel continue to trouble chart subject. Due to Pluto's life-transforming thrust, decision to confront foreigners and foreign situations should have very far-reaching effects. Possible fantasizing, over-optimism and decisions disruptive to working life during Pluto aspects—periods as set out below.

Current Pluto Effect:

Time Spans Involved for Each Transit Aspect in Current House from '84 to '89:

(1) Dec '84—April '85, Oct—Nov '85, May—Sept '86
(2) Nov—Dec '85, April—Oct '86
(3) Jan—May '91, Oct—Nov '91
(4) Jan—May '94, Nov—Dec '94

Effect of Major Operative Aspects:
Quite a mixed bag of possibilities here. Travel should aid work experience (1). But need to base all moves on practical considerations instead of dreams/fantasies (2) Repercussions likely in '91 through over-demand for personal independence, disrupting working life (3). Unrestrained optimism or trusting to luck likely to cause disputes over cultural/religious difference with foreign partner/associates in '94.

Comments in Brief: Demanding set of consequences for young adult. In this case, overseas travel could not possibly equate to mere pleasure touring. Will permanently change whole life direction. Likely to regard 1985 as a major turning point in experience.

Pluto Example Transit Sheet

FUTURE LIFE TRENDS: Years examined—

(*Reminder Note:* The planet Pluto always promotes events which *slowly* produce deep-rooted, irreversible changes in your subconscious drives and most fundamental convictions. It is a powerfully transforming influence and creates new directions in your life.)

Long-Range Pluto Effect:

Time Spans Involved in Current House Position::

Effect of House Transit:

Comments in Brief:..

....

....

....

Current Pluto Effect:

Time Spans Involved for Each Transit Aspect in Current House from:

Effect of Major Operative Aspects:

Comments in Brief:..

....

....

....

Neptune—The 'Great Illusionist' in Transit

While events provoked by Pluto's transits invariably have a 'subterranean' quality about them. . .as if they had been violently flung up from the centre of being. . .Neptune's do not. With this planet, the whole scene is 'submarine'. An impression of everything happening at full fathom five.

If you've ever tried scuba diving, you'll be better able to visualize the Neptune effect. For you'll know that beneath the sea, objects, faces, movements take on a strange, new perspective. Nebulous, out of focus, drifting, wavering. The same applies to Neptune-generated events. The planet's pull draws us down into the shadowy depths of inner experience. Slowly and silently. Away from the real world of hard facts and material goals down into the insubstantial, unreal world of dreams and illusions.

All of which explains how Neptune earned his title, too. For, once plunged into his 'undersea' domain, it is so very easy to lose touch with reality. Everything around us seems subtly changed, even distorted. Events catch us up in waves of disorientating feeling. Fantasy can be mistaken for inspiration. Deception for truth. Obviously, we cannot swim against this tide yet we must not allow ourselves to be swept away by it to sink in a sea of fanciful imaginings or wildly impractical hopes.

Neptune's transits signal the times when the search for spiritual meaning to the struggles of living intensity—even in the most hard-bitten individuals. A painful search which usually demands a higher degree of self-abnegation than the ego wishes to accept. Yet accept it we must—if we are going to survive unscathed and inspired. The journey towards enlightenment is never an easy one.

As with Pluto, Neptune's cycles are far too slow to warrant examination. This planet spends an *average* of around fourteen years in each sign so there is plenty of time for the tides of change to ebb and flow.

Check this out for yourself (as we did with Pluto house transits) by looking again at Clare Costumier's chart in Chapter 3. You'll note that Neptune crossed her tenth house cusp, thus entering her house of career/attainments in 1973—when she was 14 and at an age when adult occupation choices were demanding attention. He continues moving through her tenth house until 1989, when she attains age 30.

Thus Neptune not only heavily influences her career direction for some 16 years (formative years at that!) but further coincides with the first Saturn Return (see Chapter 3) also in the tenth. Another strand to be woven into the tapestry of her future.

Obviously then, as she develops from teenager to mature adult, Clare faces powerful planetary pressure periods while she strives to puzzle out what she wants to make of her working life.

Have events turned out like that to date? They surely have. While still at school, she began to plan a career in the creative fashion industry and by 1979 had acquired the necessary tertiary training to succeed in it. Yet the ever-present, ever-niggling sense of Neptune-style doubt as to where she was really heading and whether her successes meant anything worthwhile anyway continued to plague her.

Was she going in the right direction or wasn't she? By 1981, the glittering worlds of theatre and film (with their heavily Neptunian themes) were beckoning. In them, all is artifice, all is illusion. An imitation of life. Clare explored them both. But beneath the glamour, the greasepaint and the fantastic costumes she herself created, she found both worlds empty, even tawdry. A characteristically Neptunian revelation. True for us all. Out of the ten planets, Neptune is far and away the most adept at showing us everything that glitters is *not* gold!

Being a naturally perceptive/critical type, (Pisces Ascendant/Virgo planets), Clare soon saw that when you come close to the golden crowns, the gleaming jewels of stage kings and queens, they reveal themselves as nothing but plastic, paint and paste. Without worth or real value.

In everyday life too, this is what Neptune transits demand of us, pushing events that tangle us in 'tinsel', dangling the glittering bait till we recognize it for what it really is. If we wilfully refuse to do so, we can all too easily spend our lives chasing false goals that once attained are also found to be without worth or real value. A sad and disillusioning discovery.

Thus we observe that Neptune in his own subtle way is just as effective in inaugurating far-reaching changes in each life as Pluto. But the changes are of a very different calibre. Mysterious, elusive, unhurried, rather than violent and cataclysmic. As if the waters of Neptune were gradually wearing away the foundation stones of existence as waves erode a rocky shore.

New Avenues of Enlightenment . . . Or . . . New Dream-Worlds of Delusion

Enlightenment and delusion appear at first glance to have nothing to do with each other. In fact, they are the two sides of the same coin—currency minted by Neptune.

For Neptune-generated dilemmas invariably contain elements of both. In pursuing your dream, are you escaping into what Sagittarian-born actor/writer Noel Coward once described as 'a private dream-world of my own where everything is hilariously untrue?' Or are you steadfastly steering your course towards the beacon light that shines on a distant shore?

That *is* the question. And, like Ulysses, we have to bind ourselves to the mast of reality and stop up our ears against the siren songs of fantasy, if we're going to find the true answers to it.

To appreciate Neptunian changes in individual levels of awareness and perception, we need to remember that they flow out from the soul or spirit.

Neither psychiatry, psychology nor religions can define precisely what the human soul or spirit is. Or where it lodges in its temporary, physical vehicle—the human body. Yet all are forced to admit it exists and that it distinguishes one man from another more completely than intelligence, strength or any other easily definable, identifiable quality.

Recognition of this fact is evident in common, everyday speech. Someone is 'high-spirited' or 'mean-spirited' or even 'spiritless'. Or 'the spirit is willing but the flesh is weak'. People are 'soulful' or 'soulless'.

Thus from these types of remarks, it becomes clear that human beings never doubt that some intangible, incorporeal entity lives within each one of us. And also, that it amounts to an invisible guiding force, leading us towards the good, away from the bad and the ugly.

It is always on the spirit within every one of us that Neptune calls. Astrologically speaking then, spiritual evolution and advancement are the preserve of Neptune. But, as with Pluto, we'll understand his influence better if we glance at the mythology surrounding him.

According to Ancient Greek legends, Neptune (also known as 'Poseidon Of the Blue Hair' and sometimes depicted as a fish-tailed merman) was the god of the sea.

At his pleasure, the seas raged into tempests or subsided into gentle billows so he was plainly not a god to play games with. Sailors took utmost care to ensure they had not offended him every time they weighed anchor and sailed off to face the unknown terrors of the open sea. They also knew Neptune to be the brother of Pluto, hence never hesitant to sent them—at a wave of his trident—down into his brother's gloomy abode, the dim underworld of the dead.

At this point, in the ancient legends, we discern an intriguing connection. By making these two formidable gods brothers, the early story-tellers demonstrated their awareness of the link-ups between what is going on in the subconscious mind (Pluto) and the direction of spiritual evolution (Neptune). Indeed, as the great psychoanalyst Carl Gustav Jung once pointed out, the astrological symbolism evidenced in such mythology crystallized the summation of the psychological knowledge of the ancient world.

Assuredly, the world has changed in some 3,000 years but human beings have not. Twentieth-century hopes and fears, dreams and dreads are just the same in essence as when Socrates trod the streets of Athens. Remember the symbolism whenever you seek to assess the influence of Neptune as against other chart indicators.

Again, the naming of the planet was singularly apt. For the spirit of Man is as boundless and deep as the ocean itself. Just as a strange and different world is hidden away beneath the ever-changing surface of the sea, so is the spirit hidden away within the changing confines of the body. It is a wise man who knows his own soul.

Neptune's transits and aspects generate events which help us to catch glimpses of our spiritual selves and so sharpen our sense of rightness or wrongness. If we try to betray thise sense of rightness through actions that are unjust, unfair to others *or* untrue to ourselves, we often find a strange result occurs. We are able to navigate easily a certain distance into what look like uncharted seas, only to find that we're suddenly lost in a fog of doubt and deception. Or that life has done to us exactly what we sought to do to others.

Consider the case of a middle-aged woman with many planets in Taurus—a sign which tends to place great store on money and possessions. Following a bitter, contested divorce, she had virtually reduced her wealthy ex-husband to the point of beggary. She hated him, wanted revenge, refusing to admit that she had contributed to the marriage breakdown as much as he had. With the huge sums she gained in her divorce settlements, she invested in six, very costly paintings, planning to resell them later at an excellent profit, thereby making her revenge sweeter still.

But, at the time of the divorce and purchase, Neptune was transiting her twelfth house (self-undoing) and reaching hard aspects to two of her natal planets. The first result? She made the outrageously foolish mistake of failing to insure the six paintings. The second result? All six were stolen within three months and never recovered. Now she was financially ruined too. Neptune had given her a taste of her own bitter medicine!

That kind of lesson is an unpleasant one, not likely to be forgotten. Neptune's dream-worlds of delusion dissolve into nothingness if we try to escape into them. Yet once we perceive we *have* erred and let that revelation guide us in all future actions, the fog itself dissolves and new avenues of enlightenment open out before us.

Even in apparently ordinary, everyday decisions Neptune's hand can be seen if our decisions are reached for wrong motivations. Here's an example of Neptune 'at work' in a photographic darkroom.

A Lesson from Neptune

'God knows why but I bungled the whole process. I tried a new photographic technique and I ruined several irreplaceable negatives. I can't understand what made me do it!' The speaker was a professional photographer, who, in my view, had just experienced Neptune being ornery. . .very ornery indeed.

One of this planet's favourite ploys is to create situations where we do silly, exasperating things that afterwards appear inexplicable, irresponsible, careless, or even ludicrous. Anyone who has challenging aspects to Neptune in the natal chart will know all this only too well. Plus those who have been going through tough Neptune transits and thus been forced to observe that their usual realistic approach to life has mysteriously and confusingly deserted them.

But why? As so many of my clients ask. What's the purpose of all the muddles and mistakes? The answer is, I believe, to teach us a lesson. Not, of course, in the harsh, wake-up-to-yourself style of Saturn. Much much more subtly, gradually.

The lesson itself is peculiarly Neptunian too. And Neptune, being what the planet is, contains a spiritual message. Naturally, that's hard to put into plain words but I think it adds up to something like this:

If you do some act for the wrong reasons—for reasons that are morally and spiritually wrong for you—Neptune will turn your own hand against you and tangle you up into a weird and wonderful mess.

Fanciful as it may sound at first thought, I consider the above mentioned photographs in my first example were deliberately destroyed by a Neptunian influence. . .working on the photographer's mind. Something *was* wrong about them. Perhaps, they were not as good as they could have been. (Neptune will accept nothing but the best from us in our use of talents and everything else!) Perhaps, their subject or the motivation behind them needed rethinking.

To illustrate further: Let's take a well-known anecdote about the life of world-famous American novelist Ernest Hemingway. I cannot state what transits caused the event he recorded as he did not give its date. But Hemingway did have Mars in square to Neptune plus Saturn in wide opposition to Neptune in his natal chart.

The great writer recalled that once in Paris at the outset of his career, he lost a suitcase containing dozens of stories and manuscripts by leaving it on a train. He was furious with himself at the time because the suitcase was never returned and he had thus to start from scratch and do the work all over again. But, Hemingway himself later admitted, his writings were better the second time around.

The novelist's Neptune was in the tenth house of career: Mars was in his first house of self: Saturn was in his fourth house of home. Thus Neptune linked three of the four powerful angles of Hemingway's chart into a t-square configuration in mutables. . .an exceptionally hard-to-handle pattern!

It might also be worth mentioning that at the end of Hemingway's life, Neptune again had a hand in events. The writer died from a self-inflicted gunshot wound. Aries was on his eighth house. . .a sign which is much involved with weapons. Mars, Aries' ruler, was part of the Neptune-dominated t-square in his first house.

Several commentators later indicated from conversations with Hemingway that he believed he had passed the age when he could continue to be the man and writer he saw himself as. Since he was only around the age of sixty when he died, those views sound like a confused reaction to Neptune's influences.

All of which underlines that when Neptune sets out to teach us a lesson, we need to delve deep into the psyche to find the reasons why! Again, I've related the tales of the professional photographer and the famous writer at some length to demonstrate the very strange ways in which Neptune works in obliging us to put aside self-deception and the conscious mind's attempts to rationalize our less worthy actions. Or, in other words, Neptune requires us to look beyond the apparent, the obvious reasons for 'accidental' mistakes. To throw away the ego-camouflaged explanations of why we err. . .in major or minor ways.

Neptune's revelations are often hard to take because they *do* undermine all that is egotistical in human behaviour. Yet if we're going to move upwards towards the higher planes of existence, the ego's got to give!

Neptune House Transits—Gleams from the Depths

Wherever Neptune is situated in the natal chart, there is a curiously disorientating feeling of nebulousness and impressionability—of being caught in the undercurrents, constantly surging around the affairs of that life sector.

During his transits, Neptune sends up gleams of hope from the seemingly unfathomable depths of dreams and illusions—*if* you're willing to accept that for hopes to be realized, for wishes to come true, both must be based on a special sort of 'rightness'. They must be right, in the sense that they do no wrong to others. They must be right in the sense that they allow *you* to evolve. Not by leaning on or taking from someone else but through your own increased awareness of who you are and what you can become—(not necessarily what you had in mind!).

Neptune's influence is far more subtle, far less tangible than Pluto's . . .which naturally makes it far harder to deal with. Maybe, your natal chart shows you've tried to turn your back on the non-material world in the race for recognition. A particular Neptune transit will drown misplaced ambitions in a sea of dissatisfaction. Maybe, your natal chart shows you've been searching all your life for a dream lover (who could never exist) and thus rejecting the all-too-human partners who cross your path. A particular Neptune transit will wash away the veils of fantasy and oblige you to change. You can refuse to budge out of your castle in the clouds but you won't withstand the siege. Neptune-style events will dissolve the dream scene into nothingness before your very eyes.

When dating Neptune transits, you'll need to refer to the small blue book of *Geocentric Longitudes* mentioned in Chapter 3, remembering to blend them in with other current planetary patterns. Keep in mind as you go your mental image of Neptune as the 'Great Illusionist'. This visualized image will serve to emphasize that what you *believe* you're seeing is not always what's *actually* happening to you and around you. After all, a stage illusionist doesn't really pull a rabbit out of an empty top hat. He cunningly tricks his audience into believing he did.

Neptune can trick you like that into believing anything too. No matter how ridiculous, no matter how foolish, no matter how bizarre. *If* you continue to clutch at the straws of false ideals or egocentric aims. Yet follow the gleams of inspiration that flow up from the secret depths of your own spirit and your voyage towards self-discovery becomes a smoother passage.

As in preceding Saturn and Neptune transit sections, we'll include a 'Neptune Example Transit Sheet' for our chart subject—Clare Costumier—at the end of this section, so as to show Neptune transits at work on an actual life history. Again, you'll find a blank you can use for your own Neptune transit summaries.

Remember, of course, when you're ready to prepare completed forecasts of future trends in any life, you must blend together the effect—in events plus attitude changes—of *all* major planetary transits. Never overstress one at the expense of the others or you'll come up with an inaccurate future picture at worst, a lop-sided one at best.

If you're still unsure of the varying strengths of conjunctions, trines, sextiles, squares or oppositions between the transiting planet and any natal planet, turn back to our 'Aspect Checklist' in the Pluto section of this chapter.

FIRST HOUSE NEPTUNE TRANSIT EVENTS . . .
subtly alter self image and personal environment.

Positive Responses Promote	• Development of intuitive powers and sense of spiritual purpose. • Accomplishment through renewed inspiration and use of creative skills. • Awareness through regular meditation and quiet reflection. • Increased rapport and empathy towards others.
Negative Responses Invite	• Personal isolation and withdrawal. • Imaginary or psychosomatically based illnesses. • Loss of emotional self-control and psychological disorientation. • Escapist behaviour and gullibility towards unreliable associates.

SECOND HOUSE NEPTUNE TRANSIT EVENTS . . .
subtly alter earning power and use of own moneys.

Positive Responses Promote	• Inspired use of imagination in financial transactions. • Willingness to help those in need of support. • Benefits through charitable or philanthropic actions. • Successes in secret matters concerning money.
Negative Responses Invite	• Self-indulgent extravagances. • Losses and financial chaos through entanglements with dishonest individuals or quick-cash schemes. • Impractical spending on unnecessary luxuries. • Financial impositions by others.

THIRD HOUSE NEPTUNE TRANSIT EVENTS . . .
subtly alter mental attitudes and educational skills.

Positive Responses Promote	• Deepened intellectual interest in studies with spiritual emphasis. • Successes through applied use of creative talents. • Gain and social opportunities through kindness of close relatives and friends. • Good use of confidential information affecting mental work.
Negative Responses Invite	• Dangerous mistakes in all forms of communication. • Convoluted or self-deceptive thinking. • Evasion of responsibilities in study or mental work. • Misplaced confidence in sharing secrets with others.

FOURTH HOUSE NEPTUNE TRANSIT EVENTS . . .
subtly alter domestic circumstances and home atmosphere.

Positive Responses Promote	• Profound emotional/spiritual experiences with those sharing the home. • Heightened sensitivitity to needs of intimates/family. • Establishment of the home as a centre of spiritual retreat. • Significant, beneficial changes in place or atmosphere of residence.
Negative Responses Invite	• Hypersensitivity to behaviour of family/intimates. • Confused, chaotic conditions in

home through deliberate or unwitting deceptions.
- Serious errors or losses relating to property or home possessions.
- Secretiveness, suspicion and delusions about those with whom home is shared.

FIFTH HOUSE NEPTUNE TRANSIT EVENTS . . .
subtly alter romantic liaisons, concern with children, creative talents.

Positive Responses Promote
- Love relationships with spiritually-attuned partners.
- Good results from imaginative, creative endeavours.
- Success in speculative promotions if based on wise pre-planning.
- Heightened understanding of needs of children.

Negative Responses Invite
- Love affairs founded on fantasizing.
- Wasted efforts through wrong direction of artistic abilities.
- Entanglements in foolish investments or gambling.
- Mysterious conditions affecting children.

SIXTH HOUSE NEPTUNE TRANSIT EVENTS . . .
subtly alter working environment, health concerns.

Positive Responses Promote
- Involvement in new work areas offering opportunities to help others.
- Better co-operation with co-workers or employees through greater awareness.
- New interest in good health regimens and healing sciences.

	• Unexpected aid from social inferiors or subordinates.
Negative Responses Invite	• Depression or psychological disturbances affecting work efficiency. • Peculiar or inexplicable blocks to advancement through intrigues or underhand dealings. • Attraction to dissipated life style to escape work responsibilities. • Confinement in undesirable working conditions or loss of employment for unexplained reasons.

SEVENTH HOUSE NEPTUNE TRANSIT EVENTS . . .
subtly alter marital affairs, partnerships in love and business.

Positive Responses Promote	• Intensified rapport with partners plus understanding of their psychological make-up. • Establishment of unions with spiritually attuned partners/spouses. • Willingness to express true sentiments to love partners. • Ability to offer unstinted aid/support to partners/spouses.
Negative Responses Invite	• Attractions to unstable, deceitful or weak individuals. • Dwelling on past relationship clashes with bitterness and resentment. • Withdrawal—physically or mentally—from any union. • Commitment to new partnerships for foolish or over-idealized reasons.

EIGHTH HOUSE NEPTUNE TRANSIT EVENTS . . .
subtly alter joint/shared financial liabilities and handling of deceased estate assets.

Positive Responses Promote

- Intuitive grasp of all matters requiring financial co-operation with others.
- Benefits from acceptance of impartial, expert advice on shared money decisions.
- Resolve to adhere to high standard of morals/ethics in handling money of others.
- Better use of inherited moneys or gifts from deceased estates.

Negative Responses Invite

- Deception or underhand moves in financial sharing.
- Misplaced trust or falsified information affecting shared moneys.
- Losses through emotional blackmail or cunning manipulation by others.
- Dangers through borrowing/lending or failure to keep accurate financial records.

NINTH HOUSE NEPTUNE TRANSIT EVENTS . . .
subtly alter involvements with foreigners, travel decisions.

Positive Responses Promote

- Renewed interest in travel and personality changes through exposure to foreign cultures.
- Attractions to new religions or philosophies through association with foreign-born persons.
- Insight into coming cultural trends through gathering ideas during travel.
- Desire for religious or spiritually enlightening pilgrimages.

Negative Responses Invite	• Mental confusions through over-susceptibility to foreign ways/ideas. • Attempts to adopt false stance of spiritual or intellectual superiority. • Escapist wanderings to evade existing challenges or obligations. • Attraction to peculiar cults or occult practices.

TENTH HOUSE NEPTUNE TRANSIT EVENTS . . .
subtly alter career aims and personal status.

Positive Responses Promote	• Career changes to occupations more intrinsically satisfying. • Helpful association with prominent individuals in artistic/entertainment fields. • Improved perception of expectations of superiors/colleagues. • Attainment of recognition/fame in mysterious circumstances.
Negative Responses Invite	• Temptations to abuse confidences or use unfair means to gain advancement. • Impractical, unrealistic assessment of professional/occupational situations. • Wrong moves through sense of purposelessness or loss of motivation. • Involvement in scandal or notoriety affecting personal status.

ELEVENTH HOUSE NEPTUNE TRANSIT EVENTS . . .
subtly alter friendships and involvements in group activities.

Positive Responses Promote	• Assistance through acquisition of glamorous/talented friends.

	• Beneficial results from all types of group efforts, especially if for humanitarian purposes. • Better integrated social life and wider circle of unusual acquaintances. • Willingness to help friends without thought of reward.
Negative Responses Invite	• Entanglements with false or fair-weather friendships. • Impositions from psychologically disturbed friends/associates. • Pursuit of social pleasures as form of escapism. • Dangers through gullibility and misplaced trust in others.

TWELFTH HOUSE NEPTUNE TRANSIT EVENTS . . .

subtly alter spiritual viewpoint and capacity for self-sacrifice.

Positive Responses Promote	• Self-discovery through introspection and assessment of life goals. • Self-abnegation and willingness to put others' needs first. • Desire to aid those who cannot cope through illness or psychological difficulties. • Voluntary replacing material objectives with spiritual needs.
Negative Responses Invite	• Neurotic, unreasonable reactions to stress or other people's expectations. • Total loss of emotional restraint and fits of intense depression. • Problems through inability to think rationally or concentrate on real-world decisions.

- Sickness through self-pity, development of baseless fears and phobias.

Now, we've pursued Neptune through his transits of all twelve houses and observed their effect on the human spirit. As you can see, they require us to look down into the shadowy depths of inner experience in the search for awareness and the purpose of life.

Once again, as noted in the case of Pluto, no individual lives long enough to experience all twelve of Neptune's house transits. The planet takes approximately 165 years to pass through them all. Also, as noted earlier, check the *present* age of yourself and your chart subjects, so you can gauge what life sectors (houses) Neptune has influenced to date and those he is likely to reach in the normal life span.

On the question of past Neptunian influence, let's take another look at our specimen chart subject—Clare Costumier.

We remember that Neptune was posited in her ninth house (foreigners/travel) at birth and continued to work his way through that house until she turned fourteen in 1973. So how did the planet affect the pre-adolescent years of her life? Markedly.

While still a young child she travelled quite widely. First through Europe and then in the Pacific. Mostly in Neptune's own milieu—i.e. by sea. These early experiences stimulated her natal propensity to seek out foreign places and examine foreign life styles. As a young adult, she began travelling again and was invariably most attracted to foreign-born men.

Next, try a past-years check with your own charts, chronicling how Neptune's past house transits affected the lives in question. How the often stumbling, fumbling search for a new vision—for something deeper than mere day-to-day living—began and where it eventually led. Take your time over this. Neptune's changes are obscure, rarely discussed, sometimes not even admitted and thus can be easily missed in analysis.

Neptune Transit Aspects—New Dreams for Old

Now, on to our next consideration—Neptune's transiting aspects. While his house position prepares the background of events over lengthy periods of living, his aspects with natal planets point to times when more definitive (if such a clear-cut word can be applied to a planet as nebulous as Neptune) action must be taken.

To ensure you ascribe the appropriate emphasis to conjunctions, sextiles, trines, squares and oppositions, turn back to the 'Aspect Checklist' in the Pluto section of this chapter—if you haven't yet memorized the significance of each one.

Neptune Transit Aspects—Interpretation Table

Transiting Neptune Aspecting Natal Sun

Energy Blend: Sublimation/Personal Goals

Reminder Note: the *natal Sun* in every chart reveals the basic ego thrust . . .the true, unalterable self. . .the workings of the conscious mind.

Neptune in every chart points to the inner yearnings. . .the secret dreams and visions. . .the striving of the spirit.

Thus all contacts between transiting Neptune and the natal Sun—whether by conjunction, trine, sextile, square or opposition—create varying degrees of change and/or conflict between what *the ego* wants for itself and the way in which renewed *spiritual growth* strives to sublimate it.

The purpose of these transits is to seek out and sweep away ego-centred barriers to enlightenment. Slow yet persistent as water wearing away stone, Neptune can silently undermine all that props up a false or artificial self-image till the whole structure collapses in ruins.

Neptune/Sun Event Projection

Anyone experiencing these transits faces incidents and situations designed to:

- Recreate personal ideals and offer avenues for their expression.
- Increase intuitive perception and foresight as to coming conditions.
- Present temptations to take part in airy, over-optimistic schemes through fraudulent information.
- Invoke inflated view of own skills, leading to serious errors of judgement.

- Induce reliance on rumours, gossip or scandalous accusations through contact with dishonest or deceitful individuals.

Neptune/Sun Transit Management

Anyone experiencing these transits is strongly advised to:

- Check sources of all information for exaggeration or lack of foundation.
- Confide only in those who have proved themselves to be trustworthy.
- Avoid fantasizing about own goals or ambitions or impractical decisions.
- Act at all times according to highest principles and state views plainly.

Transiting Neptune Aspecting Natal Moon

Energy Blend: Transformation/Emotional Needs

Reminder Note: the *natal Moon* in every chart reveals the basic emotional make-up. . .the secret self. . .the imprinted response patterns.

Neptune in every chart points to the inner yearnings. . .the secret dreams and visions. . .the striving of the spirit.

Thus all contacts between transiting Neptune and the natal Moon—whether by conjunction, trine, sextile, square or opposition—create varying degrees of change and/or conflict between how *the emotions* manifest themselves and the way in which renewed *spiritual growth* strives to sublimate them.

The purpose of these transits is to dissolve self-centred motivations in emotional life, thereby enriching interchange of feeling. Attempts to resist the flow of intensifying emotional experience or failure to transcend selfish motivations leads inevitably to the dark wells of loneliness and disillusionment.

Neptune/Moon Event Projection

Anyone experiencing these transits faces incidents and situations designed to:

- Stimulate use of inspiration in dealing with all types of emotionally-based liaisons.

- Develop closer, more spiritually-satisfying relationships through renewed desire to create harmony.
- Cause confused, chaotic reactions to emotional stimuli through inability to face real issues.
- Leave the self open to trickery, dishonesty or lack of clarity in intimate associations.
- Introduce controversial attachments, leading to recrimination.

Neptune/Moon Transit Management

Anyone experiencing these transits is strongly advised to:

- Keep clear of any emotional involvement which cannot be open and above reproach.
- Use heightened awareness to act with sympathy and understanding towards those close to the self.
- Prevent mistaken attitudes in emotional/love attachments by stating feelings sincerely and plainly.
- Resist desires to escape from personal life problems by pretending they do not exist.

Transiting Neptune Aspecting Natal Mercury

Energy Blend: Sublimation/Mental Interests

Reminder Note: Natal Mercury in every chart reveals the basic mental inclinations. . .type and grade of intellect. . .powers of communications.

Neptune in every chart points to the inner yearnings. . .the secret dreams and visions. . .the striving of the spirit.

Thus all contacts between transiting Neptune and natal Mercury—whether by conjunction, trine, sextile, square or opposition—create varying degrees of change and/or conflict between how the *thought processes* operate and the way in which renewed *spiritual growth* strives to sublimate them.

The purpose of these transits is to elevate thinking habits and mental attitudes, thereby opening the mind to new inspirations, new vistas of imagination, new intellectual horizons. Refusal to allow the mind to lift itself up and beyond the merely material planes of thought produces faulty judgement, mental blockage and pursuit of spurious ideas.

Neptune/Mercury Event Projection

Anyone experiencing these transits faces incidents and situations designed to:

- Boost imagination and mental sensitivity in all intellectual pursuits.
- Evoke creative ideas through sudden flashes of inspiration.
- Cause misconceptions or mysterious problems in documents or any forms of communication.
- Introduce contacts with individuals of literary or artistic talents.
- Provoke attempts to cover too much mental territory at once, thereby resulting in confused thinking.

Neptune/Mercury Transit Management

Anyone experiencing these transits is strongly advised to:

- Subject thinking and new schemes to regular tests for practicality.
- Avoid circumstances or people who encourage disorganization or slackness.
- Apply caution in joining in occultist activities or religious sects.
- Refrain from breaking confidences or betraying secret information.

Transiting Neptune Aspecting Natal Venus

Energy Blend: Sublimation/Affectional Affairs

Reminder Note: Natal Venus in every chart reveals the basic capacities to give and receive affection. . .choice of and attraction to pleasures . . .desire for harmony.

Neptune in every chart points to the inner yearnings. . .the secret dreams and visions. . .the striving of the spirit.

Thus all contacts between transiting Neptune and natal Venus—whether by conjunction, trine, sextile, square or opposition—create varying degrees of change and/or conflict between how the *affections* operate and the way in which renewed *spiritual growth* strives to sublimate them.

The purpose of these transits is to refine and exalt affectional responses, thereby channelling the pursuit of love/friendship away from egotistical or possessive attitudes. Efforts to preserve undesirable liaisons or attractions based on selfish desires are invariably wrecked on the rocks of anger and disappointment.

Neptune/Venus Event Projection

Anyone experiencing these transits faces incidents and situations designed to:

- Bring about love or friendship links with highly individualistic or bohemian types.
- Widen circle of friends/acquaintances through renewed interest in social opportunities.
- Embroil the self with glamorous but shallow or delusive associations.
- Attract to secret or clandestine affairs with unsuitable partners.
- Offer happier relationships through the idealization of love/affection.

Neptune/Venus Transit Management

Anyone experiencing these transits is strongly advised to:

- Refrain from sentimentalizing any association.
- Resist strange fascinations or infatuations.
- Adhere to highest principles in love/friendship as an example to those cared about.
- Behave with sincerity and without overstatement of own feelings.

Transiting Neptune Aspecting Natal Mars

Energy Blend: Sublimation/Physical Desires

Reminder Note: Natal Mars in every chart reveals the basic physical strengths. . .force and direction of sexual drives. . .degree of natural vitality.

Neptune in every chart points to the inner yearnings. . .the secret dreams and visions. . .the striving of the spirit.

Thus all contacts between transiting Neptune and natal Mars—whether by conjunction, trine, sextile, square or opposition—create varying degrees of change and/or conflict between how the *physical drives* operate and the way in which renewed *spiritual growth* strives to sublimate them.

The purpose of these transits is to uplift and moderate physical urges, thereby eliminating all that is crude, base or self-seeking in sexual encounters. Pursuit of mere physical satisfaction without caring or sharing will finally set the self adrift in an ocean of misery and self-disgust.

Neptune/Mars Event Projection

Anyone experiencing these transits faces incidents and situations designed to:

- Unleash wild enthusiasms or foolishly romanticized hopes in physical relationships.
- Dissipate vitality and strength through misdirected energy.
- Offer inspiration in solving intimate relationship problems.
- Encourage elevation to new levels of mutual understanding in intimate liaisons.
- Lure into weird or dangerous sexual involvements with decadent individuals.

Neptune/Mars Transit Management

Anyone experiencing these transits is strongly advised to:

- Keep sexual urges under firm control.
- Abstain from pursuit of pointless physical pleasures or coarse behaviour.
- Resist blandishments from false lovers, leading to unfair impositions or wasteful expenditure.
- Set high standards in relationships and adhere to them.

Transiting Neptune Aspecting Natal Jupiter

Energy Blend: Sublimation/Personal Expansion

Reminder Note: Natal Jupiter in every chart reveals the basic ability to use opportunities. . .behave with optimism. . .broaden personal horizons.

Neptune in every chart points to the inner yearnings. . .the secret dreams and visions. . .the striving of the spirit.

Thus all contacts between transiting Neptune and natal Jupiter—whether by conjunction, trine, sextile, square or opposition—create varying degrees of change and/or conflict between the *innate capacity to use opportunities* and the way in which renewed *spiritual growth* strives to sublimate it.

The purpose of these transits is to replace blatant or incipient opportunism with progress through fair-minded effort, thereby directing expansion to worthwhile instead of illusory goals. Attempts to make gains at the expense of others or own ideals will soon illustrate the maxim: 'the higher they fly, the farther they fall'. . .into the black heart of Neptunian whirlpools.

Neptune/Jupiter Event Projecton

Anyone experiencing these transits faces incidents and situations designed to:

- Redirect towards new and broader designs for living through contact with influential and evolved individuals.
- Promote benefits from travel or contact with different cultures.
- Present travelling as an escape from duties or personal obligations.
- Attract to subversive intrigues or muddle-headed schemes for apparent advancement.
- Impair judgement through listening to ill-considered or sly advice.

Neptune/Jupiter Transit Management

Anyone experiencing these transits is strongly advised to:

- Maintain the highest possible level of ethics in all business or professional matters.
- Plan expansion of aims on a solidly realistic foundation.
- Consider carefully own motivations regarding travelling or involvements with foreign cultures.
- Avoid trusting to luck in speculation or committing illegal acts.

Transiting Neptune Aspecting Natal Saturn

Again to avoid repetition, for all aspects between transiting Neptune and natal Saturn, please turn back to interpretation of 'transiting Saturn aspecting natal Neptune' in Chapter 3.

Conditions, events and responses evident at such times are virtually the same. A difference in emphasis arises from the fact that Neptune/Saturn aspects during transits last far longer and thereby extend their pressure for change over much longer periods in any life.

Further, when Neptune is the directing force events produce much less immediate but more profound changes in both long-held concepts and overall life direction. At these times the nebulous, ambiguous, indistinct energies of Neptune wash over the rock-hard, unyielding disciplinarian forces of Saturn.

Transiting Neptune Aspecting Natal Uranus

Energy Blend: Sublimation/Revelation

Reminder Note: Natal Uranus in every chart reveals the basic capacity to make or adapt to drastic changes. . .exhibit independence and originality. . .free the self from restrictions.

Neptune in every chart points to the inner yearnings. . .the secret dreams and visions. . .the striving of the spirit.

Thus all contacts between transiting Neptune and natal Uranus—whether by conjunction, trine, sextile, square or opposition—create varying degrees of change and/or conflict between *innate sense of freedom* and the way in which renewed *spiritual growth* strives to sublimate it.

The purpose of these transits is to disintegrate—with the combined force of a tidal wave and a whirlwind—all that is materialistic, unimaginative or otherwise creative of impediments to spiritual growth, thereby revealing new depths of thought and experience. Attempts to struggle against the Neptunian currents of inner change are tantamount to swimming against an ocean rip. The harder the fight to get out of it, the faster the drag from the shore.

IMPORTANT NOTE: The *conjunction aspect* between transiting Neptune and natal Uranus (both slow-movers) only occurs in the charts of those who have reached the very elderly age groupings. For example, an individual born in the year 1900 would show natal Uranus between 10 and 12 degrees of Sagittarius. In the year 1975, transiting Neptune was moving between 10 and 13 degrees of Sagittarius. Thus 1900-born chart subjects would not have experienced this transiting aspect unless they had lived to age 75.

Neptune/Uranus Event Projection

Anyone experiencing these transits faces incidents and situations designed to:

- Urge pursuit of impossible dreams and magnificent visions through inspired (but not always practical) thinking.
- Induce extraordinary psychic experiences from heightened spiritual perception.
- Create errors through reliance on false information or treacherous advisors.
- Overturn mental balance, resulting in decisions based on nervous, jittery reactions.
- Reveal past improper or deceitful acts, leading to disfavour and personal downfall.

Neptune/Uranus Transit Management

Anyone experiencing these transits is strongly advised to:

- Resist moves based on fanatical or erratic ideas.
- Test inspirations against realistic assessment of existing circumstances.
- Do nothing that could be used by false friends/advisors to undermine personal reputation.
- Retain highest principles even in face of attempts to deride or oppose them by others.

Transiting Neptune Aspect Natal Neptune

Energy Blend: Sublimination/Illumination

Reminder Note: When any transiting planet makes any major aspect to that planet's natal position, the effect is one of outright confrontation. Identical energies are forced into close contact but not always comfortably. The affairs of the transit house may not suit the demands of the natal house.

Neptune/Neptune aspects during transit demonstrate this effect with events typical of this planet's pull towards change through dissolution and disintegration.

The purpose of all Neptune/Neptune transits is to oblige the changing spiritual needs and beliefs to come face to face with the natal ones. Rather like a life-raft being swept out to sea and then cast up again on the same beach from whence it came. The raft may be battered and barnacled during its sojourn in the ocean but it remains essentially the same basic structure. As Neptune's eddies and currents swirl around the individual during these transits, the inner being must come to terms with what has been often painfully learned and what was innate in the lifelong search for spiritual understanding.

IMPORTANT NOTE: The *conjunction aspect* between transiting Neptune and natal Neptune cannot occur in the human life-span.

The *opposition aspect* between transiting Neptune and natal Neptune only occurs in chart subjects who have reached their mid-eighties age groupings.

The *trine aspect* between transiting Neptune and natal Neptune does not occur until chart subjects are in their mid-fifties.

The *square aspect* between transiting Neptune and natal Neptune does not occur until chart subjects are in their early forties.

Neptune/Neptune Event Projection

Anyone experiencing these transits faces incidents and experiences designed to:

- Promote revision of long-range plans and long-cherished dreams in terms of genuine opportunities.
- Tempt into emotional or financial extravagance through aims/schemes which are not viable.
- Create atmosphere of doubt/suspicion around the self or towards others.
- Encourage, secretive, behind-the-scenes activities which cause distrust by associates.
- Allow illusions as to own motivations or delusions as to own spiritual superiority to blot out common-sense.

Neptune/Neptune Transit Management
Anyone experiencing these transits is strongly advised to:

- Look to the final outcome in real terms of intense urges/desires.
- Refuse to believe fairy stories in love/business promises.
- Show compassion through heightened empathy with needs of others.
- Stop, look and listen to the inner self's warnings before entering into final commitments.

Transiting Neptune Aspecting Natal Pluto

As before, to avoid needless repetition, please turn back to interpretation of 'transiting Pluto aspecting natal Neptune' earlier in this chapter.

Conditions, events and responses evident at such times are virtually the same. Neptune/Pluto aspects during transits are somewhat shorter in duration, although they, too, cover lengthy periods in each life. Nevertheless, when Neptune is the directing force events are seen as through a drifting mist. Their outlines are less clear, the path ahead more shadowy, the destination less certain.

Neptune Example Transit Sheet — Chart of Clare Costumier

FUTURE LIFE TRENDS: Years examined—1973 to 1989.

(*Reminder Note:* The planet Neptune always promotes events which *subtly* alter your self-awareness, spiritual growth and capacity for spiritual understanding of yourself and others. It is a gradually sensitizing influence which turns you away from materialistic aims.)

Long-Range Neptune Effect:

Time Spans Involved in Current House Position: Tenth—1973 to 1989.

Effect of House Transit: Chart subject reacted early in life (age fourteen) to Neptunian-inspired pursuit of career in the 'glamour' worlds of fashion/theatre. Natal Saturn in natal tenth assured hard effort plus discipline to obtain qualifications would be sustained. But once established in this career in early maturity, Neptune injected doubt and uncertainty as to the validity of the chosen work. Ambition wavered.

Comments in Brief: Since Neptune entered tenth at puberty when school curricula require selection of subjects to suit adult occupations, his influence over choices began at a markedly significant stage in development. Yet successes brought no steep rise in confidence. Uncertainties still continue.

Current Neptune Effect:

Time Spans Involved for each Transit/Aspect in Current House from:
From '84 to '89.

(1) Neptune conjunct Saturn and trine Venus: Jan–Aug '84, Nov '84–Jan '85, Jul '85–Nov '85
(2) Neptune trine Pluto: Feb–May '85, Dec '85–Jan '87, Jul '87–Nov '87
(3) Neptune sextile Neptune: Feb '86–July '86, Nov '86–Feb '87, Jul–Dec '87

Effect of Major Operative Aspects:
More help than hindrance here. Transit aspects further emphasize career influence of travel/foreigners. Apprehension mixes with unusual romantic liaisons (1) More inspired grasp of work/career offers (2) Added emotional rapport with foreigners plus stimulated creativity (3).

Comments in Brief: Stress on tenth, ninth and sixth houses. Events likely to emphasize career ambitions, working environment. Total change in attitude to work probable from these link-ups.

Neptune Example Transit Sheet

FUTURE LIFE TRENDS: Years examined—

(*Reminder Note:* The planet Neptune always promotes events which *subtly* alter your self-awareness, spiritual growth and capacity for spiritual understanding of yourself and others. It is a gradually sensitizing influence which turns you away from materialistic aims.)

Long-Range Neptune Effect:

Time Spans Involved in Current House Position:

Effect of House Transit:

Comments in Brief:..

....

....

....

Current Neptune Effect:

Time Spans Involved for each Transit/Aspect in Current House:

Effect of Major Operative Aspects:

Comments in Brief:..

....

....

....

At this stage, our outline of the future is beginning to take on a more definite shape. We've seen how both Pluto and Neptune—in their transits—add light or shade, depths and colour to the life plan mapped out by Saturn.

We've watched Saturn's demand for self-discipline in handling coming events. We've observed Pluto's insistence on the search for truth about our future hopes/intentions/motivations. We've looked at Neptune's urgings to pursue what is spiritually instead of merely materially best for us.

Now, in our next chapter, we face up to two more of the 'heavies' . . .Uranus, the 'Great Disrupter' and Jupiter, the 'Great Expansionist'. How did they get their titles? We'll soon see why!

Quick Reference Check-Points for Chapter 4

Looking Back to the Future

Like to see incontrovertible proof that the techniques for Future Life Trend Forecasting we've been working through in this book really work? In an actual life story? Then listen to the strange tale of a girl who only learned about her future *after* it had happened!

Here's how it came about. She was a successful young career woman with many planets in Leo. (An important fact because strongly Lion personalities invariably trust everybody and fervently believe that everybody ought to love them.)

Three weeks before she was suddenly offered a top job in a foreign country, she met, fell for and agreed to marry a young businessman. A familiar story *except* his wedding date to *another* girl was already set—for just three weeks away! He cancelled it, nevertheless, and jilted his intended bride. Only to learn his Leo love had decided to accept the overseas job, while promising to return home and marry him as soon as her new work permitted.

However, the overseas scene she found herself in proved disconcertingly problematical. She wrote at once to me (I had already interpreted her chart a year before) to request me to check the planetary influences in her life over a particular set of dates in the immediate future. She also instructed me to hand the cassette tape I'd prepared to her former fiance, adding she no longer intended to marry him but that he had agreed to pay for and collect the tape, then airmail it to her the same day.

Three years passed before I heard from her again. She rang me while on a flying visit to Sydney with the following sorry story.

All the events/problems about which both planetary transits and progressions had given strong warnings (around those now distant dates) had turned out exactly as I had described them on the tape. *And* she had made some nearly disastrous mistakes. *Because* her forsaken lover had deliberately delayed mailing the tape to her till *months after* the period she was worried about had passed. Thus, by the time she was able to listen to the planetary forecast the future had already become the past!

A cautionary tale in more ways than one. Nevertheless, it clearly puts paid to the scoffers who allege that 'predictions only come true because people have been conned into believing they will'. There was no way in the world this girl could have 'helped' the indicated events to happen since she had no prior knowledge of them. Yet happen they did. Right on cue. Just as the planetary patterns implied.

Pluto and Neptune—Sign Symbolism

Whenever you're interpreting the transits of the two heaviest and slowest of the known planets, visualize in your mind the symbols of the signs that they rule. Such images will help you appreciate the influence of the planet in pictorial form.

Pluto is the ruler of Scorpio. . .the sign symbolized by that most formidable of creatures—the death-dealing, sting-tailed Scorpion. This large insect is capable of stinging itself to death in combat. Thus it brings sharply to mind the terminal violence the planet Pluto is capable of.

Neptune is the ruler of Pisces. . .the sign symbolized by the pair of fishes, bound together but swimming in opposite directions, so portraying the endless battle between the material world of the flesh and the incorporeal world of the spirit. Thus it brings sharply to mind the 'undersea' scene of Neptune and the contrary currents within it.

The most commonly used glyph for Pluto today is ♇. This figure incorporates the initials P.L. which are those of an American professor of astronomy, Percival Lowell.

Lowell, born 13 March 1855, was the first scientist to contend that a planet existed in our solar system beyond Neptune and further that life existed on other planets. (A daring, highly controversial argument in his time!) Long after his death in 1916, but at the Lowell Laboratory in Arizona he founded, Pluto was discovered. Official date of discovery—21 January 1930. Date of announcement of discovery—13 March 1930. (Announcement was postponed to coincide with Lowell's date of birth.)

Like Pluto, Neptune is also a comparatively recent arrival in the history of astrology. Official date of discovery—23 September 1846. Neptune's glyph is ♆. This figure resembles the trident sceptre of the sea-god after which the planet was named.

Uranus, too, (to be discussed in next chapter) did not begin to figure in astrological science till late in its centuries-old story. Official date of discovery—13 March 1781.

The foregoing short sortie into astronomical and astrological history should be carefully noted. It's a reminder that the vast accumulation of recorded observations of planetary behaviour, stretching back over thousands of years, does not include Pluto, Neptune or Uranus. All are relative newcomers in the field of human experience and astrological knowledge. That does not, of course, mean these three planets did not affect human lives in past centuries. But as they could neither be observed nor their movements studied, astrologers could only surmise their existence.

Note: Interesting to observe that Albert Einstein's birthday was one day after Lowell's—14 March 1879. Though born 24 years apart, both eminent Pisceans had their natal Plutos in the sign of Taurus. Further, Lowell was born on the same date as that of Uranus' discovery—149 years earlier.

Proximity of birthdates also occurs in two other great names in physics, astronomy and astrology. Johannes Kepler was born on 27 December 1571 and Sir Isaac Newton on 25 December 1642.

All just coincidence? Chance? I don't think so!

Passing the Buck to the Stars

The rapidly escalating popularity of astrology plus the equally rapidly escalating tensions of life in the last decades of the twentieth century have produced a distinctly disturbing phenomenon. . .the emergence of people who want to shirk all personal responsibility in the decision-making process. . .who've become 'star crazy'. These types convince themselves their daily lives are literally 'written in the stars'. So when things go wrong there's always something other than themselves to blame.

Here 'in brief' are the comments of one such woman who phoned me recently:

'I never move outside my front door until I've looked up my stars in two newspapers, worked out my numerology for the day and gone over my personal horoscope', she said happily. 'Now, I don't have to think about anything. My stars and numbers make all my decisions for me!'

I barely resisted asking this poor, misguided woman how she ever managed to *get* as far as her front door each morning? *And* what she did when 'her stars and numbers' gave conflicting or wrong orders for her day? (Newspaper 'stars' columns, in any event, are so generalized as to be meaningless: one's predictions will often contradict another's). *And* what had become of her own free will, her own freedom of choice?

Always do everything possible to discourage this buck-passing attitude in your individual chart subjects. Future planetary patterns are *indicators*, not *dictators* of future events/decisions. Don't allow people seeking astrological advice to lean too heavily or too frequently on their charts or on you, yourself. If you do, you will find you're the one left holding the baby. What's more, it's a baby which cries loudly and often!

Pluto Transits: Compulsion Plus Propulsion

Undoubtedly, one of the best examples of Pluto-style compulsions leading to 'jet-propelled' actions was the case of an amateur astrologer, who arrived in my office some years ago with briefcase so crammed with calculation sheets he could barely carry it.

He was in his mid-forties, and well and truly in the grip of transiting Pluto's square to natal Pluto which occurs in most lives between age 40 and age 50.

'I've never been married', he said breathlessly. 'Now, I feel I must be. As soon as possible. I think I've found someone. She's living with another man and she says she loves him. But. . .', he paused to extract a wad of papers from his bulging case, '. . .I've worked out our synastry and we're perfect for each other!'

I checked over the relationship/compatibility patterns as he'd set them down. They looked ominous—to say the least.

'What makes you think these are perfect? And what about the fact that the lady in question loves and lives with another man?'

'Oh,' he laughed. 'I'm not worried about that. See! Our Moon's Nodes match!'

Stark realisation of wasted years and lost opportunities strike us all with cataclysmic force as youth departs forever and transiting Pluto climaxes the mid-life crisis by arriving at the square to his natal position. At this time, a feeling of desperation may take over, forcing desperate measures in the houses linked by the square.

In this case, Pluto's recent entry into the seventh house of marriage/unions by transit had struck natal Pluto in the fourth house of home/early conditioning. Both highly significant angular houses, the net result of the impact of such mighty forces was compulsion. Our man felt compelled to initiate radical, life-transforming changes in these two life departments.

But—with the added impetus of an awkwardly-aspected natal Neptune, which had always induced romantic fantasizing—he had contrived to convince himself that a totally incompatible female, who had plainly shown no interest and already had a long-established live-in lover, was about to become his ideal bride.

This impossible 'dream girl' was the latest in a long line of inaccessible women—stretching back to his adolescence—yet when I remarked on his difficult natal Neptune, he stared at me in open-mouthed astonishment. He obviously did not know what I was talking about although he stated he'd been studying astrology for ten years.

Thus this story serves as a warning on three counts:

1. All the pages of complicated calculations in the world won't get you anywhere if you haven't thoroughly grasped the basics of chart interpretation. (Our man was undoubtedly at the top of the class for his maths: at the bottom for his analysis.)
2. When interpreting your own chart, you must look at it as if it belonged to a stranger. Unless you strive for the highest possible degree of emotional and intellectual detachment, you will make our man's mistake of stressing comforting fallacies at the expense

of unpalatable facts. (He'd pounced on the link between the Moon's Nodes, a minor factor at best, so as to blind himself to the numerous indicators of incompatibility between his impossible 'dream girl' and himself.)

3. Pluto transits demand change based on calm self-assessment instead of desperation. Otherwise Pluto-style compulsions can amount to propulsion into disastrous and hopeless situations.

Thus, once in the grip of Pluto, you can be sure—to transpose a famous sentence of novelist John Steinbeck—'this ain't going to be no little mouse-squeak of a party!'

Weighing Up Neptune

Perhaps, the stickiest trick Neptune pulls out of his bottomless bag of illusions, delusions and deceptions is the one labelled 'spiritual conceit'. The totally false conviction that lures some individuals into boasting that they have reached heights of spiritual evolution far beyond the reach of ordinary mortals. Sometimes they keep this dangerous belief to themselves. More often they parade it to impress the gullible.

As witness the example of one such man, encountered by an astrologer colleague of mine at a party. He was introduced by the host as the founder of a new religious sect in Europe, an occultist, a spiritualist and (astonishingly!) an astrologer. He was also so eye-stoppingly obese he overflowed the large chair on which he was seated.

In conversation, he raised the subject of astrology and later my friend remarked that she found Neptune's energy the hardest to handle.

'Do you.' The mountainous man smiled benignly. 'If you're as highly evolved as I am, Neptune is never a problem. I. . .'

At that moment, he broke off in mid-sentence as supper was announced. He rushed to the buffet, returning with a piled-high plate which he quickly ploughed through before collecting a second helping of everything. Later in the evening, when the supper table was empty, my friend saw him raiding his host's refrigerator.

Since Gluttony is named as one of the Seven Deadly Sins in Christianity as well as several other religions and this man was holding himself out as a spiritual leader, my friend found his behaviour even more appalling. She told me later she would have loved to examine his horoscope chart. Such shocking self-deception could only have been the work of a very badly placed and aspected Neptune, mixing as it did totally unrestrained self-indulgence with spiritual conceit.

Equally, one shudders to think what this man taught his sect followers. Nevertheless, this story does illustrate how totally Neptune can mislead us and how unrelentingly we have to struggle against his negative manifestations in personality. So beware! Take care! When Neptune makes tough tansits either in the natal chart or during his transits, religious delusions of all shapes and sizes abound. The more so today when the search for spiritual meaning in our hi-tech world has intensified to the point where we can all too easily fall under the spell of false gurus and phoney prophets.

Your 'Tapestry' of the Future. . .Stitching in the Colours

An analogy I regularly use in teaching natal chart interpretation as well as future forecasting is to advise students to think of both as a tapestry. A very long and detailed one. Rather like the famed Bayeux Tapestry which relates in narrative picture form the Norman Conquest of England in 1066.

Imagine the major planetary influences as coloured threads. Deep brown threads for Saturn, typifying his earthy, disciplinary action. Dark red threads for Pluto, typifying his capacity for waging bloody battles between the subconscious and the ego. Sea-green, threads for Neptune, typifying his revelations of the unfathomable depths of the human spirit. Electric blue threads for Uranus, typifying his crashing through resistance like a flash of lightning.

Next think of the horoscope chart as the blank frame into which you'll stitch your coloured threads according to the designated pattern. This analogy will serve to remind you that each individual thread and colour must be worked into its appointed place—*before* the whole picture can be seen and examined. None missed. None over-used.

So far, we've gathered our store of coloured threads for Saturn, Pluto and Neptune. Our calculations will show us where to put each one and how much of the coloured thread to use. In the next chapter, we'll add Uranus and Jupiter to our tapestry of the future.

CHAPTER FIVE

The Faster-Moving Planets—Their Role in Switching Life Directions

We've compared Pluto's transits to shock waves of earthquake proportions as they shake the foundations of the subconscious mind. And Neptune's transits to tidal waves of changing sensations, sweeping away old illusions to bring about spiritual enlightenment. In the same style, we'll now compare Uranus' transits to whirlwinds, rushing up out of nowhere to blow away crystallized habits of thought and living.

Just as huge trees are ripped up like matchsticks and flimsy houses flattened like matchboxes when a tornado hits, so Uranus tears down deep-rooted, well-entrenched attitudes and poorly-constructed plans. Far more drastic in effect and immediate in impact on events than the transits of the other two heavy planets, Uranus goes for instant action. With him there are no yesterdays and no tomorrows. Everything is now. Right now! Scenes and situations are switched before your astonished eyes. One set of circumstances is whisked abruptly away to be replaced—just as summarily—by a completely different set. The need to act becomes imperative. Something's *got* to give! And something invariably does! Then and there!

This effect is in sharp contrast with life changes instigated by Pluto and Neptune. Their impact may not be fully felt and understood by yourself or your chart subjects until some years after the crisis points have passed. This is because the changes are taking place at deeper levels of consciousness. With Uranus, his sudden pressure on events cannot be mistaken or ignored.

Naturally, this speeds up responses and speed can add up to danger—especially in natal charts which show marked tendencies towards rashness/impetuosity. In such cases, Uranian transits demand one foot on the brake and both eyes on the road ahead. Otherwise, the result is not unlike driving a car with the accelerator jammed at full on and a cliff top in front of you. You'll be over the edge before you know it!

As happened in the case of a 40-year-old male executive (with several planets in Leo), who flung himself recklessly into a love affair with his 18-year-old secretary as transiting Uranus entered his seventh house of marriage and shortly after arrived at an opposition aspect with natal Uranus. (A not uncommon story with this particular Uranus aspect: see 'Planetary Switch-Points' section in Chapter 2. Everyone experiences it around age 40. Some handle it constructively, others don't.)

This man let it run wild. He deserted his wife and two teenage children, set up house with the girl, trying to pretend he was young again and 'starting over'. Predictably, it didn't take reality long to raise its spiky head.

His teenage son and daughter refused to see him or even speak to him. His youthful new partner wanted marriage and children of her own, rejecting outright the role of prospective stepmother to a boy and girl, who were not only hostile but almost the same age as herself. His wife, still hoping to save her 18-year-old marriage, begged her husband to have his chart analysed.

He agreed, but as both the natal and future planetary patterns relentlessly exposed the realities he was striving to ignore, he became increasingly more tight-lipped and antagonistic.

Further, since Uranus' hard aspects (in both natal links and transits) imply stubborn adherence to wrong-headed ideas, this man refused to pay any attention at all to the planetary warnings. Instead, he discarded his analysis on the seat of his wife's car with an angry note, concluding with: 'Astrology's a load of old rubbish!'

Meanwhile, as he rushed further along his collision course with trouble, his new romance was showing signs of crashing down to earth. Financial problems were piling up fast. Upkeep of two homes, maintenance payments, division of marital assets and property. Talk of further children he didn't want at 40 plus and couldn't afford anyway.

The final outcome? Virtually a foregone conclusion. The girl left him for a man closer to her own age. His wife and children rejected his overtures towards reconciliation. He was out in the Uranian cold with nothing but bills to keep him company.

Without moralizing over the rights or wrongs of his actions, this man was neither an inexperienced youth nor an uneducated simpleton. Nor did he need to be clairvoyant to foresee some, if not most, of the disastrous consequences of his rashness. That is, provided he'd stopped to think at all. But having allowed himself to be caught up in a series of Uranus-style errors—more easily because he was a naturally impulsive individual through the heavy stress on fire in his natal chart—he looked only at the moment, the 'now'. His yesterdays no longer existed: the pay-offs of tomorrow would never come. Uranus had no trouble in pushing him over the precipice. Remember this case when interpreting Uranus transits yourself. Look ahead *before* you leap into action.

Uranus—the 'Great Disruptor' in Transit

Speed in motion as well as action is one of Uranus's distinguishing features too. Compared to Pluto and Neptune, he literally dashes through the twelve signs of the Zodiac, spending approximately seven years in each as he transits them. (Thus giving planetary backing to the old saying— the 'Seven Year Itch'.)

Astronomically too, the number seven is associated with Uranus. The planet is the seventh from the sun with an orbit lying between that of Saturn and Neptune.

Once again, to more fully understand Uranus' role in both the natal chart and during transits, we'll need to take a closer look at the appropriate mythology.

Here, Uranus stands high above—in more ways than one—all the other ancient Greco-Roman deities who have given their names and traits to the eight planets. For starters, he was the progenitor of most of them with his private domain being the limitless sky itself. Uranus was also the first of the male deities to appear on the scene in the role of the chosen bridegroom of Gaea, the Great Earth Mother. Hardly had the marriage got under way however, than she presented him with a veritable horde of children. The very worst—out of an exceedingly bad bunch in Uranus' view—was Saturn.

Uranus solved this problem simply and permanently. At least that's what he thought. He dumped the lot, without consulting his formidable wife, into a bottomless pit at the most distant point in the universe.

Failure to consult the wife on important family decisions is usually a fatal error for any husband. And, supreme god though he was, so it proved to be for Uranus.

Gaea, infuriated at her consort's obvious lack of fatherly feeling, rescued Saturn and stood calmly by while he, chopper in hand, despatched his unsuspecting parent to enthrone *himself* as Lord of the World. For the time being, that satisfactorily settled the issue. Then Saturn in turn took a wife and sired Jupiter plus numerous other offspring, two of whom were Neptune and Pluto. Predictably, it didn't take long for Saturn to discover that 'all his troubles were little ones' too, since heavenly history promptly repeated itself.

Following established paternal precedent, Jupiter (with the aid of his siblings) soon made short work of Saturn and installed *himself* as the Chief of the Gods. In grateful appreciation of services rendered, he handed over rulership of the Underworld to his dark brother Pluto and the Oceans to his aquatic brother Neptune.

Understandably, the foregoing long, tangled and bloody saga of unceasing domestic warfare, conducted with gusto and on a depressingly grandiose scale by all his nearest and dearest, did nothing to convince Uranus that wives, children or grandchildren for that matter, were worth the trouble they caused. He came to the inevitable conclusion that if he'd kept himself to himself. . .if he hadn't married anybody or sired anybody. . .he'd still be running the universe *his* way.

It is exactly this method of thinking which underlies reactions encouraged by Uranus' natal position and/or events instigated by his transits. Both are highly separative, directed at severing permanent ties of all kinds, much inclined to promote the 'Do-Your-Own-Thing-And-To-Hell-With-Everything—Else!' stance. This approach explains why Uranus earned his title of the 'Great Disruptor!'

Footnote: Readers interested in studying comparative mythology should note that almost identical tales of ferocious family blood-letting among the gods occur in many, diverse ancient cultures. The scene of the action changes but plot and characters remain very nearly the same.

In this book, I have used the Roman names for the gods involved since these remind us at once of the planets to which they are linked. But in Ancient Greece, for example, Saturn and Jupiter were known as Cronus and Zeus respectively. In Ancient Egypt, Uranus appears in much the same scenario as the god Osiris, his wife as Isis with the fearsome Set taking over Saturn's role.

American analyst, Dr Edward C. Whitmont, in his excellent book, *The Symbolic Quest—Basic Concepts of Analytical Psychology* explains at length the great significance of ancient mythology in comprehending the complexities of human relationships and the unending battles for power and survival. Not only in the distant past but right now at the end of the twentieth century. Over those many thousands of years, Man has changed his world, not necessarily for the better. He has never been capable of changing himself in any but material ways. Thus, in just the same manner as narrated by the myths of the ancients, the deadly power struggles go on and on. American intellectual Gore Vidal put it this way:

> 'It is not possible to regard our race with anything but alarm. . .the majority of mankind take delight in our predatoriness: that's how we made it!
>
> From primeval ooze to the stars, we killed everything that stood in our way, including one another.
>
> War is our natural state with one another, with environment, with space, with other worlds where live—what else?—formidable beings whom we must eliminate.'

Sobering thoughts, those! But then Vidal is a Libran—born 3 October 1925 (with Mercury and Mars as well as the Sun in Libra)—so his civilized horror of violence may have caused him to overreact to the human story.

New Flashpoints of Innovation. . .Or . . .New Flare-ups of Rebellion

Innovation and insight, rebellion and perversity, brilliance and invention, brutality and chaos—all these show up on the debit and credit sides of the Uranian ledger. This planet spells out 'FREEDOM' in capital letters and lets loose explosive events, wild reactions in the individual pursuit of liberty, usually with little care for consequences.

As a result, individuals with Uranus powerfully placed in their natal charts or experiencing important Uranus transits are capable of exhibiting behaviour that appears reckless at best, destructive at worst. For Uranus never plays it by anybody's rules but his own and never dances to anybody else's tune.

Further, his mythological eminence as ruler of the sky, standing far above and totally detached from earthly affairs, tells us a great deal about Uranian-inspired actions. As does his consequent symbolic link with the element of air. That cool, blowing intangible element which is attached to nothing, cannot be grasped or seen yet is capable of changing its gentle breezes to the gales of hurricane force in minutes.

Air is, of course, a predominantly mental element. Hence Uranus works on the thinking mind, the intellect, in his push for freedom, demanding detachment from mundane obligations, responsibilities, duties, promoting a heady sense of god-like power and superiority. A dangerous view as we saw with the case of the erring husband earlier in this chapter.

Such reactions are naturally more marked when Uranus is transiting any one of the four angular houses or activating major natal planetary configurations.

In the first house, he suddenly blows the whistle for personal *freedom* so that flight from restrictions on self-expression and self-presentation ensues.

In the fourth house, he suddenly produces new notions of *freedom* as possible tools for breaking up the happy home.

In the seventh house, he suddenly pushes *freedom* from irksome familiarity as the excuse for replacing existing partners with new ones.

In the tenth house, he suddenly urges *freedom* from routine as the reason for adventuring in search of new occupational interests and high-flying objectives.

The recurrence of three words—'suddenly', 'freedom' and 'new'—in the foregoing examples of Uranus transits emphasizes the effect of them. Uranus-style changes are invariably sudden, invariably freedom-oriented and invariably discount what is old/established in favour of all that is new/novel.

Nothing wrong with that in essence. We cannot confine ourselves for ever to our safe, well-cushioned ruts: we cannot dwell in the vanishing world of the past.

If we are going to evolve and develop as thinking beings, we must sometimes risk a ride on the whirlwinds of change. Yet this must not be taken to mean that Uranus' demand for freedom at any price should be answered heedlessly. Pursuit of freedom without an attendant sense of responsibility is not true freedom at all. It is plain licence.

One of the most memorable examples of transiting Uranus at his most disruptive is that of a female cookery teacher who—to use an old-fashioned phrase—threw her bonnet over every windmill in sight as the planet entered her seventh house.

On first thoughts a classic Cancer type, she had, until then, been a pillar of society. Mother of two, a respectable family-minded traditionalist, who even taught Sunday School at her local church. *And* she looked the part. Shortly before Uranus struck, she had had her chart interpreted and been warned of possible and imminent perils to marital stability. These warnings she had dismissed with a polite smile and a demure shake of the head.

How long did it take transiting Uranus to turn her neat, well-ordered existence upside down and inside out? Less than 12 months. Leaving her husband at home as a live-in babysitter, she tossed out her button-down collars for plunging necklines and tight jeans, hit the local discos like a brunette bombshell and jumped into bed with every good-looking male who asked her.

How did Uranus so swiftly accomplish such a staggering turn-about? By battering down her carefully-tended Cancer demeanour to arouse her Sagittarian Ascendant and Sagittarian Moon—both of which she had been conditioned to squash since childhood. Set free at last, they leapt into action with wild abandon. Had it not been for the opportune arrival of a stabilizing Saturn transit, she too could have gone over the edge of the Uranian precipice.

As it was, she stopped just short of the point of no return. Certainly her existing marriage had fallen apart under the strain of what for her was bizarre behaviour. But the divorce was fair and amicable, followed by a new marriage to a partner more suited to her contradictory Sagittarius/Cancer personality.

Thus, here, Uranus wrought changes which, though disruptive, were necessary to release heavily-repressed traits in this young woman's psychological make-up. Had something as drastic as this not happened, repression could have gone on laying the groundwork for future mental and/or physical disorders later in her life.

(Although the result is rarely as startling as the case just cited, overstressing Sun sign traits and hence repressing those of the Ascendant and Moon signs is always risky. . .in daily life and close relationships. If you're not fully aware of this danger, read my two companion books—*How to Astro-Analyze Yourself and Others* and *Astro-Pick Your Perfect Partner*.)

Uranus House Transits—Bolts from the Blue

Wherever Uranus is situated in the natal chart, there is an inextinguishable dread of anyone or anything coming too close and crowding personal space. . .a kind of inner claustrophobia. Packaged with this is a concomitant wilfulness, a desire to shock and resist conformity—to cut cold at the first hint of constraint or restriction. Naturally, these qualities are more emphasized in those whose natal charts are markedly Aquarian or where Uranus holds a dominating position.

Genius composer Wolfgang Amadeus Mozart (whose birth patterns were discussed at length in my first book in this series) is a perfect example. Born 27 January 1756 and with four planets in Aquarius, Mozart consistently displayed his brilliance and simultaneously wrecked his opportunities through his wildly Uranian behaviour.

Another world-famous Aquarian, this time of the twentieth century, was the man still called 'The King' of Hollywood and decades after his death is still remembered as every woman's idol of rugged and raffish American masculinity. Clark Gable, born 1 February 1901 – died 1960. Gable's willingness to shock and flout convention is immortalized in two reported incidents.

The first: At a glittering gala dinner, his society hostess remarked she had always admired his beautiful teeth.

'Why, thank you', replied the dress-suited 'King', smiling broadly. 'Would you like a closer look?' Whereon he deftly slipped out his dentures and offered them for inspection across the festive table!

The second: While replying to journalists' questions about his acting technique which caused leading ladies 'to melt under his lusty lingering gazes', he said:

'I get the effect by thinking about a piece of prime juicy steak.' No mistaking the voice of Uranus in comments like those.

During his transits, Uranus arouses in everyone—whether naturally meek or naturally wild—this desire to rebel and resist convention, throwing it up in stark relief, like lightning flashing over a dim landscape. The effect is startling, unsettling. Simmering discontent boils over. Limitations on freedom, whether they be people or circumstances, are suddenly seen as useless stumbling blocks which must be pushed aside, smashed or blasted out of the path to progress. Caution is forgotten, long-established routines become intolerable.

The dash for freedom is on and the devil take the hindmost. Yet handled skilfully, Uranus transits can turn the improbable into the actual. For instance, it was highly improbable that a 49-year-old housewife would wake up one morning and decide to write a film script. It was even more improbable that this script would win her enrolment in the most sought-after film school in the country against hot competition from much younger, more experienced candidates. But that's what happened as Uranus entered her fifth house, connected with natal planets and thus boosted creative skills which had lain dormant and neglected since childhood.

Now for another Uranus-type question. Stop here—this very minute—and ask yourself *why* you decided to read this book? What sparked your interest in astrology—now or in the past? Whatever you consider to be the reason, one glance at your chart will show Uranus himself playing a leading role in the story.

If you believe you've always had a natural 'feel' for astrology, check the position of Uranus in your natal chart. Most leading professionals have this planet occupying a dominant position in their chart patterns. For from Uranus come the flashes of insight, the grasp of scientific method, the sense of the rhythms and timing of life. And the unflagging determination to battle bigotry, ignorance and prejudice which—like the poor—are always with us.

If you've suddenly become attracted to astrology, go over your natal chart carefully plus current transits and progressions.

If you've been studying astrology for years, turn back to the time when you first began to take a serious interest and examine the planetary pictures current then.

In both cases, you'll observe Uranus at work, for astrology is his own science. Whether right now or in your distant past, sudden interest and the speed with which that interest gathers force is an unmistakable characteristic of Uranian transits as they activate your natal planets. . .particularly those affecting intellectual preoccupations or career directions.

Again, many leading practitioners agree that powerful Uranian transits ignited the first flames of enthusiasm which led them eventually to abandon other careers in favour of astrology. That's certainly how it happened for me when Uranus dropped astrology into my life in his typical crash-bang style by dumping twelve books of it on my front doorstep one afternoon in the mid-sixties.

The bearer of the books was as bizarrely Uranian as you could wish for. An ancient ship's captain (retired), complete with snowy beard and brass buttons, who roared in a voice you could have heard from the bridge of an aircraft carrier, that he'd learned I was a qualified psychologist and author. The astrology books, he said, he'd picked up in America. They were cheap, highly-coloured trash about love, sex and the stars. Would I accept his commission to write a new set of twelve, aimed at readers with minds? And applying my psychological training in describing the tastes and traits of the twelve Zodiac signs in love and marriage?

I was obliged to decline his offer because at that time I knew virtually nothing about astrology. He told me to keep the books anyway and swiftly the spark of interest took fire. Despite the bad writing and trite commentaries on the Sun signs, I saw tiny embers of truth, glowing among the ashes. Gold among the dross. I had to find out more and soon I did. But some 20 years were to pass before I felt ready to write my book on synastry, a companion title to this one—*Astro-Pick Your Perfect Partner*.

Your own introduction to astrological science may be a trifle less odd than mine but you'll invariably find an important Uranian transit or aspect or both acted as the triggering devices. (Both Uranus and Pluto were transiting my tenth House (career/attainments) and making powerful aspects to natal planets situated therein at the date the captain landed on my doormat.)

Still, that little anecdote certainly illustrates Uranus' habit of hurling bolts from the blue into everybody's life and thus blasting it off in an entirely new, often startlingly unexpected direction.

Once again, as in earlier chapters, we'll include a 'Uranus Transit Sheet' at the end of this section, so you can also check Uranus Transits creating their customary flashpoints and flare-ups. *But*—and that 'but' can never be repeated often enough—handle Uranus with care. A great deal of care! Otherwise, as we saw in our case histories, if you respond too rashly, too recklessly and without thought for the practical consequences of your acts, Uranus' wild winds of change can blow you over the precipice on to the rocks of regret.

FIRST HOUSE URANUS TRANSIT EVENTS . . .
drastically alter self image and personal environment.

Positive Responses Promote	• Broadening of scope of personal interests. • Progressive changes in private environment. • Expression of boosted individuality and originality. • Release from restrictions and wise use of new freedoms.
Negative Responses Invite	• Set-backs through imprudence or selfish pursuit of own ends. • Futile rebellion against necessary duties/ties. • Nervous disorders through fear of change. • Irresponsible, erratic behaviour.

SECOND HOUSE URANUS TRANSIT EVENTS . . .
drastically alter earning power and use of own moneys.

Positive Responses Promote	• Sudden successes through use of ingenuity in finances.

	• Opportunities to branch out into new ways of earning. • Gains from technological skills/interests. • Freedom from financial liabilities/restrictions.
Negative Responses Invite	• Errors of judgement from impatience, erratic thinking. • Stubborn adherence to unrealistic, ill-conceived planning. • Losses through wilful, uncooperative behaviour. • Money worries from refusal to accept wise advice.

THIRD HOUSE URANUS TRANSIT EVENTS . . .
drastically alter mental attitudes and educational skills.

Positive Responses Promote	• Original, broad-minded thinking, creative of new intellectual activities. • New manners and methods of communication. • Attraction to new forms of study, educational courses. • Eradication of old thinking habits, outdated ideas.
Negative Responses Invite	• Restless switching from one new interest to another. • Inability to concentrate in pursuit of knowledge. • Errors/bad judgement in choice of advisors or teachers. • Pointless trips or travelling.

FOURTH HOUSE URANUS TRANSIT EVENTS . . . ***drastically alter domestic circumstances and home atmosphere.***

Positive Responses Promote	• Beneficial changes in location of residence and/or conditions within the home. • Attraction to progressive, interesting individuals with which to cohabit. • Sudden insight into needs of family members. • Freedom from long-standing domestic-type restraints.
Negative Responses Invite	• Continuing, restless dissatisfaction with partners, home situatoins. • Inability to maintain domestic harmony through erratic attitudes. • Upsets through high-handed, uncooperative reactions within the home. • Tension from intolerably provocative behaviour.

FIFTH HOUSE URANUS TRANSIT EVENTS . . . ***drastically alter romantic liaisons, concern with children, creative talents.***

Positive Responses Promote	• Sudden, stimulating romantic interests/attachments. • Attraction to new pleasures/amusements, sometimes of a more daring nature. • Fresh insights into relationship with children and their needs. • Unexpected chances to demonstrate creative/artistic/design skills.

Negative Responses Invite	• Callous termination of love affairs in search of thrills and freedom from ties. • Involvement in sports/pleasures that are either risky or obviously dangerous. • High-handed tactics with children, causing clashes and lack of understanding. • Constant changing of love partners or links with erratic, non-commital individuals.

SIXTH HOUSE URANUS TRANSIT EVENTS . . .
drastically alter working environment, health concerns.

Positive Responses Promote	• Innovative, new work methodology. • Opportunities to branch out into different, less routine-oriented occupations/professions. • Greater appreciation of original ideas by co-workers/employers. • Search for work with challenges and offering increased personal freedom.
Negative Responses Invite	• Rebellion against onerous work duties/obligations, creating censure. • Erratic changing from job to job without thought of security. • Provocative, irritable reactions in work-place. • Problems arising out of overexpectation of work effort from others.

SEVENTH HOUSE URANUS TRANSIT EVENTS . . .
drastically alter marital affairs, partnerships in love or business.

Positive Responses Promote	• Opportunities to revitalize—through new insights—relationships suffering from familiarity or routine. • Encounters with potential new life partners who are themselves stimulating, unusual types. • Decisions to break free of futile, stultifying marriages/unions. • Breaks in business partnerships to make way for better use of skills.
Negative Responses Invite	• Problems from rash pursuit of new love experiences, leading to break-ups/divorce. • Attempts to evade or escape from responsibilities towards those once cared about. • Attraction to partners who are married, unavailable or unreliable. • Condemnation by others, conflicts with past partners/intimates who have become open enemies.

EIGHTH HOUSE URANUS TRANSIT EVENTS . . .
drastically alter joint/shared financial liabilities and handling of deceased estate assets.

Positive Responses Promote	• Improved capacities to handle sudden changes in partnership finances/joint assets. • Surprising opportunities to gain greater financial authority over others.

- Sudden availability of credit in monetary matters.
- Clever use of monetary gifts, legacies leading to beneficial changes in life style.

Negative Responses Invite

- Involvement with unreliable or erratic business partners with possible financial losses.
- Erratic moves to break free of restriction/obligation in all forms of financial sharing.
- Sudden upsets/clashes over inherited moneys or division of assets.
- Unwelcome disruption to life style relating to shared property.

NINTH HOUSE URANUS TRANSIT EVENTS . . .
drastically alter involvements with foreigners, travel decisions.

Positive Responses Promote

- Radical changes in attitude/aims through travel or contact with foreigners.
- Sudden elimination of obstacles or blocks to personal development, resulting from new philosophy.
- Beneficial changes from contacts with progressive minds, often through travel.
- Unexpected chances to broaden education connected to travelling.

Negative Responses Invite

- Attraction to travel as means of evading responsibilities/studies.
- Accidents/disturbances connected to travelling or in communication with foreigners.
- Mistakes arising from rigid refusal to

consider others' opinions, especially if not own compatriots.
- Inability to integrate willingly with totally different life styles.

TENTH HOUSE URANUS TRANSIT EVENTS . . .
drastically alter career aims and personal status.

Positive Responses Promote	• Sudden, total changes in career direction/job opportunities. • Offers to engage in innovative enterprises with better understanding of new techniques. • Chances to express own originality through promotion and increased authority. • Abrupt removal of people/problems in path of career progress.
Negative Responses Invite	• Rash, ill-advised termination of present job/occupation in favour of irresponsible, worthless pursuits. • Dramatic drops in power/status through rigid adherence to outmoded precepts. • Over-assertion of independence, damaging to reputation and impressions made on others. • Assumption of rebellious, high-handed response to bosses/authority figures.

ELEVENTH HOUSE URANUS TRANSIT EVENTS . . .
drastically alter friendships and involvements in group activities.

Positive Responses Promote	• Startling changes in definition of former significant hopes/wishes.

	• Arrival in life of progressive, free-thinking friendships, promising profitable results. • Upsurge in social life with challenging opportunities for new group efforts. • Introductions to individuals of status with forward-looking ideas.
Negative Responses Invite	• Problems through refusal to co-operate willingly in group efforts/decisions. • Attraction to uncaring, irresponsible individuals in friendships. • Abrupt breaks with important contacts due to rejection of traditional views. • Involvement in erratic, impractical activities through foolish, misguided friendships.

TWELFTH HOUSE URANUS TRANSIT EVENTS . . .
drastically alter spiritual viewpoint and capacity for self-sacrifice.

Positive Responses Promote	• Emergence of new spiritual values and benefits from helping those unable to cope with life. • Sudden destruction of situations/environments which limit self-development. • Discovery of new understanding through changed perception of past actions/liaisons. • Appearance of new, more broadly-based intellectual interests, capable of changing source of income.

Negative Responses Invite	• Depressing periods of introspection and brooding over past history. • Self-recrimination through sudden exposure of previous misconduct in private or business affairs. • Sudden emergence of heavily-repressed feelings/needs in disturbing incidents. • Losses through hidden enmities or false friends.

Having watched Uranus blazing his trail through the twelve houses, we can see how his flashpoints and flare-ups set each life flying off in new and sometimes startlingly different directions. Once again, remember that although Uranus is the fastest of the super-slow movers, even he rarely completes a full circuit of any chart in the average lifetime since the majority of human beings do not live to reach 84 years.

Obviously, as we noted earlier in this book, the age of each chart subject should be carefully considered when assessing the impact of Uranus transits. An individual reacting to a first house Uranus transit, for example, at age 25 is undoubtedly much more likely to throw caution to the winds of change than a 55-year-old experiencing the same type of Uranian pressure. There's no gainsaying the fact that as we grow older our options do become fewer and the weight of experience heavier. At 25, we can drastically change jobs, partners, hair-dos, habits in a flash if the fancy takes us. At 55, we're likely to baulk even on the hair-do!

But, now it's time for another glance at the Uranian influence on our specimen chart subject—Clare Costumier. We recall from her natal chart that she began life with Uranus, sitting in her sixth house. So what happened when he moved into her seventh house (marriage/unions) in 1963 as she reached age four and continued transiting that house until 1970 when she was approaching age 11? Plenty!

Her parents' mismatched marriage, itself a Plutonic power struggle, began to founder. By 1963, it was already listing badly; by 1970 it had run aground on the rocks of barely-suppressed anger, occasional violence and insuperable incompatibility. Uranus had given her a sneak preview of exactly what happens when the wrong people marry each other—a lesson she never forgot. As the planet established himself in her eighth house (shared moneys) in 1970 she witnessed the final break-up plus the consequent unpleasant and recriminatory squabbling over matrimonial property.

As she matured from adolescent to young adult between 1975 and 1982, Uranus traversed her ninth house (foreigners/travel) and she completed her tertiary education, had a brief, unsettling affair with a foreign-born male, began working and spent her earnings on travel.

In late 1982 with Uranus crossing her tenth house (career/attainment) cusp, she suddenly resigned her job, changed her working environment drastically and for the first time in her life began to think of training for an *entirely* different profession.

All in all, a vivid portrayal of Uranus transits at work. Virtually straight out of the textbook.

Now, as before, do a past-years check with your own chart subjects, plotting the periods of Uranus' house transits and chronicling the events which accompanied them. Watch to see whether each individual raced off along the perilous path of reckless rebellion and thus skidded towards a collision course with events. Or if he/she used those sudden lightning flashes of Uranian insight to light the unfamiliar and possibly stony track ahead.

Uranus Transit Aspects. . .New Worlds for Old

Next, we look to Uranus' transiting aspects as they place sudden and often disruptive pressure on the houses (or life sectors) through which the planet is moving. Remember, as set out earlier, to give greatest weight to powerful aspects—conjunctions, trines, squares and oppositions—in postulating events.

Uranus Transit Aspects—Interpretation Table

Transiting Uranus Aspecting Natal Sun

Energy Blend: Innovation/Personal Goals

Reminder Note: the *natal Sun* in every chart reveals the basic ego thrust

. . .the true, unalterable self. . .the workings of the conscious mind.

Uranus in every chart points to the sense of self-reliance. . .the desire for personal freedom. . .the search for newness.

Thus all contacts between transiting Uranus and the natal Sun—whether by conjunction, trine, sextile, square of opposition—create varying degrees of change and/or conflict between what *the ego* wants for itself and the direction in which *the boosted drive for independence* strives to push it.

The purpose of these transits is to blow away the ego-based fear of the new and unfamiliar. Efforts to hold on to whatever is narrow, overly conservative or dulling to the self's skills lead to explosions and enforced new starts.

Uranus/Sun Event Projection

Anyone experiencing these transits faces incidents and situations designed to:

- Force new directions in life style and occupational concerns.
- Break routines in pursuit of stimulating activities.
- Induce a more progressive, forward-looking approach to private/business problems.
- Create tension and serious errors of judgement if reacting to impulse or over-expectation.
- Cause disruptively uncooperative behaviour, damaging to both personal and public affairs.

Uranus/Sun Transit Management

Anyone experiencing these transits is strongly advised to:

- Base all decisions on sound, well-considered planning.
- Avoid provoking controversy through erratic, exaggerated attitudes.
- Be prepared to risk a more adventurous approach in reaction to sudden opportunities.
- Seek new avenues of personal expression to respond to need for fundamental changes in environment/interests.

Transiting Uranus Aspecting Natal Moon

Energy Blend: Innovation/Emotional Needs

Reminder Note: the *natal Moon* in every chart reveals the basic emotional make-up. . .the secret self. . .the imprinted response patterns.

Uranus in every chart points to the sense of self-reliance. . .the desire for personal freedom. . .the search for newness.

Thus all contacts between transiting Uranus and the natal Moon—whether by conjunction, trine, sextile, square or opposition—create varying degrees of change and/or conflict between how *the emotions* manifest themselves and the direction in which the *boosted drive for independence* strives to push them.

The purpose of these transits is to break down emotional constraint and allow the feelings to flow freely and openly. Attempts to cling to the past and force emotions to remain in long-established channels are dealt with summarily by Uranus. If the needed changes are not made, he thrusts them into the life through severed ties and inner turmoil.

Uranus/Moon Event Projection

Anyone experiencing these transits faces incidents and situations designed to:

- Instigate original, inventive methods of solving private life problems.
- Bring sudden opportunities for emotional stimulation through creative or progressive individuals.
- Encourage rashness, excess speed or even eccentric behaviour in emotional liaison contacts with females.
- Cause sudden mood swings/inner tension in any intimate relationship.
- Stimulate urges to break ties through attraction to new partners.

Uranus/Moon Transit Management

Anyone experiencing these transits is strongly advised to:

- Steer clear of entanglements with unstable/unreliable types.
- Eradicate ingrained, dull or dreary responses, stemming from childhood conditioning.
- Abstain from unconventional, separative actions.

- Welcome changes where based on realistic acceptance of obligations instead of evasion of them.

Transiting Uranus Aspecting Natal Mercury

Energy Blend. Innovation/Mental interests

Reminder Note: Natal Mercury in every chart reveals the basic mental inclinations. . .type and grade of intellect. . .powers of communication.

Uranus in every chart points to the sense of self-reliance. . .the desire for personal freedom. . .the search for newness.

Thus all contacts between transiting Uranus and natal Mercury—whether by conjunction, trine, sextile, square of opposition—create varying degrees of change and/or conflict between *how thought processes operate* and the direction in which the *boosted drive for independence* strives to push them.

The purpose of these transits is to set the winds of change blowing through the cobwebby recesses of the mind. Refusal to switch the thinking patterns into new and broader channels leads to disoriented, muddled or confused communication.

Uranus/Mercury Event Projection

Anyone experiencing these transits faces incidents and situations designed to:

- Develop original, inventive methods of handling work/mental concerns.
- Boost self-reliance and willingness to take the initiative in decisions.
- Create disputes or sudden conflicts with reactionary or temperamental individuals in the work-place.
- Cause unfavourable reception of plans through sarcastic or harsh forms of communication.
- Accentuate over-forceful even belligerent expression of new ideas.

Uranus/Mercury Transit Management

Anyone experiencing these transits is strongly advised to:

- Think before speaking or leaping into action to test effect on others.

- Be prepared for unexpected developments, sudden news which can totally alter decisions.
- Apply enterprise and drive in pushing through to success in business/studies/publicity planning.
- Listen to contrary views calmly without attempting to contradict or overbear them.

Transiting Uranus Aspecting Natal Venus

Energy Blend: Innovation/Affectional Affairs

Reminder Note: Natal Venus in every chart reveals the basic capacities to give and receive affection. . .choice of and attraction to pleasures . . .desire for harmony.

Uranus in every chart points to the sense of self-reliance. . .the desire for personal freedom. . .the search for newness.

Thus all contacts between transiting Uranus and natal Venus—whether by conjunction, trine, sextile, square or opposition—create varying degrees of change and/or conflict between *how the affections operate* and the direction in which the *boosted drive for independence* strives to push them.

The purpose of these transits is to break the fetters of old, outworn feelings/habits in love and affection to reveal the path into new ways of responding. Unwillingness to open the prison door and release repressed desires for love/understanding lets loose a Uranian hurricane of discord, self-recrimination and lost opportunities.

Uranus/Venus Event Projection

Anyone experiencing these transits faces incidents and situations designed to:

- Cause sudden, seemingly inexplicable attraction to off-beat types as friends/intimates.
- Spark off new directions in social life and widened circle of unusual acquaintances.
- Boost search for excitement and challenge in love or pleasures, sometimes heedlessly.
- Bring about clashes with those cared about through over-demand for own freedom.

- Evoke disapproval of or ambiguity in new relationships.

Uranus/Venus Transit Management

Anyone experiencing these transits is strongly advised to:

- Keep a check on restlessness or impulsive moves which can break relationships/friendships.
- Maintain a flexible attitude and avoid exhibitions of possessiveness or jealousy.
- Adopt a fresh approach in assessing existing ties/involvements.
- Avoid pursuing partners who are already married, unpredictable or inclined to make false promises.

Transiting Uranus Aspecting Natal Mars

Energy Blend: Innovation/Physical Desires

Reminder Note: *Natal Mars* in every chart reveals the basic physical strengths. . .force and direction of sexual drives. . .degree of natural vitality.

Uranus in every chart points to the sense of self-reliance. . .the desire for personal freedom. . .the search for newness.

Thus all contacts between transiting Uranus and natal Mars—whether by conjunction, trine, sextile, square or opposition—create varying degrees of change and/or conflict between *how the physical drives* operate and the direction in which the *boosted thrust for independence* seeks to push them.

The purpose of these transits is to revivify waning or jaded energies till they break themselves free of intolerable, deadening restraints. Attempts to drive underground the explosive, urgent demand of the Uranus/Mars team-up can create physical or mental health problems, suppressed anger leading to accidents, broken relationships and overstrain of physical resources.

Uranus/Mars Event Projection

Anyone experiencing these transits faces incidents and situations designed to:

- Invigorate powers of self-assertion and ability to attract/impress others.
- Cause rebellious, over-intense behaviour, thereby causing conflict and lack of co-operation.
- Stimulate sexual urges to the point that relationships are smashed or seriously disturbed.
- Boost ingenuity and daring in pursuit of own desires.
- Encourage aggressive, quarrelsome attitudes and disregard of conventions.

Uranus/Mars Transit Management
Anyone experiencing these transits is strongly advised to:

- Control irritability, harsh comments and overexcitable responses.
- Direct boosted physical/sexual capacities wisely instead of overstraining or overdoing them.
- Use increased personal magnetism to break through obstacles or opposition.
- Avoid creating enmity through rude, brusque or autocratic actions.

Transiting Uranus Aspecting Natal Jupiter

Energy Blend: Innovation/Personal Expansion

Reminder Note: Natal Jupiter in every chart reveals the basic ability to use opportunities. . .behave with optimism. . .broaden personal horizons.

Uranus in every chart points to the sense of self-reliance. . .the desire for personal freedom. . .the search for newness.

Thus all contacts between transiting Uranus and natal Jupiter—whether by conjunction, trine, sextile, square or opposition—create varying degrees of change and/or conflict between the *innate capacity to utilize opportunities* and the direction in which the *boosted thrust for independence* seeks to push them.

The purpose of these transits is to throw open the high road to opportunity and advancement, to replace narrow, routine objectives with bigger and brighter goals. Efforts to keep the life within its accustomed groove bring a Uranian avalanche of wasted chances, lost hopes and strained relationships.

Uranus/Jupiter Event Projection

Anyone experiencing these transits faces incidents and situations designed to:

- Offer sudden advancement of projects through optimistic planning.
- Bring about sweeping changes in business/educational interests, possibly involving long distance travel.
- Encourage over-exuberant attraction to schemes or ideas which are based on foolish risk-taking.
- Threaten periods of unexpected demands on finances, requiring prudence and economy.
- Create advantages through increased independence.

Uranus/Jupiter Transit Management

Anyone experiencing these transits is strongly advised to:

- Build a broader, brighter and more philosophical approach in utilizing opportunities.
- Take pride in accomplishments so as to benefit from possible publicity.
- Maintain a realistic, never over-expansive, assessment of financial schemes/offers.
- Avoid abandoning security for apparent but possible insubstantial gains through misplaced trust in others.

Transiting Uranus Aspecting Natal Saturn

Again to avoid repetition, for all aspects between transiting Uranus and natal Saturn, please turn back to interpretation of 'transiting Saturn aspecting natal Uranus' in Chapter 3.

Conditions, events and responses at such times are virtually the same. A difference in emphasis arises from the fact that Uranus/Saturn aspects during transits last far longer and thereby extend their pressure for change over much longer periods in any life.

Transiting Uranus Aspecting Natal Uranus

Energy Blend: Innovation/revelation.

Reminder Note: When any transiting planet makes any major aspect to that planet's natal position, the effect is one of outright confrontation.

Identical energies are forced into close contact but not always comfortably. The affairs of the transit house may not suit the demands of the natal house. Uranus/Uranus aspects during transit demonstrate this effect with events typical of this planet's pull towards change through mutiny against restriction and defiance of convention.

As Uranus' lightning flashes of insight strike any life, the twin bogs of boredom and monotonous routine are shown up in all their ugly, stultifying futility. Failure to make wise use of such startling insights create events which can instigate blind Uranus-style rebellion not only against constricting circumstances but also against reason and responsibility.

IMPORTANT NOTE: The *conjunction aspect* between transiting Uranus and Natal Uranus cannot occur until individuals are well into their eighties so few experience this one.

The *opposition aspect* between transiting Uranus and natal Uranus occurs in every life around age 40 and thus heralds the 'Middle Life Crisis'.

The *Trine Aspect* between transiting Uranus and natal Uranus occurs twice in the average life-span. Firstly in the late 20's and again in the early 60's.

The *square aspect* between transiting Uranus and natal Uranus occurs twice also in each life. Once around age 20 and again around age 60.

Uranus/Uranus Event Projection

Anyone experiencing these transits faces incidents and experiences designed to:

- Eliminate abruptly people and situations that have served their purpose.
- Stimulate a new urge to achieve unhampered freedom and independence from former work/personal ties.
- Introduce stiff competition from forceful, progressive individuals.
- Create crises as to personal identity and life direction.
- Force a search for new forms of self-expression.

Uranus/Uranus Transit Management

Anyone experiencing these transits is strongly advised to:

- Control the demand to throw overboard established standards of behaviour without forethought as to consequences
- Examine own motives to ensure pursuit of challenges and liberation is not based on self-centredness.
- Update personal views and outlook to keep pace with progressive thinking among rivals.
- Assess accomplishments and direct them into new avenues.

Transiting Uranus Aspecting Natal Neptune
Transiting Uranus Aspecting Natal Pluto

As both of these sets of aspects have already been dealt with in preceding Neptune/Uranus and Pluto/Uranus transit interpretation sections, please refer back to appropriate table in Chapter 4.

Conditions, events and responses at such times are virtually the same. However, in these cases—as Uranus travels more quickly than either Neptune or Pluto—Uranus/Neptune and Uranus/Pluto aspects are somewhat shorter in duration than Neptune/Uranus or Pluto/Uranus transits.

On the next page, you will find a blank Uranus Transit Sheet. Test your skills by completing it for our chart example girl — Clare Costumier. Refer first to her natal chart in Chapter 3 and comments on her life in this section.

Uranus Example Transit Sheet

FUTURE LIFE TRENDS: Years examined—

(*Reminder Note:* The planet Uranus always promotes events which suddenly break up ingrained habit patterns in your life and increase your urge for total independence. It is a dramatically individualising influence which pushes you towards unconventional behaviour.)

Long-Range Uranus Effect:

Time Spans Involved in Current House Position:

Effect of House Transit:

Comments in Brief:...

....

....

....

Current Uranus Effect:

Time Spans Involved for each Transit/Aspect in Current House:

Effect of Major Operative Aspects:

Comments in Brief:...

....

....

....

Jupiter—the 'Great Expansionist' in Transit

Whirling silently in space, 775 million kilometres from the Sun and with a diameter nearly eleven times that of Earth, lies the largest planet in our solar system. . .the red-spotted giant Jupiter. 'Giant' *is* the operative word for Jupiter in more ways than one. Encyclopaedias state the planet's mass is about two-and-a-half times the mass of *all* the other planets combined. Further, that its dense, cloudy atmosphere of hydrogen, helium, methane and ammonia is so impenetrable some astronomers suggest that 'beneath no definite surface may exist'.

Whenever I look up these astronomical descriptions of Jupiter, I can't help thinking how apt they are in considering this planet astrologically as well as astronomically. For whether it be through his effect on the natal chart or by his transits, Jupiter is forever wrapping up opportunities in gassy, glorious rainbow-coloured clouds of enthusiasm which ignore hard facts and beneath which 'no definite surface (of feasilibity) may exist'.

Which, of course, explains how he gained his title of the 'Great Expansionist'. And why those born under Sagittarius, Jupiter's own sign, are often accused by their more pragmatic associates of promising far, far more than they could ever hope to deliver. Yet 'Promises! Promises!' are inevitably part of Jupiter's style and since he's the swiftest-moving of the five heavy planets, he circuits the chart in the fast lane, completing each trip in a mere 12 years. That means, of course, he doesn't stay in one place long enough to be called to account for his high-flying promises as well as repeating the same sign/house transits and transiting aspects regularly as clockwork—approximately every 12 years.

Take a moment now to look through your ephemeris and check Jupiter's movements out with your own chart subjects. You'll observe, at once, he returns to his natal position at around ages 12, 24, 36, 48, 60, 72, 84, 96 etc. Obviously, the last pair of returns are only experienced by very few and very long-living individuals. Yet, these days with life-spans of 80-plus becoming more common, many of us will see at least six Jupiter returns, for instance, though not so much as one Uranus return unless we make it past age 84.

I stress this difference in planetary speeds because newcomers to astrological science are often not fully aware of its effect. And its consequence. That is, that the length of time planets spend in any specific house transit or transiting aspect is certain to add mightily to their impact not only on possible events but also in individual responses to them from the point of view of forecasting.

Thus, by comparison with the far longer periods Uranus, Neptune, Pluto and even Saturn spend in signs, house and aspects, Jupiter's quite brief contacts do not warrant the same detailed attention being paid to them. Certainly, they *do* offer opportunities, boost optimism and build a not always solidly-based sense of confidence in handling the events they indicate but no more. Yet, the opportunities *have* to be grasped and carefully tended. The helping or hindering energies of the slower planets *have* to be taken into account if a constructive result is to be achieved.

Again, check this blend of planetary energies out with our specimen chart of Clare Costumier in Chapter 3. We'll look at the year 1984. She was then approaching age 25 and was engaged in work that she found dull and unfulfilling.

In March 1984, Jupiter entered her eleventh house (friends/group activities/hopes and wishes) where he would remain until the end of March 1985. Right on cue, an old *friend* invited her to take part in an exciting, highly-paid film project, which meant plenty of *group activity* and had been a secret *wish* of hers for years.

She hesitated. Why? It was a golden opportunity. Let's look for the answers among what the other heavy planets were doing in 1984.

There was Saturn, still in her ninth house (see Chapter 3), prodding thoughts of travel but also insisting on the practical fact that large sums of money had to be found to finance it.

There was Uranus, very visibly on the scene too. He had moved into her tenth house (career/attainment) back in December 1982 where he would remain until 1990. He had already caused notable disruption to her career plans.

There was Neptune (see Chapter 4) who had been travelling through her tenth house since her early secondary schooldays began in 1972 and would not leave that life sector till she reached 30 in 1989.

There was Pluto (see Chapter 4) again poised on the brink of her ninth house in December 1984, adding his pressure to Saturn's on the desire to travel.

Hence all major career decisions were not going to be easily made. Some 12 years of Neptune's foggy concoction of inspiration, uncertainty, illusion and confusion had left its mark on her attitudes. Another 15 months of Uranus's favourite blend of sudden, surprising stops and starts, twists and turns in professional matters had had its effect, too. Whereas Pluto was now so close to his entry into the ninth, his influence was growing stronger and stronger in her subconscious mind.

From this thumbnail sketch of the interplay of planetary energies on Clare's life in 1984, her 25th year, we can see—using transiting house positions alone—more clearly why the following events ensued:

- She accepted the film job. (Jupiter's opportunity.)
- More of the same soon followed. (Jupiter again.)
- The higher salary ensured she could soon save several thousand dollars. (The Saturn demand.)
- As soon as possible thereafter, she refused further offers and set off on her travels. (The Uranus thrust for new experiences and experimenting with work in new environments.)
- But the questions as to whether the life she was leading and the work she was doing were really worthwhile and really satisfying remained unanswered (Neptune's questions).

By the time her trip was nearing its end in the latter months of 1985, Pluto had also finally established himself in her ninth house (foreigners/travel) forcing her to reflect long and deeply on what she had learned.

Jupiter, too had moved on—into her twelfth house in 1985. She began to wonder again if her present career in the film world of make-believe, play-acting and imitations of real life was in fact the right choice for her. Thoughts of training for entirely different work in psychology or one of the social sciences where she could help others began to dominate her thinking. (The desire to help others is a typical reaction to Jupiter transiting the twelfth house.)

From this further instalment of Clare's story, we can observe how one particular Jupiter-inspired opportunity was used and how it developed against the background of the changes being urged by the transits of the other heavy planets.

Now, as before, look at your chart subjects and sketch in the effect of Jupiter-style opportunities and how they blended with other planetary energies to postulate the result.

New High Roads to Opportunity. . . Or . . . New Low Roads to Folly

'All that glitters is not gold!' is an ancient proverb which we need to keep in the forefront of our minds when transiting Jupiter gives us a glimpse of his cornucopia of glittering prizes, all looking so close we need only stretch out our hands to claim them. That first piece of advice should be specially earmarked by those whose natal charts show large helpings of optimism, enthusiasm *and* opportunism. Yet, the converse equally applies for which we can quote another proverb: '*He who hesitates is lost*.' That second piece of advice should be particularly noted by those whose natal charts suggest lack of confidence, timidity or innate pessimism.

For, in the first instance, if we grab for the opportunities Jupiter offers too hastily and heedlessly, we're likely to find—to our cost— that the only person who 'gets rich quick' from somebody's 'great, new, get-rich-quick' scheme is the same somebody who dreamed it up in the first place. While, in the second instance, if we let our once-in-a-lifetime chances for love, happiness or advancement pass us by just because we are too fearful to grasp them, we'll be left at the starting-post, bemoaning our unhappy fate and with nothing before us but vain regrets.

Hence, when assessing the effect of Jupiter transits in any chart, it is vital to look both ahead and around at other planetary energies affecting the issue. And, of course, at the natal chart too, to see if its patterns predispose towards rashness in the face of important choices. Or towards more judicious consideration of the hard facts beneath the burgeoning bubbles of enthusiasm. In other words, to see if Jupiter is offering a smooth ride along the high roads to opportunity instead of a very rough one along the low roads to folly.

To appreciate why Jupiter-inspired changes create an urge to do it not only 'high, wide and handsome' but also 'in the biggest way there is', we need to inspect the mythological background of the Greco-Roman deity after which this planet was named.

Zeus to the Ancient Greeks, Jupiter (or Jove) to the Romans, he was unquestionably the supreme father god of both his celestial and mortal flocks and looked the part. Big, bearded and beneficent, he interpreted his parental role quite literally too, siring impressive numbers of offspring (two of whom were the Geminian twins) during his amorous encounters on earth as well as in and about his court on Mount Olympus. When not in pursuit of love, he applied himself to such fatherly duties as meting out instant justice, rewarding good deeds, punishing the bad, hurling down thunderbolts when displeased and spreading the skies with sunshine when favourably impressed.

This commanding position of Jupiter in the hierarchy of the gods no doubt explains why the Ancients chose to name the biggest planet they could see in the heavens after him. It further explains why the best and worst manifestations of Jupiter's influence on both personality and events lead to expansion or exaggeration, generosity or improvidence, optimism or boastfulness, exuberance or indulgence. Each positive has its negative.

The positive manifestations allow us to take the tide at the full, to risk our all for a just possible dream, to raise ourselves to our place in the sun. The negative manifestations of Jupiter-style responses lead to trusting to luck that verges on the lunatic, to pursuing hopes that have no footing in reality, to bury ourselves in a trough of debts and disappointments.

Hence, although Jupiter's role in Future Life Forecasting is not as heavily indicative of life-changing events as those of Saturn, Pluto, Neptune and Uranus, his transits still require to be checked and handled with wisdom.

Let's look now at a case in point: JUPITER 'JUNKIES'.

In the older astrology texts, Jupiter is often referred to as the 'Great Benefic'. But *sometimes* his beneficience is less than beneficial. . .particularly if he makes a square aspect to Neptune in a chart, natally or by transit. Then you'll find individuals who simply can't resist, absolutely must have, whatever it is that turns them on. Often the result is not much more than spending sprees although, because the aspect can denote various forms of addiction, its effect can be more sinister.

I was amused recently to hear a client of mine, whose Jupiter squares Neptune, state:

'I'm a record 'junkie'. If I pass a second-hand record shop, I can't stop myself from buying as many records as I can carry. . .then, may be I'll never play them. Something just gets hold me. Something I can't control and I spend up big despite the fact that I haven't got the money to spare.'

All of which goes to show that you need to keep an eye on Jupiter, both his natal aspects and his transits, if you want to be sure that you and your money are not soon parted! The more so when—like the client just quoted—you already have one or more dodgy Jupiter aspects in your own natal chart and Jupiter transits are activating it. As had happened in this case. The record-buying spree had got suddenly and totally out of control as transiting Jupiter moved into this man's second house.

Agreed, wasting comparatively small sums of money on useless purchases is not a devastating result. But what if this irresistible impulse to indulge one's desires had attached itself to drugs or alcohol? Then, the effect could have been catastrophic, even fatal!

The drugs or drinking problem must never, of course, be taken as a simple Jupiter influence. Life-destroying addictions stem from groups of hard natal aspects, often linked to Neptune and thus create the urge to escape from the real world into drink-or-drug-type fantasies.

It's well worth noting too that Jupiter's expansion of the dimensions of opportunities is not restricted to the mind. He's just as adept at expanding the physical body as well! At piling on the killer kilos. Both film mega-star Marlon Brando and Rock king Elvis Presley exemplify this point.

Brando swiftly hit the peaks of the acting profession but as his horizons expanded so did his girth. Compare him figure-wise in the 1955 musical 'Guys and Dolls' and then in the 1979 Vietnam epic 'Apocalypse Now!' By 1979, the salaries he commanded per film were vast as was his bodily bulk.

Born on 3 April 1924 with a Sagittarian Ascendant, Jupiter in his first house (physical body) plus Sun/moon in close conjunction in Aries, Jupiter's role in Brando's life story was obviously a leading one. Especially as Aries is not a sign which commonly produces heavyweights.

Elvis shared with Brando a Sagittarian Ascendant, his correct birth time being 4.35 a.m. (verified from the records of the doctor who delivered him and his stillborn twin) on 8 January 1935, although some reference works wrongly state the time as 12.20 p.m. Elvis, too, shot from penniless obscurity to world-wide fame overnight but died at only 42 on 16 August 1977, his once slender body bloated to a horrifying 114kg (18 stone).

Here Jupiter-inspired indulgence, exacerbated by other chart factors, in both drugs and overeating had exacted a fatal price. (Those readers interested in learning more about Elvis' contradictory personality as shown by his natal chart will find a detailed analysis of his birth patterns in my companion book—*How to Astro-Analyze Yourself and Others*.)

Jupiter House Transits—Gifts from the Gods

Wherever Jupiter is situated in the natal chart, *there* is the spot where hope springs eternal. Where no matter how many set-backs, knock-backs and flashbacks to past failures, the belief survives that somewhere way over the rainbow, the streets really are paved with gold. And that someday, one day it *will* all come right in the end. For those who hope hard enough (and work hard enough) it usually does. Eventually.

Or as Oscar Hammerstein II, born 12 July 1895 with Sun, Mercury and Jupiter in Cancer and song-writer for many of America's greatest film musicals, once put it in 'South Pacific.' 'You've *got* to have a dream. If you don't have a dream, how are you going to make that dream come true?' There's no doubt that Hammerstein worked hard and long on making his own dreams of fame and success come true but never lost sight of the fact that one swallow does not make a summer. One record-breaking success doesn't guarantee you stay top of the heap for all time.

Testimony to this Cancer-style wariness of the vagaries of fortune is enshrined in a greeting card he once sent to selected friends. On it were listed *not* his smash hits but his most shattering flops, together with the succinct message: 'I have done it before. I can do it again!'

Hammerstein's realistic comment is worth framing and staring at long and hard whenever Jupiter transits are in the offing—particularly if you or your chart subjects are what Hammerstein also described in another of his songs as a 'cock-eyed optimist'.

Jupiter loves to give the impression that whatever he's promoting at any given time is as easy to achieve as falling off the proverbial log. Alas, not so. Hopes and dreams of glory are only attainable if they fit within the range of each individual's training, knowledge, natal abilities *and* capacity to work unceasingly towards their achievement. After all, it goes without saying that you'll never set the world on fire as a latter-day Hammerstein if you have no ear for music or way with words—no matter how much you hope and dream. But, handle Jupiter transits wisely and put your back into your own private success story and they'll help you become a much more successful performer in your own special field. Possibly even point you in the right direction if you feel you've been a square peg in a round hole too long.

Nevertheless, since Jupiter moves so much more swiftly round the chart than the other slow-moving planets, too much store cannot be placed on either his house transits or transiting aspects. Both can give a quick boost to plans and life direction but in a very short time by comparison, they're gone again. In a sense, therefore, they can be likened to someone offering you a leg-up to a high wall or tall tree. The leg-up surely helps but you need much more in strength and skill if you're going to get to the top of your wall or scale your tree.

In the following section, we'll list short-form interpretations of Jupiter's house transits and transiting aspects together for two reasons.

Firstly, because they belong in the 'Brief-Effect Basket' like the transits of the faster-moving planets, Sun, Moon, Mercury, Venus and Mars. An important rule to remember is: The shorter the house or sign transit of any planet in its duration, the less effect it will have on any life. That fact is virtually axiomatic and needs to be borne constantly in mind so that short-term transits are never over-emphasized in Future Life Trend Forecasting.

Secondly, because modern, psychologically-based astrological interpreting is pulling strongly away from what is called 'event-oriented predicting'. The outdated 'good day for this'. . .'bad day for that' approach, which relies on planetary transits of very short duration, lasting maybe no more than a single day, and thus with a minimal effect on any life—an impact that is equally slight and short.

Further, this 'predicting' fosters the erroneous impression that hopes/ plans will go right or wrong merely because brief, passing planetary pictures around a specific date or dates are helpful or hindering to a particular purpose. As if the client had no control over his/her actions and regardless of what he/she does, thinks or feels at the time. Often too (and even worse), regardless of what the natal chart has to say concerning the matter on which advice is sought.

This type of 'Pick-Your-Day' predicting is the kind where a client is advised for instance, 'To go to the races this Saturday' merely because a passing Jupiter transit might be favouring luck in gambling. And quite irrespective of the fact that such client's natal chart may show no success whatsoever in any kind of gambling. Or even a tendency to plunge heavily and heedlessly.

Of course these days, the individuals who go in for this type of predicting are rarely, if ever, well-qualified astrologers. More often, fortune-tellers holding themselves out as astrologers. Yet, sadly, gullible people believe their 'prophecies' and hence the damage done can be shocking. Not solely to the individual concerned but to the science of astrology itself.

I recall one case told to me by a German businessman visiting Sydney that his mother would not even get out of bed if her 'astrologer' told her it was 'a bad day'. Not even to answer the door or the telephone. You can easily imagine what *he* thought of astrologers! Certainly, in that case, the foolish old lady had lost nothing more than the odd day but irresponsible 'predicting' could have cost the woman in our next example her share of a considerable family inheritance.

She rang in a panic to state she had visited a 'clairvoyant astrologer' and further that she was a beneficiary in a will over which serious controversy existed. The 'clairvoyant astrologer' had advised her thus: 'It's hopeless. Everything is against you. You'll lose all that money. You won't get a cent of it!'

Not surprisingly, this had placed the above-mentioned phone caller in a highly negative frame of mind to the point that she was prepared to throw in the towel without so much as seeking expert legal advice. I told her to see a good lawyer at once. Then, if she so desired, to seek the services of a competent and responsible astrologer, who would be able to reassure her that nothing is ever hopeless. Never is everything against you. And there is a positive, as opposed to a negative, method of handling all future events. As shown by our next example.

Here, one of my own clients asked among other questions 'when would be the best date to take a lottery ticket as I want to be sure of winning the huge first prize'. Such a question was patently naive for if astrologers could answer it with *any* degree of accuracy, everyone (including the astrologers themselves) could become overnight millionaires—simply by asking it.

However, over-hope, over-confidence, overstatement and exaggeration represent all the negative expressions of Jupiter-style traits when the planet is awkwardly placed natally or makes problem aspects during his transits. So let's elaborate on Jupiter in action a little more.

One instance refers to an astrologer who specialized in horse-racing forecasts of the 'Pick-The-Winners-By-The-Stars' variety. He spent his days hovering on the brink of bankruptcy because his winners were left at the post far more often than they romped home. A case of over-hope and over-confidence here.

Another instance: A newly-trained astrologer was cajoled by a sceptical journalist (despite warnings from more experienced practitioners) into attending a big race meeting and 'proving' astrology by predicting the names of the winning horses.

This was a further example of more misplaced confidence than common sense. For, not unexpectedly, the experiment was no more successful than if the winners had been picked with a pin! Added to that, it gave the newspaperman the opportunity to write one more story in which astrologers were held up as a joke.

That is why I always warn students to steer well clear of this kind of predicting. Astrology was never designed for it. The chances of being correct are small and it hands weapons to those who would deride the science.

But back to our lottery lady. Certainly, she had a well-placed natal Jupiter which had convinced her she was a 'lucky' sort of person. And in many ways, she was. But *not* from any kind of gambling. I told her this while further pointing out her chart showed a marked degree of creative talent—possibly in the field of photography. Plus the fact that particular transits, one of them being a Jupiter link-up, promised good opportunities if she was prepared to handle them purposefully.

Four years later, she wrote to me. In the intervening time, she had trained herself and become an outstandingly successful commercial photographer. Not only was she much happier and more fulfilled in earning from her own skills, but I think this case supports my view that behind every so-called 'good luck' story is a solid foundation of determined effort.

Jupiter House Transits with Transiting Aspects—Short-Form Interpretation Table

Reminder Note: Since Jupiter travels through the twelve signs in about 12 years, he spends roughly 12 months in each. Precise periods vary due to retrograding. For example, in 1986-87, Jupiter was moving through Pisces from 21 February 1986 to 2 March 1987—slightly more than one year. Whereas his stay in Gemini in 1988 – 89 covers 21 July 1988 to 30 November 1988, then from 11 March 1989 to 30 July 1989, the intervening months being taken up by a retrograde movement back into Taurus. Thus total period in Gemini in above years was only about 9 months. Jupiter's transiting house positions and aspects are consequently also much briefer in duration than the other heavy planets.

Aspects during transits can be as long as two months or as short as two weeks. Remember, Jupiter's influence through his transits is aimed primarily at presenting opportunities and expanding the scope of activities.

Used wisely, the result will be just that. A sense of having caught the main chance as it flies. A feeling of confidence and well-being. Conversely, over-reacting to Jupiter overdoes the whole performance. Can show up in the forms of opportunism, greedy grasping for more money, more pleasure, more everything, magnification of meagre molehills of achievement into mighty mountains of attainment.

Remember, however, any short-term Jupiter transit can pass without its subject becoming aware of any noticeable effect on his/her activities—especially if other heavier, much more slow-moving planets are creating major changes in different life sectors.

FIRST HOUSE JUPITER TRANSITS. . .

concentrate attention on:

- Physical body.
- Personal environment.
- Self-image.

HELPFUL ASPECTS to natal planets during first house transits prompt events which encourage optimism in personal concerns and thus boost benefit through:

* Increased self-esteem.
* Better opportunities to impress others.
* Added sense of physical well-being.

TROUBLESOME ASPECTS to natal planets during first house transits prompt events which urge overemphasis in personal concerns and thus threaten mistakes through:

* Self-important behaviour.
* Overindulgence in physical activities, including eating and drinking.
* Pretentious claims and false pride.

Positive result quote: 'I began a get-fit programme. Now, I look better, feel great.'

Negative result quote: 'I've been eating too much and drinking a lot after work. My weight's shot up alarmingly.'

SECOND HOUSE JUPITER TRANSITS. . .

concentrate attention on:

- Income and earning power.
- Material possessions.
- Personal prosperity.

HELPFUL ASPECTS to natal planets during second house transits prompt events which encourage optimism in monetary matters and thus boost benefit through:

* Skilful use of financial opportunities.
* Generosity towards others.
* Better ability to perceive economic trends.

TROUBLESOME ASPECTS to natal planets during second house transits prompt events which urge overemphasis on monetary matters and thus threaten mistakes through:

* Fits of foolish extravagance.
* Gambling on ill-considered money-making schemes.
* Entanglement in business problems of others.

Positive result quote: 'I got a promotion I've been working hard for since last year. Big salary increase too.'

Negative result quote: 'I bought a big slab of shares, about $5,000's worth. The company turned out to be non-existent. Its promoters were con-men.'

THIRD HOUSE JUPITER TRANSITS. . .

concentrate attention on:

- Intellectual abilities.
- New educational/cultural interests.
- Communications of all types.

HELPFUL ASPECTS to natal planets during third house transits prompt events which encourage optimism in mental skills and thus boost benefit through:

* Positive, more broad-minded thinking.
* Further studies in present or new fields.
* Better ability to communicate ideas in speech/writing.

TROUBLESOME ASPECTS to natal planets during third house transits prompt events which urge overemphasis in mental skills and thus threaten mistakes through:

* Overstatement of qualifications or abilities.
* Intellectual posturing and pomposity in letters, statements.
* Enrolment in fake or futile study courses.

Positive result quote: 'I was a university drop-out. Now, I've resumed my degree studies and am doing well.'

Negative result quote: 'I was only a law clerk at the time but I started telling people I was a fully-qualified solicitor. I got into a heap of trouble when my boss found out.'

FOURTH HOUSE JUPITER TRANSITS. . .

concentrate attention on:

- Domestic arrangements/family affairs.
- Home improvements and location of residence.
- Persons sharing home.

HELPFUL ASPECTS to natal planets during fourth house transits prompt events which encourage optimism concerning domestic scene and thus boost benefits through:

* More harmonious sharing with partner/family.
* Much improved living conditions.
* Advantageous change of home, investment in real estate.

TROUBLESOME ASPECTS to natal planets during fourth house transits prompt events which urge overemphasis on domestic scene and thus threaten mistakes through:

* Over-expenditure on home either in cost of purchase or renovations/additions.
* Accommodation with unreliable or free-loading individuals.
* Desire to impress others with living standards beyond own means.

Positive result quote: 'I had to find a smaller home after my marriage ended. I was amazed to get something that was just right and I could afford.'

Negative result quote: 'I moved to a glamorous flat in an up-market area. The person who was going to share the rent didn't pay up. There was a lot of unpleasantness and expense before I got rid of him.'

FIFTH HOUSE JUPITER TRANSITS. . .

concentrate attention on:

- Romantic involvements and social life.
- Creative and artistic interests.
- Matters concerning children.

HELPFUL ASPECTS to natal planets during fifth house transits prompt events which encourage optimism concerning love affairs and pleasures and thus boost benefit through:

* Better social opportunities.
* Harmony with lovers/children.
* Recognition of artistic/creative work.

TROUBLESOME ASPECTS to natal planets during fourth house transits prompt events which urge overemphasis on love affairs and pleasures

and thus threaten mistakes through:
* Heedless pursuit of empty amusements.
* Extravagance towards love partners/children.
* Wasted effort through mistaken faith in own talents.

Positive result quote: 'I'd been writing short stories for ages. At last a top magazine accepted one.'

Negative result quote: 'I put up the money for a new business for my son. He didn't work at it the way I hoped. I had to sell it at a heavy loss.'

SIXTH HOUSE JUPITER TRANSITS. . .
concentrate attention on:
- Employment and job opportunities.
- Working environments and co-workers.
- Health and diet.

HELPFUL ASPECTS to natal planets during sixth house transits prompt events which encourage optimism concerning work and health concerns and thus boost benefit through:
* New avenues of work/job change.
* Help from employers/colleagues.
* Better health and physical condition.

TROUBLESOME ASPECTS to natal planets during sixth house transits prompt events which urge overemphasis on work and health concerns and thus threaten mistakes through:
* Irresponsibility and reckless behaviour.
* Belief in baseless promises of work benefits.
* Poor health from overdoing effort or over-indulgence.

Positive result quote: 'I decided to allow my employees more say in the running of my business. Work output improved remarkably.'

Negative result quote: 'I was miserable at work and started to eat whenever I felt low. Raiding the fridge at night. That sort of thing. The more weight I put on, the worse I felt.'

SEVENTH HOUSE JUPITER TRANSITS. . .
concentrate attention on:
- Marriage/partnership opportunities.
- All forms of close, co-operative associations.
- Search for affluence through union.

HELPFUL ASPECTS to natal planets during seventh house transits prompt events which encourage optimism in permanent relationships and thus boost benefit through:
- ⋆ Choice of supportive, prosperous partners in love/business.
- ⋆ Enthusiastic development of shared objectives.
- ⋆ Elevation in social financial status with help of partners.

TROUBLESOME ASPECTS to natal planets during seventh house transits prompt events which urge overemphasis on permanent relationships and thus threaten mistakes through:
- ⋆ Over-expectation of love/business partners.
- ⋆ Procrastination and reluctance to share responsibilities.
- ⋆ Unrealistic hopes, based on poor judgement of close associates.

Positive result quote: 'My wife received a good-sized legacy. She put the money into my business and became a sleeping partner—both senses of the word. Our marriage is better than ever.'

Negative result quote: 'I got personally involved with my boss. He was much older than I am and married. He said he'd leave his wife for me but I found that was all talk.'

EIGHTH HOUSE JUPITER TRANSITS. . .
concentrate attention on:
- Shared moneys, partnership finances, inheritance.
- Loans and borrowing for business or self.
- Bequests or monetary benefits from relatives.

HELPFUL ASPECTS to natal planets during eighth house transits prompt events which encourage optimism in handling inheritances/shared assets and thus boost benefit through:

* Improved credit standing, individually or with partners.
* Judicious borrowing to expand business or own life style.
* Profitable partnerships with fair sharing of resources.

TROUBLESOME ASPECTS to natal planets during eighth house transits prompt events which urge overemphasis on handling inheritances/shared assets and thus threaten mistakes through.

* Allowing partners to indulge in excessive spending.
* Attempts to win status or popularity by buying them.
* Unexpected opposition or competition.

Positive result quote: 'I had wanted to started my own business for a long time. I met someone then I got along well with and we shared the expenses. It's been a success from the day we opened our doors.'

Negative result quote: 'An old aunt left me quite a sum of money. My husband talked me into buying a little holiday cottage with it, saying he'd get all the legal work done. When we broke up several years later, my solicitor found my husband had put the cottage in his name only. That meant it was all his. I couldn't sell it to get my money back.'

NINTH HOUSE JUPITER TRANSITS. . .

concentrate attention on:

- Long-distance travelling.
- New viewpoints through exposure to foreign cultures.
- Search for knowledge and higher education.

HELPFUL ASPECTS to natal planets during ninth house transits prompt events which encourage optimism in travel and dealings with foreigners and thus boost benefit through:

* Profitable trips for business or personal reasons.
* New links with foreigners in private or occupational affairs.
* Broadened outlook from travel or further qualifications.

TROUBLESOME ASPECTS to natal planets during ninth house transits prompt events which urge overemphasis on travel and dealings with

foreigners and thus threaten mistakes through:
* Travel undertaken to avoid commitments/obligations.
* Slackness in learning foreign and cultural differences/customs.
* Failure to apply self and sustain interest in higher studies.

Positive result quote: 'At that time, my mother won a big bet at the races. She gave me $12,000 to tour Europe. It changed my whole thinking.'

Negative result quote: 'I'd had a lot of trouble with a girl friend, who wanted us to get married. I went and lived in another country for a few months to get away from her. That cost me all my savings and the problem was still there when I went home.'

TENTH HOUSE JUPITER TRANSITS. . .
concentrate attention on:
- Career advancement and recognition.
- Achievement of personal goals.
- Professional prominence and popularity.

HELPFUL ASPECTS to natal planets during tenth house transits prompt events which encourage optimism in career and occupational planning and thus boost benefits through:
* Favourable notice from superiors.
* Work which improves status and reputation.
* Acquisition of additional accomplishments/skills.

TROUBLESOME ASPECTS to natal planets during tenth house transits prompt events which urge overemphasis on career and occupational planning and thus threaten mistakes through:
* Inflated opinion of own abilities.
* Mismanagement and trusting to luck in decisions.
* Boastfulness and exaggeration of achievements.

Positive result quote: 'I was told my forward-looking policies had earned me a directorship in the company.'

Negative result quote: 'I wanted a more glamorous career and pretended I had experience in a field which I knew almost nothing about. I got the job but only lasted a month.'

ELEVENTH HOUSE JUPITER TRANSITS. . .

concentrate attention on:

- Group activities, friendships.
- Attainment of long-held aspirations.
- Humanitarian interests

HELPFUL ASPECTS to natal planets during eleventh house transits prompt events which encourage optimism concerning group efforts and private hopes and thus boost benefit through:

* Meetings with kind, like-minded friends.
* Interest in social reforms and helping others.
* Generous aid from associates.

TROUBLESOME ASPECTS to natal planets during eleventh house transits prompt events which urge overemphasis on group efforts and private hopes and thus threaten mistakes through:

* Hoping for the impossible or unattainable.
* Choice of friends for social-climbing purposes.
* Involvement with groups whose aims are suspect or impractical.

Positive result quote: 'I'd always wanted to travel but was afraid to do it alone. At this time, an old friend reappeared and we went overseas together.'

Negative result quote: 'A friend persuaded me to join what she said was a new religious movement. I gave its leader a large amount of money before I realized he was a phoney.'

TWELFTH HOUSE JUPITER TRANSITS. . .

concentrate attention on:

- Spiritual needs and contemplation.
- Understanding of own life purpose.
- Support and assistance to those in need.

HELPFUL ASPECTS to natal planets during twelfth house transits prompt events which encourage optimism concerning spiritual directions and thus boost benefits through:

* Unselfishness and expanded awareness.
* Voluntary service and financial aid to charities.
* Periods of relaxation and introspection.

TROUBLESOME ASPECTS to natal planets during twelfth house transits prompt events which urge overemphasis on spiritual directions and thus threaten mistakes through:

* Dwelling on past troubles and self-pity.
* Allowing others to impose or make unfair demands.
* Deliberate self-isolation.

Positive result quote: 'I'm retired and felt lonely, unwanted. I joined a society which helps with rehabilitating prisoners. It gave me great satisfaction and made me see others were far worse off than I.

Negative result quote: 'About that time, I suffered from what my doctor called "Agoraphobia". I've always been timid and it got so I was scared even to go out and shop.'

Now, we've examined Jupiter in action and effect, we've come to the last of the heavy planets whose orbits lie beyond those of the 'personal planets'. . .i.e. Sun, Moon, Mercury, Venus and Mars.

We've noted that Pluto is the slowest and therefore exerts the longest-term influence on each life and its story. We've seen that in comparison the speedy movements of Jupiter consign his passing influence to the 'Brief-Effect Basket'.

Therefore, the types of events and quotes set out in preceding sections are never solely due to Jupiter's influence. Back-up pressure from other more significant planets will invariably be observed as well.

To illustrate: You *may* receive a handy windfall from the estate of Great-Aunt Abigail as Jupiter transits your eighth house and makes helpful aspects while so doing. But since, he repeats the same patterns roughly every twelve years, you'd need a whole team of ancient, wealthy relatives to hit the Jupiter jackpot every time!

In our next chapter, we'll consider the effect of the five 'personal planets' themselves so we can weave them into our 'tapestry' of the future.

Quick Reference Check-Points for Chapter 5

Foreign Correspondence

Jupiter is a planet associated in forecasting with long-distance travel from the earliest writings in astrology. Most people think of this as travel into foreign countries and introduction to new life styles. Often it is. But distance here is the operative word. In very big countries like America or Australia, you can travel thousands of miles without changing the language or culture around you.

The word 'foreigner' needs a quick comment too. Astrologically, every one is a foreigner to you unless they are your own compatriots. An Englishman is a foreigner to an Australian, for example, even though they share the common language of English and the same cultural roots. So travel doesn't necessarily mean leaving your own country.

Prophesying Parrot-fashion

Long after I'd qualified as a psychologist but right at the time those 1960's Uranian transits (mentioned earlier) began pressing me to learn astrology, I decided to have my chart interpreted by one of the local exponents and was referred to an elderly woman, who claimed to be the best ever.

Her fees were high but her manner, appearance and method did little to inspire confidence. Astrological symbols all over the place and a well-rehearsed line of patter, bristling with 'prophecies' which were so far beyond the bounds of probability they verged on the ridiculous. Later, after I'd made a thorough study of astrological science myself, I understood why she was so wide of the mark.

To begin with, she plainly had no comprehension of the psychology of the natal chart. Therefore she did not understand how to relate the future movements of the planets to it in forecasting and so parroted off her prophecies—straight out of the pages of outdated textbooks. Two of her silliest statements I never forgot. They were: 'At the end of next year, you will put on a lot of weight. You'll get fat.' 'Before 18 months have passed, you will go to Europe. You'll be working in films.'

Still slim, still in Sydney and very definitely not in films, I recently came across some notes I'd made of that long ago interview. (She put nothing in writing.) I compared them to my chart, searching for the planetary source of her 'prophecies'.

The 'get fat' bit looked like an old textbook interpretation of a Jupiter transit, then current. She had picked that out, ignoring or not skilled enough to perceive the factors in my natal chart which categorically denied excess weight in any stage in life. The 'film travel' bit seemed to come from the same source and relate to a Neptune/Jupiter transit, since—if talent, training and interest exist—Neptune does attract to the film world. I had none of these prerequisites as my natal chart plainly showed. Neither did I have the time nor opportunity with three young children to visit Europe in those days for any purpose.

Thus, this story underlines several points I've been stressing throughout this book. Firstly, that the natal chart remains the dominant factor in forecasting. No transit will bring about anything which that chart does not support. Secondly, the perils of repeating blindly textbook interpretations of transits. These must be regarded as guidelines only. Thirdly, the use of the word 'will' in forecasting. This not only gives the impression that the hearer has no control over his/her actions but also surrounds the astrologer with an aura of god-like authority and infalliblity. And that's very dangerous indeed!

Cauldron! Cauldron! Boil and Bubble!

It never ceases to astonish me that in our Aquarian Age of space probes, super computers and mass literacy, that some people still harbour the absurd and fantastic notion that astrologers are a variety of latter-day sorcerers. For example, I heard recently of a couple of cases where telephone callers asked an astrologer for: 'Something that will make my wife come back to me and get rid of my mother-in-law.' *And* 'Can you give me something to stop my husband from trying to leave me?' *What* on earth did these misguided characters expect? A potion? A set of spells? And what made them think astrologers were in the spell-binding business anyway?

What's more this equally weird view seems to be held by some television scriptwriters. Around a year ago, I caught a snatch from a popular soap in which the miscreant (when apprehended by police) blandly announced that he had stolen special things from a christening, a wedding and a funeral 'because my astrologer told me I must do so!' Mind-blowing, isn't it? I can't imagine any judge listening to anything as far-fetched as that by way of a defence.

Nevertheless, these examples should bring home to all of us who seek to uphold the great science of astrology the need to aim for the highest professional standards at all times. To impress upon laymen that astrology has nothing whatsoever to do with magic or fortune-telling. To do everything we can to blow away the cobwebs of ignorance, superstition and prejudice through which too many people still view the science *and* those who practise it.

Falling in Love by Numbers

On the vexed question of future forecasting, one of the founding fathers of the Federation of Australian Astrologers once gave the following excellent advice to students.

1. Never underestimate the gullibility of your clients *and* never exploit it or play upon it.
2. Never use astrology as a form of self-aggrandizement. Don't claim qualifications you haven't got. Don't give yourself fancy titles.

I thought of those wise words recently when an astrologer colleague related this incident as an example of what happens when the above precepts are ignored.

A middle-aged neighbour of my astrologer friend had requested him to construct his chart some time before, then called one day in mid-1984 to say he was now obtaining a divorce. Since the man's chart had shown both marked incompatibility with the wife plus the imminence of a break-up as well as the fact that he passing through the dangerous years between forty and fifty when the heavy planets hit hard, the astrologer nodded.

'I'm not surprised. Have you found a new girl friend yet?' His former client smiled mysteriously, then announced: '1985!'

'Who on earth told you that?'

'I've been to a metaphysician. A wonderful woman. There's a lovely young girl for me in 1985!'

'I thought metaphysics was a branch of philosophical theology. It's the first time I've heard of clairvoyants calling themselves metaphysicians.'

'No,' said the client firmly. 'She's not a clairvoyant. She did it by adding up a lot of numbers.'

The astrologer told me this man's gullibility astounded him, especially as he was a well-educated person with two university degrees. Worse, he seemed to imagine 'the lovely young girl' would materialize one day in 1985 on his doorstep without any effort to meet suitable partners himself. And, of course, the so-called metaphysician was plainly no more than a numerologist.

The glum finale to this story was that long after 1985 had passed into history, the poor man was still single and sadly disillusioned. Assuredly, planetary indicators current in his chart in 1985 may have pointed to the possibility of a new and happier union. But no astrologer worth his/her salt would have stated it as a certainty. Or implied it would happen without even trying.

On Charting the Path Ahead. . .Advice from an Imperial Aquarian and an Ancient Oracle

You rarely find the crowned heads of history casting themselves in the role of soothsayers and coming out with prophetic utterances, but some *have* done it. And with notable success.

One such was the Roman Emperor Hadrian, who was born in the same century as Christ, in the year AD 76, under the sign of Aquarius, and who died in AD 138, having ruled Rome's far-flung and turbulent territories for a hectic 21 years. In his diaries, he observed that he believed himself fortunate to have been born in the sign of the Water-Bearer and further that he had planned his life in accordance with his birth chart's guidelines. What's more, he ascribed his skill—in staying alive *and* on top of the intrigues and back-stabbings (literally!) around his court—to his ability to forecast the future. Not by any variety of clairvoyance but by examining the present.

Here is a translation of his wise words: 'I could foretell the future with some accuracy, a thing possible after all, when one is informed on a fair number of the elements which make up the present.'

That statement is as true and instructive as it was nearly 2,000 years ago. Which is why I recommend it to students, anxious to try their hands at forecasting. After all, the future does not rear up in front of us—out of the blue and without warning. Its events, successes and failures, are inevitably the product of what has gone before.

Think about *why* you are *where* you are at this point in time. You're there because you chose this occupation or that one. Teamed up with this person or avoided that one. Grasped that opportunity and let another go by. In short, because you are *you* and nobody else. So consider the present as Hadrian advised and look back at the past. In both, you'll find the story of the future.

Another famous crowned head who also followed Hadrian's advice, perhaps without realizing it, was Queen Elizabeth's grandfather, King George V, born like Queen Victoria under the sign of the Twins. I ran across one of his well-documented prophecies recently when reading a biography of his eldest son, the late Duke of Windsor. The chapter dealt with the year 1936 in which George V died, his son became briefly king, then abdicated to marry the then notorious, twice-divorced Mrs Wallis Simpson.

King George had obviously been well 'informed on a fair number of the elements which make up the present' when he predicted the future in these words: 'After I am dead, the boy will ruin himself in twelve months.' In actual fact, his prediction erred only in its estimate. His son's rise and fall had taken slightly less than twelve months. He succeeded to the throne in January 1936 and left it in December.

How could the old king have spoken so surely of the future? He had only to look around him. At the type of personality his son was. At the expectations of the British people of monarchy. At the endless indiscretions of flaunting an intimate relationship with a number of other married women before Mrs Simpson. At the certain opposition of the Church to marrying a divorced person. From this summing-up of past and present, he well knew that once his restraining hand was gone, the future was a sad and foregone conclusion. So, when forecasting the future yourself, follow the royal lead.

More Wise Words. . .from the Delphic Oracle

Anyone interested in the history of the ancient world will have heard of the famous oracle at Delphi in Greece, presided over by priestesses, the chief of which was always called Pythia. Emperors and rulers, lovers and power-seekers thronged Delphi in search of advice from the oracle. Some got it. Some did not. All had to attempt to puzzle out the meaning of the cryptic prophecies.

Again, while delving into translations of ancient documents, I came across the following comment from one of the succession of Pythia priestesses. 'Most of the oracles that come out of Delphi are nothing but good common sense, done up in puzzling mysteries. The people would pay no attention otherwise. But set a mystery before a man and he will worry it until he unravels it. Then he will proclaim Pythia wise and himself no less for discovering what could be told him in a few, blunt words.'

Although I have never believed that astrologers should see themselves in the role of oracles or clairvoyants for that matter, Pythia put it in the proverbial nutshell when she described advice on the future as 'nothing but good common sense'. And, it is much easier for any intelligent, skilled individual who is acting in the role of counseller/advisor to see a client's problem *and* its solution in terms of 'good common sense'.

Why? Mainly, because the counsellor is not personally involved. He/she is outside the problem and thus can consider it dispassionately from all sides. In the round, so to speak. Indeed, sometimes the answer to a client's problem is so obvious it stands out like an iceberg in an empty ocean. Yet, due to emotional turmoil, the subject simply cannot see it.

As to Pythia's advice on clothing counsel in puzzling mysteries, cryptic words. . .I don't think that should be applied to astrological guidance. Statements should be kept clear and as free from jargon as possible. Most laymen find it mysterious enough that a piece of paper with a circle and a set of odd-looking symbols on it can reveal the innermost secrets of their lives to the well-trained eye in any case.

Some Quick Quotes from Future 'Seekers'

Despite growing public awareness of what serious astrology is all about, the belief that it's tied up with the 'cross-my-hand-with-silver' brigade still sadly persists. Here are a few recent instances mentioned to me.

Female phone caller: 'I've been told that if I keep on going to the races, I'll meet a Frenchman. Can you confirm this?'

Personally, I can't imagine any qualified astrologer who would. That statement is a piece of plain, old-fashioned fortune-telling.

Male phone caller: 'I read in the paper a woman from the past is about to re-enter my life. Can you tell me when that will happen?'

Another male phone caller: 'I tried to talk to a girl I like yesterday but she brushed me off. Then I read in my "stars", it was bad day for me. Can you tell me when's the right day?'

These last two quotes illustrate the perils of taking mass-produced newspaper 'forecasts' to heart. Further, both men seemed to think astrologers could supply the answer to those very curly questions on the spot *and* on the phone *and* without having first constructed the individual chart in each instance. Even assuming both callers imagined that astrologers were all automatically clairvoyant, it would have to be an incredible soothsayer who could pull the answers out of the air in the way they were obviously expecting. And in a flash!

Certainly, if the first man's chart had given suitable indications, it might have been possible to postulate the resumption of a past love affair. But, in no way, could that be done from his Sun Sign alone. (Sun signs are all that are used in newpaper forecasts.) As for the second man, the truth of the matter—unpalatable as it clearly was to him—was the girl he liked simply did not like him. His 'stars' had no hand in that scene!

CHAPTER SIX

Forecasting with the Fastest-Movers—Sun, Moon, Mercury, Venus and Mars

Planetary Progressions

Up to this point, we've kept our future 'telescope' firmly focused on the planetary movements termed 'transits'. And, we've concentrated on the longer-term effects of the slower-moving planets. . .Pluto, Neptune, Uranus, Saturn and Jupiter. The transits of the fast-movers—Sun, Moon, Mercury, Venus and Mars can be examined as well but as these are very brief by comparison, their effect is consequently very short-term. Such transits can be useful in highlighting conditions likely to prompt individual decisions or actions around a particular day or week for better or worse, but they don't tell us what is the prevailing direction of any life as do those of the slow-movers. Further, although long-term transits do supply important clues to the background of coming events plus the intervention of others in each life, transits are not the only performers in the future story.

Behind the scenes, other forces are at work which explain to some extent why one individual will make the best use of new chances and changes while another person will miss them or muff them. . .even when the natal charts of the two are fairly similar. These other future response indicators are termed 'progressions' and represent changes in inner states—mental, physical, emotional. They explain why you're 'in the mood to make it' at one specific time when progressing planets may be fuelling physical energy and emotional equilibrium. And why you're 'not in the mood to do anything more than gnash your teeth' when they may be creating depression and dropping physical vitality down to zero.

Of course, as I've stressed throughout this book, no single transit or progression should be pounced upon and overemphasized. That's rather like cutting one face out of a group photograph and looking at it as if it represented the whole picture. If you do that, you'll find you're only seeing the 'face' of the Sun, for instance, and ignoring the very different 'faces' of all the other planets ranged alongside it in your future pictures.

I recall one case where a girl was emphatically and quite wrongly told to drop her present career and become a psychiatric nurse—simply because planets were currently emphasizing her twelfth house. This house, does sometimes imply involvements with hospitals/institutions but in the above case, the astrologer had made the dangerous mistake of failing to observe other contraditory natal patterns and other transiting and progressing planetary influences. Had due attention been paid to these factors, it would have become immediately apparent that psychiatric work would have caused ruinous consequences in this girl's life. She patently did not have the stamina or calm emotional make-up to deal with the mentally disturbed.

In another story, a woman was 'accused of being an alcoholic' (her own words) because of a Sun/Neptune progression and due to the fact her speech was slightly impaired following a car accident. These cases serve as warnings as to the perils of irresponsible or incompetent forecasting. But back to the problem of working out planetary progressions.

Using them is a little more difficult for new students than in the case of transits since they have to be calculated. Instead of merely being listed from the appropriate planetary ephemeris for the future year/years being studied. Added to this, several different methods of calculation exist. Nevertheless, the system most commonly used today is the one termed 'A-Day-For-A-Year'.

Since this book is concerned primarily with interpretation, if you want to learn more about the astrological mathematics of planetary progressions, pick up a good textbook devoted to that subject. If you'd rather dodge the maths altogether, you can buy computer charts with progressions already calculated for you from firms specializing in chart print-outs.

Later, in this chapter, you'll find interpretation tables for all major progressed aspects of the 'Personal Planets', i.e. Sun, Moon, Mercury, Venus and Mars. Minor ones are not included since—in common with most teachers—I've noted that students tend to err on the side of *quantity* instead of *quality* when handling aspects. The result then adds up to pages upon pages of calculated aspects, many of which are so minor their psychological effect on any life is minimal, yet which confuse the outline of future trends. The secret of success in this area of astrological interpretation is exactly the same as in natal chart work.

Look for the most powerful energies, (the leading actors) in your scenarios for the future. Don't waste time on the minor ones, (the bit players) or you'll finish up with 'a cast of thousands!' Interpretation tables herein are set out in a concise but comprehensive, quick-reference format, designed for easy checking by students and should fill the gap left by many textbooks. For, in recent inspection of astrology textbooks available in specialist bookshops, I have observed that most modern authors apply themselves conscientiously to discussing the mathematics and methods of working with progressions but few offer much in the way of easy-to-follow interpretation tables for progressed aspects.

This situation, doubtless, explains why the works of two early twentieth century authors on progressions are still being reprinted and still appear on bookshop shelves. These authors are Mrs L.H. Milburn, author of the 170-page book'*The Progressed Horoscope Simplified*' (published 1928) and Alan Leo, author of the 353-page book '*The Progressed Horoscope*' (published 1905). Agreed, these authors were sincere, responsible practitioners. Also agreed, human nature hasn't changed any in the many decades that have passed since these works were written. *But*—and this is a very big '*but*'—social conditions, morals and personal expectations of life and love have. Enormously. Which makes these authors' interpretations not so much wrong, but out of step with the world of the last years of the twentieth century.

Take this important fact into consideration whenever you read textbooks more than 60 or 80 years old. Discard the fortune-teller-like, old-style terminology in vogue in those ancient times, such as 'in evil aspect' etc. It, too, is out of keeping with modern research. More importantly still, remember little or no understanding of the *psychological* changes brought about by progressions existed in those far off days. Indeed, the science of psychology itself was then still very much a closed book to the general public. No authors, trained as either psychologists or psychoanalysts, had so much as begun to write serious books devoted to the blending of their own sciences with astrology. (In 1905, the great Swiss-born psychoanalyst, Carl Gustav Jung, who later became one of the most remarkable pioneers in such investigatory fields, was only a couple of years out of medical school.)

As an illuminating flash-back to public attitudes to astrologers in late Victorian times, it now seems sad and strange that Alan Leo—in common with many other practitioners of that period—felt it risky to write under his real name of W.F. Allen. He used instead that pseudonymn, chosen from his own Leo Ascendant. Nevertheless, (and unbelievably now) he was twice hauled into court for 'fortune-telling'. The last case, heard not long before his death in 1917, resulted in a fairly modest fine. Perhaps, it is fear of such dire consequences ensuing these days should anyone take their 'predictions' seriously, which prompts certain varieties of 'pop' astrologers to conceal their true identies behind assumed and often outlandish names even in late 1980's.

Never ever be tempted to use anything other than your own name in your chart work. Today there is neither need nor excuse for so doing. What is more, if you call yourself by false, phoney or fanciful names, you will automatically and instantly fuel the suspicion which many outsiders still harbour about astrology in general. *And* attach it to yourself in particular. *And* rightly so!

Can you imagine anybody trusting for a moment a doctor who listed himself as Dr Marvel S. Medico in the telephone directory? Of course not! Yet false names just as weird and wonderful have been and still are being used by some astrologers. (This foolish practice hit new peaks of absurdity in the 1970's but thankfully nowadays there are fewer and fewer of those types still operating. Here in Australia or overseas.)

But when you run across one of those extraordinary names, you can't help feeling they leave astrology open to immediate ridicule by intelligent readers. For example, I've never forgotten flipping through an English magazine once in which the weekly 'predictions' were served up by an individual, styling himself as 'Gypsy' somebody or other. He had dressed up in headscarf, neckerchief and gold earrings for the cameraman but his cockney face looked as if it would be more at home behind an old clothes barrow in Petticoat Lane! You'd have to be a very simple soul indeed to take such a character as anything but a joke. But, now let's get down to the calculation side of progressions.

Working Out Progressions (1)— Progressed Birth Date (PBD)

Briefly the 'DAY-FOR-A-YEAR' method uses the principle its name implies. To find what is termed the 'Progressed Birth Date' (PBD for short) for each chart subject, you merely add *one day* to the actual birth date for each year of life. . .i.e. 10 days for a child of 10 years, 30 days for an adult of 30 years, and so on.

If, however, the GMT birth time for a chart subject puts the birth date a day *ahead* or a day *behind*, the GMT birth date is the one to count your day-for-a-year from. *Don't ever forget this point or your calculations for future progressions will be one whole year out.*

Now, let's work out the PBD for a male born at 4.35 p.m. on 26 November 1962 in London, England. Since Greenwich is in fact within the city of London, and London is on Greenwich Mean Time, neither birth time nor birth date change. We want to find his PBD for 1987, a year in which he celebrates his 25th birthday.
So. . .

* We list his birthdate as. . .26.11.62
* We add his age in 1987. . 25
* We obtain a total of . . . 51.11.62

No month contains 51 days and his birth month of November has only 30 days. So we subtract the number of days in November from the 51.11.62 figure to find our man's PBD for the year 1987 is . . .21.12.62. (ie. 21 days into the next month—December).

* We look up our Noon Ephemeris for 21.12.62 and note the signs and degrees of the planets on that day from which we can estimate the underlying changes in his mental, physical and emotional attitudes during his 25th year of life.

If we want to examine his 26th year, we simply add one more day to our PBD, another for his 27th year and so on. However, that's not quite the end of calculating. We must now find what is termed either 'Adjusted Calculation Date' or 'Perpetual Noon Date'. (They both mean exactly the same thing.) Here ACD is used for short.

Unless we have the appropriate ACD, all the PBD supplies are the progressed planetary positions for anybody and everybody born on a given date in any given year. That would not be good enough. We must know exactly *when* the changed planetary positions will most affect our subject's life. We want a definite date.

We could, of course, go back to scratch and construct a complete new chart, using the PBD as a sort of notional 'birthday'. But that would waste a lot of time and the process would have to be repeated for each different future year we wish to consider. Obtaining the ACD cuts out all that unnecessary work.

Working Out Progressions (2)—Adjusted Calculation Date (ACD)

So, we'll work through the appropriate steps and an example, observing that—by using Margaret Hone's method—the ACD is obtained by the simple arithmetical process of *division*, followed by a *subtraction* or *addition* as the case may be. Other textbook authors suggest different methods, but, in my view, these are much harder for new students to comprehend. Using a *Noon Emphemeris*, the steps are:

1. Note GMT birth time and birth date. (i.e. Greenwich Mean Time.) Don't forget that if GMT birth time is an a.m. time, the hours and minutes are the difference between that time and noon. (e.g. 1.30a.m. GMT birth time is 10 hours 30 minutes before noon. So you'd be dividing 10 hours 30 minutes in Step 2.)
2. Divide GMT birth time *in half* and list figures as *months and days* instead of *hours and minutes* (e.g. 6 hours converts to 3 months).
3. If the GMT birth time was a.m.—i.e. *before noon*—*add* the months and days figure to GMT birth date. If the GMT birth time was pm that is *after noon*—subtract the months and days figure from GMT birth date.
4. The final date thus obtained is the ACD.

The concept here is anything but easy for new students to comprehend and takes pages of astrological maths and theory to explain—both of which are often terrifying to beginners. However, if you want to study in detail the entire theory and technique see Margaret Hone's classic 320-page work '*The Modern Textbook of Astrology* which devotes a full chapter to the subject of progressions. Luckily, as with music, you don't have to understand fully the theories of harmony to be able to pick up an instrument and play. The same applies to working out Adjusted Calculation Dates so we won't go into all the whys and wherefores.

The process will become clearer if you check through our following example, referring again to the male born on 26 November 1962 at 4.35 p.m. (GMT) in London, England and using a *Noon* Ephemeris.

Step 1. List his GMT birth date. . .26 November 1962.
Step 2. List his GMT birth time. . .4.35 p.m. (i.e. 4 hours 35 minutes *after noon*)
Step 3. Subtract from his birth date. . .2 months and 9 days.
Step 4. List his ACD. . .17 September.
Step 5. List his PBD for the year 1987 (as shown earlier). . . 21 December 1962.

From these processes, we now know we can list our man's planetary positions for the year 1987 in which he turns 25—straight from the Noon Ephemeris. We also now know the date when such planetary influences will exert the strongest effect on his life and behaviour. (The ACD.)

Traps for Beginners. . .At a Glance

Unless you have a thorough understanding of *natal* chart calculation and astrological maths, you can easily make mistakes with progressions which will throw your forecasts out by *years*. If you doubt your skills, refer to my companion book—*How to Astro-Analyze Yourself and Others* or any other reliable astrology text to brush up technique. *Or*, obtain a computer natal chart print-out with progressions shown thereon.

GMT Birth Date

When you convert your subject's birth time to GMT, remember the birth date may *also* change. For example, subject born at 5.20 a.m. on 16 June in Sydney, Australia: GMT birth time here becomes 7.20 p.m. (because Sydney time is 10 hours *ahead* of Greenwich) on *day previous* to birth date. GMT birth date so becomes 15 June and such date is always used in calculating progressions.

Division of Hours and Minutes of GMT Birth Time into Months and Days

When working out the ACD, the division *by half* of hours of birth time into months is easily grasped. For example, 6 hours equals 3 months. The minutes of GMT birth time may be a little harder to follow. This short table will help. In practice round off your figures to nearest day.

- 60 minutes in GMT birth time = ½ of a month (about 15 days).
- 30 minutes in GMT birth time = ¼ of a month (about 7½ days).
- 15 minutes in GMT birth time = ⅛ of a month (about 3¾ days).
- 5 minutes in GMT birth time = $^1/_{16}$ of a month (about 1¼ days).

Let's say our subject's GMT birth time was 1.30 a.m. This time is 10 hours 30 minutes *before noon* on GMT birth date. We divide the above figure as shown. It becomes in months and days. . .5 months and 7½ days.

Adding or Subtracting the ACD

* Always *add* the ACD figure of months and days to GMT birth time, where this birth time is a.m.
* Always *subtract* the ACD figure of months and days to GMT birth time, where this birth time is p.m.

Set this rule in your memory with a piece of alliteration, using the letters 'a' or 'p'.
'a' = a.m. = *add* the months and days.
'p' = p.m. = *peel* off the months and days.

When the ACD Changes the Year

Sometimes when you either add or subtract the ACD figure of months and days, you will find it takes you back to the *year previous* to subject's birth or ahead to the *year after* the subject's birth. Remember, in cases like this:

* *Add one day* to the PBD where the ACD *moves back* to previous year.
* *Subtract one day* from the PBD where the ACD *moves ahead* to the following year.

Work through this example to observe this rule in action. Take subject with GMT birth time of 1.23 a.m. on 16 September 1955. We wish to consider the year of 1988 when the subject will reach age 33. Add 33 days to our GMT birth date to find the PBD is 19 October 1955. Note: GMT birth time is a.m.

Convert GMT birth time to *months* and *days*. Here 10 hours and 37 minutes, convert to 5 months (10 hours) 7½ days (30 minutes) and 2 days (7 minutes). Total equals 5 months and 10 days.

As it is an a.m. time we add 5 months and 10 days (in round figures) to GMT birth date of 16 September 1955. This means we move ahead into the next year, arriving at an ACD of 23 February. Therefore we must *subtract one day* from the PBD of 19 October 1955 to make it 18 October 1955.

Sign Interception in Chart Houses

Don't forget that when a sign is intercepted in any house of the natal chart, any progressing (or transiting planet) will spend much longer moving through such house. For example, let's say a subject's natal chart shows 26 degrees 49 minutes of Aquarius on the first House cusp and 0 degrees 40 minutes of Aries on the second House cusp. This situation means that the sign of Pisces is intercepted (i.e. 'trapped') in the first House between Aquarius and Aries, and hence has no cusp of its own.

In our example, therefore, any planet progressing or transiting this subject's first House would remain there from the time it reached 26 degrees and 49 minutes of Aquarius until it had passed through Pisces and travelled on to 0 degrees 40 minutes of Aries.

Planetary Progressions—Looking Within the Self

First and foremost, remember these are *inner* states. Hence, in many ways, they are less easily identifiable when observing or forecasting behavioural responses. Of course, it's easy to spot when your partner or boss is in a good mood or a bad one. But, often, there seems to be no apparent reason why.

The answers can be found in helpful or disturbing events (planetary transits) or in reassuring or upsetting inner states (planetary progressions) which prompt positive or negative behaviour. Sometimes either, sometimes both together. If the mood or reactions appear to be comparatively short-term, the progressions of the Moon require closest inspection. For the Moon, linked as she is astrologically to individual emotional make-up, reveals by her progressed aspects and house positions the origin of a prevailing 'mood'.

Using the ACD as the focal point of intensity, you can judge as the Moon approaches this date, the 'mood' developing, reaching full effect, then dissipating as she moves on again. With Moon progressions, you can usually allow *about 3 months* for the above process, since she is the fastest-moving of the planetary indicators. The other personal planets—Sun, Mercury, Venus and Mars—are all much slower-moving than the Moon, so can be taken in progression interpretations as having a consequently longer-term and thus more significant effect. The allowance of *approximately 18 months* is advisable, taken from 1 year before the ACD's focal point of intensity and then about 6 months afterwards. As the progressing planet begins to approach the progressed aspect, the inner state of the individual experiencing it begins to react to it. As the progressing planet passes the ACD and moves on again, the reaction slowly dies down.

The areas of response progressing planets symbolize are exactly the same as in natal chart and transit interpretation. Still, as a reminder for new students, we'll list them hereunder. But, first, when considering the effect of progressions, check again the basic rules for all forms of interpretations.

1. The *nature* of each planet indicates the *traits* of personality which it will stress. For example, Mars stimulates sexual drives/physical energies.
2. The *house* any planet occupies determines the specific *life sector* where the planet's influence will be most apparent. For example, Mars in the seventh house stimulates a forceful pursuit of relationships/partnerships.
3. The *aspects* made by one planet to another reveal how their respective energies *blend*, comfortably or contrarily. For example, Mars in a tough aspect to Saturn depletes energy, drops sexual drives.

Therefore, when considering the effect of progressed aspects between the planets, we must always allow for the three factors set out above. . .

* The *nature* of the progressed planet, making any aspect.
* The *house* such planet is occupying.
* The *blend* of its energy with that of the natal planet it is aspecting.

And, as always, we must look back to the natal chart every time. *Do not quote verbatim* interpretations for progressions from this book or any other. Each one must be linked back to the personality potentials shown by the birth patterns themselves. It would be ludicrous, for instance, to assert that a chart subject with heavy natal planetary emphasis on self-control, practicality and caution would suddenly become an all-night rager—just because a Mars progression was currently stimulating sexual appetites. Some change of attitude in this life sector would assuredly show but to nothing like the extent it could in an individual who was characteristically passionate and impetuous.

Age of your chart subjects, again as noted earlier, must be allowed for too. Middle-aged or elderly subjects are not incapable of passions through the weight of years alone, but they're considerably less likely to give way to them than the young.

House Meanings—At a Glance

* First House: The self; physical body; personal environment.
  Second House: Income; earning power; personal financial status.
  Third house: Intellectual concerns: parental influences.
* Fourth House: Home; domestic concerns; parental influences.
  Fifth House: Children; romantic interests; pleasurable activities.
  Sixth House: Work environment; employment; health concerns.
* Seventh House: Marital affairs; partnerships; co-operative efforts.
  Eighth House: Inherited assets; joint property; money of others.
  Ninth House: Travel; foreigners; higher education.
* Tenth House: Career; attainments; professional status
  Eleventh House: Friendships; social activities, hopes.
  Twelfth House: Sacrifices; Isolation; hidden enmities.

NOTE:

(a) Houses marked with 'star' are angular houses. Planets progressing through them therefore have greater impact on any life.

(b) With the solitary exception of the Moon, none of the other progressing planets moves fast enough to change signs or house to any notable extent during the average human life-span. Remember always that with progressions 10 *days* equals 10 *years* of life, 30 *days* equals 30 *years* and so on. Check this concept with your ephemeris and you'll see it clearly demonstrated, but don't confuse it with the manner you work out transits where both signs and houses can change many times during each human lifespan.

Planetary Meanings. . .At a Glance

Sun:	Life force: desire to shine: leadership capacities.
Moon:	Emotions: responsiveness: core of feeling.
Mercury:	Mind: intellectual skills: communicative powers.
Venus:	Love: displays of affections: all forms of caring.
Mars:	Physical vitality: sexuality: impetuosity.
Jupiter:	Expansiveness: optimism: generosity.
Saturn:	Industry: concentrated effort: conservatism.
Uranus:	Originality: independence: search for freedom.
Neptune:	Spirituality: imagination: intuition.
Pluto:	Gut consciousness: regeneration: compulsion.

Interpretation Table for Progressed Aspects

Key: Herein *harmonious* means the two planetary energies joined in the aspect are compatible. For example, some conjunctions, trines, sextiles.

'Inharmonious' means the two planetary energies joined in the aspect are incompatible. For example, some conjunctions, squares and oppositions.

(If you don't thoroughly understand how to decide which aspects are which—please refer to my companion title—*How to Astro-Analyse Yourself and Others* or any other reliable textbook.)

Progressed Aspects of the Sun

NB Progressed Sun aspects show whether other planets are assisting or hindering the thrust of the will and the direction of the life purpose.

---

(1) *Progressed Sun aspecting Natal Moon*

If harmonious: Brightening influence. Will and emotions integrate comfortably. Aids achievement and sense of self-esteem. Gives good impression of benevolence and generosity in daily activities.

If inharmonious: Exaggerates above. Generates tension and inner frustration. Gives bad impression of lowered self-worth and agitation in daily activities.

---

(2) *Progressed Sun aspecting Natal Mercury*

If harmonious: Mentally stimulating influence. Will and mind work well together. Aids demonstration of reasoning power and personal skills. Gives good impression of quicker-wittedness and adaptable thinking in daily activities.

If inharmonious: Exaggerates above. Generates jitteriness and indecisive behaviour. Gives bad impression of restlessness and uncertainty in daily activities.

---

(3) *Progressed Sun aspecting Natal Venus*

If harmonious: Attracting influence. Will and affections blend appealingly. Aid relationships. Gives good impression of willingness to please and enjoy life in daily activities.

If inharmonious: Exaggerates above. Generates over-eager displays of affection, slackness. Gives bad impression of pleasure-seeking, dilatory behaviour in daily activities.

---

(4) *Progressed Sun aspecting Natal Mars*

If harmonious: Energizing influence: Will and physical drives fire each other. Aids energy and sexual vitality. Gives good impression of enterprise and boldness in daily activities.

If inharmonious: Exaggerates above. Generates rashness and lack of control. Gives bad impression of over-assertiveness, aggressive behaviour in daily activities.

---

(5) *Progressed Sun aspecting Natal Jupiter*

If harmonious: Confidence-building influence: Will and optimism reinforce each other. Aids advancement and grasping of opportunites. Gives good impression of open-mindedness, greater tolerance and generosity in daily activities.

If inharmonious: Exaggerates above. Generates misplaced self-confidence and self-indulgence. Gives bad impression of exaggerated self-importance and faulty judgement in daily activities.

---

(6) *Progressed Sun aspecting Natal Saturn*

If harmonious: Disciplining influence: Will and sense of duty stabilise conduct. Aids ambition and self-reliance. Gives good impression of steadiness and acceptance of responsibility in daily activities.

If inharmonious: Exaggerates above. Generates pessimism and narrow-mindedness. Gives bad impression of selfishness and suspicious attitudes in daily activities.

---

(7) *Progressed Sun aspecting Natal Uranus*

If harmonious: Individualizing influence: Will and dynamic energy thrust together. Aids new enterprises and search for exciting experiences. Gives good impression of forward-looking, progressive viewpoints in daily activities.

If inharmonious: Exaggerates above. Generates erratic and/or autocratic behaviour. Gives bad impression of rebelliousness and foolhardiness in daily activities.

---

(8) *Progressed Sun aspecting Natal Neptune*

If harmonious: Enlightening influence: Will and sensitivities serve inspiration. Aids realization of private dreams and intuitive understanding. Gives good impression of kindness and sympathetic attitudes in daily activities.

If inharmonious: Exaggerates above. Generates muddle-headed thinking and impracticality. Gives bad impression of weakness and gullibility in everyday affairs.

---

(9) *Progressed Sun aspecting Natal Pluto*

If harmonious: Regenerating influence: Will and subconscious drives act cohesively. Aids single-minded pursuit of most deeply-felt needs. Gives good impression of inner strength and renewed vitality in daily activities.

If inharmonious: Exaggerates above. Generates compulsive behaviour and over-assertiveness. Gives bad impression of being obsessed with self and own desires in daily activities.

Progressed Aspects of the Moon

NB Progressed Moon aspects show whether other planets are assisting or hindering emotional expression and the type of intimate liaisons sought.

---

(1) *Progressed Moon aspecting Natal Sun*

See Sun/Moon in preceding section, but allow much shorter-term effect.

---

(2) *Progressed Moon aspecting Natal Mercury*

If harmonious: Diversifying influence: Emotions and mind work flexibly together. Aids all forms of intellectual activities and communications. Gives good impression of versatility and lighter, less intense reactions in emotional affairs.

If inharmonious: Exaggerates above. Generates restlessness and fickleness in attachments. Gives bad impression of unreliability and fretful behaviour in emotional affairs.

---

(3) *Progressed Moon aspecting Natal Venus*

If harmonious: Heartening influence. Emotions and affections stimulate pleasurable feelings. Aids friendships, social contacts, love attachments. Gives good impression of charm and being at ease in emotional affairs.

If inharmonious: Exaggerates above. Generates overly demonstrative behaviour and misplaced sentimentality. Gives bad impression of laxity and inertia in emotional affairs.

---

(4) *Progressed Moon aspecting Natal Mars*

If harmonious: Vitalizing influence: Emotions and physical drives balance each other. Aids sexual satisfaction and successes through daring. Gives good impression of heightened animal energy and courage in emotional affairs.

If inharmonious: Exaggerates above. Generates lustfulness and physical excesses. Gives bad impression of egocentricity and over-assertiveness in emotional affairs.

(5) *Progressed Moon aspecting Natal Jupiter*

If harmonious: Encouraging influence: Emotions and hopes of fulfillment prompt happy responses. Aids satisfaction and confidence in taking the necessary chances. Gives good impression of cheerfulness and zest in emotional affairs.

If inharmonious: Exaggerates above. Generates show-off attitudes and obvious opportunism. Gives bad impression of boastfulness and imprudence in emotional affairs.

(6) *Progressed Moon aspecting Natal Saturn*

If harmonious: Trust-building influence: Emotions and sense of duty work in unison. Aids application of common sense to private life issues and a search for practical answers. Gives good impression of seriousness and reliability in emotional affairs.

If inharmonious: Exaggerates above: Generates melancholy and rejecting behaviour. Gives bad impression of narrowness and severity in emotional affairs.

(7) *Progressed Moon aspecting Natal Uranus*

If harmonious: Magnetizing influence: Emotions and dynamic energy stimulate each other. Aids progressive decisions and inventive answers to personal problems. Gives good impression of friendliness and originality in emotional affairs.

If inharmonious: Exaggerates above. Generates autocratic, high-handed attitudes. Gives bad impression of perversity and wilfulness in emotional affairs.

---

(8) *Progressed Moon aspecting Natal Neptune*

If harmonious: Idealizing influence: Emotions and sensitivities combine happily. Aids inspiration and empathy in private life issues. Gives good impression of gentleness and imagination in emotional affairs.

If inharmonious: Exaggerates above. Generates woolly-headedness and hypersensitivity in making moves. Gives bad impression of sloppy sentimentality and self-deception.

---

(9) *Progressed Moon aspecting Natal Pluto*

If harmonious: Motivating influence: Emotions and subconscious drives urge action. Aids perception and powers of observation in private life choices. Gives good impression of awareness and avoidance of subterfuge in emotional affairs.

In inharmonious: Exaggerates above. Generates violent, bloody-minded behaviour. Gives bad impression of resorting to force and outrageous demands in emotional affairs.

Progressed Aspects of Mercury

NB Progressed Mercury aspects show whether other planets are assisting or hindering intellectual activity in all fields and the manner in which it is being channelled.

---

(1) *Progressed Mercury aspecting Natal Sun*

See Sun/Mercury in preceding section.

---

(2) *Progressed Mercury aspecting Natal Moon*

See Moon/Mercury in preceding section but allow a longer-term effect.

---

(3) *Progressed Mercury aspecting Natal Venus*

If harmonious: Communicative influence: Mind and affections co-operate pleasantly. Aids ability for persuasion and sharing of ideas/feelings. Gives good impression of cleverness and charm in expression of intellectual concerns.

If inharmonious: Exaggerates above. Generates loquacity and over-anxiety to please. Gives bad impression of mental laziness and attempts to placate opponents in intellectual concerns.

---

(4) *Progressed Mercury aspecting Natal Mars*

If harmonious: Vigour-boosting influence: Mind and physical drives thrust energetically. Aids driving home of views and dynamic decision-making. Gives good impression of passionate conviction and directness of speech in intellectual concerns.

If inharmonious: Exaggerates above. Generates pugnacious pushing of ideas and rude demands. Gives bad impression of aggressive behaviour and lack of consideration in intellectual concerns.

---

(5) *Progressed Mercury aspecting Natal Jupiter*

If harmonious: Jovial influence: Mind and optimistic expectations blend favourably. Aids broadly-based enterprises and enthusiastic planning. Gives good impression of open-mindedness and eager use of opportunities in intellectual concerns.

If inharmonious: Exaggerates above. Generates improvidence and trust-to-luck attitudes. Gives bad impression of carelessness and overstatement in intellectual concerns.

---

(6) *Progressed Mercury aspecting Natal Saturn*

If harmonious: Practicality-boosting influence: Mind and sense of duty control decisions. Aids conscientious effort and sober pre-planning. Gives good impression of self-control and strong sense of justice in intellectual concerns.

If inharmonious: Exaggerates above. Generates mean-spirited attitudes and dogmatism. Gives bad impression of lack of inspiration and fearfulness in intellectual concerns.

---

(7) *Progressed Mercury aspecting Natal Uranus*

If harmonious: Free-thinking influence: Mind and dynamic energy underlie thought processes. Aids unorthodox enterprises and reforming zeal. Gives good impression of unusual ideas and breaking free of convention in intellectual concerns.

If inharmonious: Exaggerates above. Generates wild fancies and aims without feasibility. Gives bad impression of eccentricity and detachment from reality in intellectual concerns.

(8) *Progressed Mercury aspecting Natal Neptune*

If harmonious: Imagination-building influence: Mind and sensitivities broaden perspective. Aids creative work and subtlety in communication. Gives good impression of pliability and heightened understanding in intellectual concerns.

If inharmonious: Exaggerates above. Generates self-deceptive thinking and gullibility. Gives bad impression of vagueness and drifting aimlessly in intellectual concerns.

(9) *Progressed Mercury aspecting Natal Pluto*

If harmonious: Reformative influence: Mind and subconscious drives delve deep for answers. Aids ability to break through subterfuge and/or camouflage and reveal the truth. Gives good impression of refusal to accept falsehoods or dissembling in intellectual concerns.

If inharmonious: Exaggerates above. Generates outpourings of anger and inability to see other side of problems. Gives bad impression of irascibility and unrestrained force in intellectual concerns.

Progressed Aspects of Venus

NB Progressed Venus aspects show whether other planets are assisting or hindering affectional needs and indicate how love behaviour is being channelled.

---

(1) *Progressed Venus aspecting Natal Sun*
See Sun/Venus in preceding sections.

---

(2) *Progressed Venus aspecting Natal Moon*
See Moon/Venus in preceding sections, but allow longer-term effect.

---

(3) *Progressed Venus aspecting Natal Mercury*
See Mercury/Venus in preceding sections.

---

(4) *Progressed Venus aspecting Natal Mars*

If harmonious: Warming influence. Affections and physical drives seek out satisfaction. Aids love affairs and social successes. Gives good impression of companionable attitudes and willingness to heal breaches in affectional concerns.

If inharmonious: Exaggerates above. Generates misplaced ardour and uncontrolled impulses. Gives bad impression of alternating languor and demand in affectional concerns.

---

(5) *Progressed Venus aspecting Natal Jupiter*

If harmonious: Attracting influence: Affections and hopes of fulfillment allow easier grasping of opportunities. Aids sociability and attempts to improve status. Gives good impression of easy-going behaviour and a more philosophical approach in affectional concerns.

If inharmonious: Exaggerates above. Generates misplaced faith in self or others and lack of discrimination. Gives bad impression of letting things slide and hoping for the impossible in affectional concerns.

---

(6) *Progressed Venus aspecting Natal Saturn*

If harmonious: Wisdom-promoting influence: Affections and sense of duty promote trustworthiness. Aids advancement of aims by calm, supportive conduct and closer bonding of ties. Gives good impression of solidarity and maturity in affectional concerns.

If inharmonious: Exaggerates above. Generates coldness and

distancing of the self from others. Gives bad impression of stiff, inhibited reactions in affectional concerns.

---

(7) *Progressed Venus aspecting Natal Uranus*

If harmonious: Ingenuity-oriented influence. Affections and dynamic energy break through barriers. Aids sudden revelations of feelings and exciting attachments. Gives good impression of liveliness and independence in affectional concerns.

If inharmonious: Exaggerates above. Generates inner tension and erratic behaviour in affectional concerns. Gives bad impression of heartlessness and wayward responses in affectional concerns.

---

(8) *Progressed Venus aspecting Natal Neptune*

If harmonious: Intuition-promoting influence: Affections, sensitivities combine enticingly. Aids popularity and handling of delicate issues. Gives good impression of joyfulness and romanticism in affectional affairs.

If inharmonious: Exaggerates above. Generates low moral standards and self-gratification. Gives bad impression of abandoned behaviour and lack of principles in affectional affairs.

---

(9) *Progressed Venus aspecting Natal Pluto*

If harmonious: Forthright influence: Affections and subconscious drives eliminate artifice. Aids recognition of needs of others and determination to overcome obstacles. Gives good impression of faith in self and integrity in affectional affairs.

If inharmonious: Exaggerates above. Generates disruptive reactions and attempts to overbear. Gives bad impression of compulsive demand for own way and intolerance in affectional affairs.

Progressed Aspects of Mars

NB Progressed Mars aspects show whether other planets are assisting or hindering sexual and physical needs and the manner in which physical energies are being channelled.

---

(1) *Progressed Mars aspecting Natal Sun*
See Sun/Mars in preceding sections.

(2) *Progressed Mars aspecting Natal Moon*
See Moon/Mars in preceding sections, but allow longer-term effect.

(3) *Progressed Mars aspecting Natal Mercury*
See Mercury/Mars in preceding sections.

(4) *Progressed Mars aspecting Natal Venus*
See Venus/Mars in preceding sections.

(5) *Progressed Mars aspecting Natal Jupiter*

If harmonious: Enthusiasm-boosting influence: Physical energies and hopes of fulfilment ignite each other. Aids speed and thrust in gaining objectives and taking chances. Gives good impression of exuberance and speed in physical activities.

If inharmonious: Exaggerates above. Generates wastefulness and extravagance in promoting the self. Gives bad impression of over-assurance and one-upmanship in physical activities.

(6) *Progressed Mars aspecting Natal Saturn*

If harmonious: Patience-building influence: Physical energies and sense of duty come together well. Aids constructive planning and new projects with solid foundations. Gives good impression of well-directed energy and stamina in physical activities.

If inharmonious: Exaggerates above. Generates quarrelsomeness and ill-disciplined actions. Gives bad impression of truculence and boorishness.

(7) *Progressed Mars aspecting Natal Uranus*

If harmonious: Action-oriented influence. Physical energies and dynamic energy join forces. Aids overthrowing opposition and sexual attraction. Gives good impression of surging energy and resilience in physical activities.

If inharmonious: Exaggerates above. Generates disconcerting behaviour and belligerence in physical activities. Gives bad impression of irritability and bloody-mindedness.

---

(8) *Progressed Mars aspecting Natal Neptune*

If harmonious: Replenishing influence: Physical energies and sensitivities illuminate each other. Aids co-operation and aims based on idealistic principles. Gives good impression of refinement and reduced tension in physical activities.

If inharmonious: Exaggerates above. Generates equivocation and duplicity. Gives bad impression of trickiness and uncontrollable urges in physical activities.

---

(9) *Progressed Mars aspecting Natal Pluto*

If harmonious: Reinvigorating influence: Physical energies and subconscious drives combine effectively. Aids display of initiative and well-timed moves. Gives good impression of renewed strength and forcefulness in physical activities.

If inharmonious: Exaggerates above. Generates fanaticism and antagonistic behavour. Gives bad impression of lawlessness and disregard for others in physical activities.

Now that we've worked through interpretations for progressed aspects among the personal planets, let's assume we're applying them to individuals. What could we expect from the progressed Sun in harmonious aspect to natal Moon?

Here follow a range of possible consequences flowing from this aspect: Better health, less worrying, career advances, better relationships. All because this aspect heightens the sense of inner harmony and better integration between the will and emotions.

What if it were an inharmonious Sun/Moon progression? Possible consequences then would be: Frustration of aims, failures, self-doubt, unsatisfying contacts with others.

This time because such an aspect upsets inner harmony and causes a clash between the will and emotions.

Progressions of the Slow-Movers—Jupiter, Saturn, Uranus, Neptune and Pluto

Once again remembering that with progressions we are calculating with the *Day-For-A-Year Method*, you'll appreciate that most of the above-named slower-moving planets will not get all that far from their natal positions during any lifetime. Hence, the aspects they form by progression often simply signify their arrival at a closer point of contact with each other than an aspect already shown in the natal chart. Such contacts, when they occur, certainly intensify the reactions/capacities which existed at birth and can thus be considered in that light.

However, don't forget all the slower-movers affect to a far lesser degree the overall personality structure of each individual in natal charts. Some such natal aspects (between the very slow-movers) are what are termed 'Generation Aspects', meaning the charts of vast numbers of persons born around a certain date and year contain these. Thus they signify a kind of mass reaction to certain stimuli, rather than a markedly individual one. (To perceive this in action, compare the response to war and soldiering shown by the youth who enlisted in the armed services in World War II. Then, look at how young people feel about going to war today. The contrast is startling.)

Of course in this book, we're looking for a 'relief map' of the future—so to speak—with greatest emphasis on its most noticeable 'mountain peaks' and 'chasms'. Therefore aspects between the slow-movers will not be discussed in any detail. Still, if you wish to check progressions of the slow-moving planets to the faster-moving 'personal' planets, you can do this merely by referring back to preceding sections. For example, for Saturn/Mars progressions see (as before indicated) Mars/Saturn.

You may also use, by altering their emphases, excerpts from the transit interpretations set out for the slow-moving planets in earlier chapters when examining progressions. Indeed, you'll see—if you look through textbooks devoted solely to either planetary transits or planetary progressions—almost identical wording is used by their authors for the interpretations of both types of change indicators. Personally, I think the vital difference to note is that with progressions we are looking for changes wrought by changing *inner* needs/responses rather than changes in behaviour prompted by changing *exterior* circumstances.

To illustrate: Let's assume we want to check progressed Saturn square natal Uranus. We look up in Chapter 3, 'Transiting Saturn Square Natal Uranus'. But now, as we're examining inner responses, we observe that deep within the self is where Saturn is exerting his greatest pressure. Arousing feelings of doubt/depression/inflexibility. Striking head-on Uranus' demand for freedom and love of drastic change. The effect, felt within the self, is one of great strain and tension.

Before we begin to apply the techniques discussed in this book to a pair of VIP's, whose adventures and misadventures are documented in any public library and thus can be easily checked, a couple of final points about Future Life Trend Forecasting are worth noting.

Firstly, we are not concerned with 'prediction' in any sense of the word. Derived as it is from two Latin words meaning 'before' and 'say', the Oxford Dictionary defines 'To predict' as 'To foretell, to prophesy'. Or to translate it literally to '*say*' something will happen '*before*' it does. As noted earlier in these pages, many leading astrological groups and societies issue the strongest warnings to their members about the making of 'predictions'. And so do I. Astrologers should not see themselves as prophets.

Secondly, the simplified forecasting techniques I've set out in this book are not the only ones. Some professionals also use New and Full Moons, Solar and Lunar Returns, and Harmonic Directions to mention but a few. This is a matter of your own personal choice. Nevertheless, I do not suggest you attempt to work with any of these unless you are already a fully qualified and experienced practitioner. Otherwise, you can easily lose your way in a labyrinth of calculations or make dangerous errors. Whether in books or magazines, I always aim my writings primarily at new students, keeping recommended methods of calculating and technique as clear and easy-to-follow as possible. If you understand the theories in this book thoroughly, the map of the future which emerges will reveal to you and your chart subjects the paths to follow and the dead-end roads to avoid.

Further, the purpose of this book throughout has been to search the astrological chart for the *major* guidelines which can show us how and where to focus our energies and efforts to the best advantage. To become future winners instead of losers in the race for happiness and fulfillment. The birth patterns of ourselves and our chart subjects will clearly state what these private hopes and dreams actually are. Maybe, they're as modest as love on the dole in a caravan park. Maybe, they're as high as a permanent niche in the Hall of Fame. Maybe, they're not what we once thought they were at all. One thing only is certain. The future movements of the planets offer us opportunities to make the best of our natal potentials. *When* the time is ripe. *And* if we're prepared to expend the effort.

In our next and final chapter, we'll apply all we have learned and focus our microscope on the lives of two people who have been very, very important persons in the arena of world fame. Or, in other words, we'll play a game of 'Headliner Hunting'. This is a game I always recommend to new students as it will develop your skills at an astonishing rate and allow you to test them against documented facts.

In effect, 'Headlines Hunting' means: Pick a celebrity, dead or alive, chart their birth patterns, read biographies and encyclopaedias, then pick the most significant turning point or the greatest crisis in their lives and calculate the planetary transits and progressions current at the time such event occurred. 'Headliner Hunting' is a game that takes a great deal of time and heaps upon heaps of reading but it's well worth the effort. Not only will it deepen enormously your understanding of astrological science. It will also prove beyond doubt that birth patterns *never* lie. That the tangled bundle of goods and bads, talents and vices, hopes and fears which combine to establish the individual psychological make-up of each human being are visible in the birth chart for all to see—*if* the eye has been trained to detect them.

And it will show that—whether kings or presidents, superstars or physicists—beneath the ballyhoo and the glamour, they have precisely the same needs and urges, joys and disappointments as ordinary people. Or, as the old saying goes—'The Colonel's lady and Judy O'Grady are sisters under the skin.' And *under* that 'skin' of fame and status is where the natal chart allows us to look.

Quick Reference Check-Points for Chapter 6

On 'Talking Astrology' to Friends, Family, and Casual Enquirers

Whether you're studying astrology for pleasure or planning one day to become a practitioner, you'll find that (as soon as the word is out), friends, family or even total strangers will start asking you questions about their lives and loves. In my experience, these questioners fall into two main 'bundles'. The ones who are having love troubles and want you to sort them out on the spot—so to speak. Or, the ones who have a future-oriented problem and want you to solve it for them . . .then and there.

I always warn new students to avoid the temptation of saying *anything* without an accurately-calculated chart in hand. And, to make sure the birth data proffered is correct. Some casual advice-seekers have been known to lop a few years off their ages, for example. . .especially if they've teamed up with a partner considerably younger than themselves. In cases like that the planetary positions you check in the ephemeris will, of course, be quite wrong.

Attempting to give advice based on your questioner's sun sign is equally risky. To begin with, the sun sign is only one facet of personality. And, further, you'll invite the favourite criticism of catch-you-out sceptics who'll cry triumphantly: 'Rubbish! My girlfriend and I are both Scorpios and we're nothing like each other.' No two personalities are identical, certainly, although there are invariably basic similarities in behaviour when two individuals belong to the same Sun Sign. However, these can be masked or diverted by other planetary indicators so that to the untrained mind and eye the two people *appear* as different as chalk and cheese.

If you've progressed as far as constructing charts for friends and family, here are a few more tips on how to handle the various types of questions you're likely to encounter. Remember, there is still a great deal of uncertainty among the general public about what astrologers do and don't do—and about what the science can and can't offer in the way of advice/guidance. The questions listed below represent some of the most frequent people ask me plus the answers I give.

Q. 'I've heard there are some really awful people who call themselves astrologers. How can you tell who's a good, reputable astrologer and who isn't?'

A. If a particular practitioner has been recommended to you by a friend whose opinions you trust, that's a good start. Nevertheless, I always suggest that you ask the following questions before ordering your horoscope chart.

1. Is the astrologer a member of the leading astrological society in your country? This is a valuable safeguard against falling into the hands of charlatans or incompetents. Astrological societies do not accept as members anyone whose qualifications fail to reach the required standard.
2. How much experience and how many years of practice has the astrologer had? Sad as it is to relate, nowadays individuals with little or no training advertise themselves as astrologers. The mistakes these types make—especially in giving advice—is nothing short of horrendous!

So, if you don't get the right answers to these questions, look elsewhere!

Q. 'I'd like to have my fortune told. Do astrologers do that?'

A. Not reputable, well-qualified practitioners. Indeed, the Code of Ethics of the Federation of Australian Astrologers (and presumably those of its counterparts elsewhere), expressly prohibits making statements which can be construed as 'fortune-teller-type' predictions. The horoscope chart offers clear guidelines as to future possibilities in every life but does not predict the future in the sense of defining what *will* happen. The chart never denies the role of your own free will in making the best use of future opportunities and avoiding future trouble spots.

Q. 'Some of my friends say astrology's a load of garbage and I'm stupid to believe in it. What do you say to that?'

A. I suggest you ask your 'knowledgeable' friends how many years they've devoted to studying astrology to make them competent to offer an opinion. You'll quickly discover that none of them has so much as opened a serious astrology textbook and wouldn't know one end of the horoscope chart from another. I often wonder too how the intellectual qualifications of the sceptics and scoffers would fare when measured up against such outstanding exponents of astrology as psychoanalyst Carl Gustav Jung, one of the world's greatest authorities on human behaviour and an expert astrologer; Professor Stephen Arroyo, MA, one of America's leading psychologist/astrologers and marriage counsellors; psychologist Noel Tyl, Harvard University graduate and author of a 12 volume treatise on scientific astrology.

Q. 'I have a tremendously important decision to make very soon. Can an astrologer tell me what to do and what *will* happen if I do or don't make that decision?'

A. In my personal view (and I would think that of all well-qualified practitioners) the astrologer's role does not amount to making your decisions for you. The horoscope chart will show the possible results which are likely to ensue from a specific action made at a certain time. And a good astrologer will explain precisely which planetary patterns are influencing your range of choices. . .through studying your natal chart plus progressions and transits current at the dates you're concerned about. These indicators may add up to a 'green light' for your project or show a warning 'red'. Or even a cautionary 'yellow'. But that's it. Don't ask an astrologer to sit in the driving seat and take over the wheel for you. After all, it's *your* car!

Q. 'Is it true that astrologers do tarot cards, numerology and palmistry as well?'

A. A few do use tarot readings and numerology etc. Most leading practitioners do not. I have never felt the horoscope chart needs any help from other systems if it is correctly interpreted and understood. Astrology should not be confused with clairvoyance.

Q. 'I have a serious problem in my personal life. Would an astrologer be able to help me?'

A. Yes, if you're willing to listen to advice and the astrologer you choose is qualified in personal counselling. In any case, although the horoscope chart will invariably reveal the origin of the problem and how to overcome it, you've got to be prepared to make the effort to change your personality minuses into pluses.

Q. 'I'd like to consult an astrologer but I'm frightened. A friend went to one and was told she'd be lonely all her life, never have a family and never get anywhere. She's been terribly depressed since. Will I be told those sort of things too?'

A. Not by astrologers who know what they're talking about. *And* understand the virtually irreparable damage this type of irresponsible 'predicting' can do. All the 'predictions' you quote are nonsensical, unprofessional, and ludicrously negative. No horoscope chart would ever indicate such circumstances. Certainly, the chart may show that a person like your friend was going through a difficult period (through certain transits or progressions) and/or that her personality was such that she may unconsciously reject offers of love and friendship. It may even show that she was less likely to have children or had no real urge to become a mother. *But*—and this is a very big *but*—a responsible, experienced practitioner would clearly state when difficult times end (as transiting or progressing planets move away from awkward aspects) *and* how to manage personality traits affecting her attitudes to love relationships and motherhood. In my view, your chart interpretation should offer you new hope, new confidence, and heightened awareness of your innate potentials. Not, of course, by skipping or glossing over your failings but by showing you how to overcome them.

Q. 'I rang an astrologer advertising in my local newspaper, whose fees were $150. For this, I received a cassette that was obviously mass-produced and my personal horoscope chart was not included. What can you do when you find you've been ripped-off' like that?'

A. Firstly, you can report the case to your local astrological society or organization for investigation. These bodies do the best they can to police the activities of charlatans and phonies. You could also seek advice from a solicitor. But, as mentioned in Question 1, you'll save yourself money and worry, if—when approaching a practitioner you don't know or have not been recommended to—you ask if he/she is a member of any astrological organization. Members are required to abide by its strict code of ethics.

I must say that whenever I hear of bad work or bad practices by astrologers, I feel angry and disgusted. Angry because the trust of a client has been abused and the great science of astrology has been dragged in the mud. Disgusted because I find it incredible that anyone could even begin to study astrology and remain so unaffected by its truths as to deny them by adhering to mercenary or irresponsible attitudes. For example, just recently a man rang me and told how he'd fallen for a confidence trick by consulting an 'astrologer' he knew nothing about. 'If that's how astrologers work, I think the whole business stinks!' said he. I told him that I sympathized with him but the individual he saw was anything but typical of a conscientious, well-qualified practitioner. Still, that little story proves my point. One rotten apple can ruin the whole barrel!

Q. 'I've read that many scientists condemn astrology as "mumbo jumbo". How do you answer that?'

A. There's no doubt that certain scientists leap into furious print at the mere mention of the word 'astrology'. Back in 1975, nineteen of them issued a statement deploring 'the uncritical dissemination of horoscopes by otherwise reputable media.'

Most leading practitioners would wholeheartedly agree with the scientists on the matter of mass-produced newspaper 'stars' columns or radio/television daily 'predictions'—to which that statement obviously refers. Each individual's astrological chart is as unique as his/her thumbprint, as to the personality traits it reveals *and* the future life directions it indicates. Hence, no generalized statements about horoscopes can be valid.

On the other hand, there is a growing group of scientists—physicists as well as psychologists—who have been making thorough, long-term studies of astrological science and have found evidence to support its doctrines. Last, without studying a subject, how can anyone be remotely competent to comment—for or against? Assuredly, astrologers do make mistakes but so do scientists. Both are only human.

Here's an example of an earth-shattering (literally!) mistake which happened during a planetary alignment in 1982—known at the time as 'The Jupiter Effect'.

A lengthy book on this alignment was published in the 1970's in which it was predicted that the whole earth would go up in smoke on 10 March 1982. Much ominous burbling about this began in the national media as the dread day grew near. When nothing at all notably celestial happened. . .here's a 10 March 1982 quote from a leading metropolitan daily:

'Contrary to popular beliefs of astrologers, prophets of doom and assorted cranks, the world did not come to an end today.'

The news story then went on to state that the originators of the doomsday, Armageddon or whatever-you-call-it prophecy were not astrologers at all. But—wait for it—*two British Scientists*! ! ! Not one single, solitary reputable astrologer had made any such blood-curdling prediction.

Yet, presumably because our science is based on planetary movements, the above-mentioned report writer felt safe in falsely inferring astrologers were being quoted and dropping them—without any substantiation whatsoever—into the bin labelled 'prophets of doom and assorted cranks'. Astrology-bashing is still a favourite sport among some 'smart-alec' type media commentators.

Q. 'Are future forecasts by astrologers always right?'

A. If the practitioner is competent, qualified and experienced, the general outline of future life directions which the individual natal chart supplies will be correct in essence.

However, future life forecasts by astrologers can be compared to future weather forecasts by meteorologists. Both search the skies—so to speak—for indications of changes in life conditions (astrologers), in weather conditions (meteorologists). Both may issue forecasts for 'sunny periods' or 'storm warnings' ahead. Nevertheless, there are always times when you take your umbrella to town for the expected 'rainy day' and find a cloudless, blue sky instead because something in the weather pattern has surprisingly changed. So it is with astrological forecasts. Further, a chart subject, who takes care to prepare for and handle constructively life's stormy spots, will find he/she can navigate them successfully. Then the 'heavy weather' will seem more like 'calm seas.' On the other hand, chart subjects who ignore 'storm warnings' may find they've overturned their 'boat'. There are always some people who *refuse* to be warned. Just like those inexperienced sailors who put to sea when the barometer's falling and a hurricane has been forecast. Short of a miracle, they'll go down with their ship!

Again, in the same manner as weather forecasters, astrologers point out *not what will happen* in times ahead but what *is likely to happen*. Neither can do more than that. It's up to everyone to listen to the advice or do the opposite. The choice itself and the free will to decide is theirs alone. Happily for meteorologists, they don't have to suffer the cries of condemnation and accusations which astrologers sometimes do when forecasts do not turn out the way their hearers hoped.

Q. 'What does it take to become a professional astrologer?'

A. As interest in astrology soars to the top of the board, more and more people are asking questions like that, so I thought a short outline of the path to professionalism could offer readers a few handy clues.

To begin with, there are *no short-cuts to success.* No 'Learn To Play The Stars In Five Easy Lessons!' Whatever method you choose to study astrology—whether by classes, private tuition or textbooks—you'll never get to grips with its fundamental truths until you prove them for yourself. Again and again and again. This process adds up to working your lonely way through calculations and chart interpretations literally by the barrel load. Before you throw your doors open to a waiting world. *And* before you begin to charge for your services.

Many years ago now I did this myself and I'm still convinced it's the only way there is. Good textbooks and/or good instructors will teach you the mathematical techniques and the basic rules of chart interpretation. But once you have all those so well imprinted on your memory you barely have to stop and ponder—it's very definitely over to you. For the final fruit of unrelenting study is the ability to *synthesize.* To blend effectively together all the contrary data the chart offers. As to personality type, emotional needs, mental attitude, life direction etc., etc. Only plenty of personal experience can teach you that.

Take care, of course, if you're just starting out on your studies to choose books or instructors with the greatest of care. The sheer junk written about astrology would fill the Albert Hall or the Sydney Opera

House. If you tangle with that stuff, you'll be off to the worst possible start. Some so-called teachers are just as hopeless. Thus I always advise beginners seeking tuition to check out the picture with the leading astrological society in their country. Better to be sure than sorry you wasted your money!

Most such groups or societies only accept practitioners whose standards and qualifications reach the required criteria. Membership is graded according to individual expertise.

These days an initial check-up on the qualifications of anyone offering tuition is even more advisable. For, as astrology's popularity grows so does the number of individuals who bring shame and ridicule to it through incompetence, shoddy work or pursuit of the fast buck.

Further, I believe you need to be reasonably mature. . .to have built up a sizeable amount of life experience yourself. . .to have acquired at least a basic understanding of human psychology. . .to make a good professional. Remember—whether they state it or not—most clients seek the aid of astrologers when they have a genuine problem. They look to the practitioner for good advice and wise guidance. Qualities which rarely manifest in early adulthood.

Lastly, never make the mistake of thinking that practising as a professional astrologer is a lucrative job. Not only does it take years to build a reputation, it also requires hours of work on each chart you erect and interpret. Even if you use a computer to do your calculations, you can't turn out good work like sausages from a sausage machine!

Thus, I felt like roaring with laughter when I ran across this statement in a book by a scientist who spared a few lines for the sole purpose of knocking astrology. 'Astrology is one of the many easy ways of making a living' said he. (Thus also proving he hadn't the faintest knowledge of what he was pontificating about.)

However, I felt somewhat mollified after reading a further quote from Professor Hans Eysenck (a world-famous name in the field of psychology) commenting in his book—*Astrology: Science or Superstition?*; 'Many of the people in the scientific establishment would have fitted well into the panel which condemned Galileo!' Galileo, it will be remembered, was the great Italian physicist who was tried by the Inquisition in 1633 for demonstrating that the earth revolved around the Sun—instead of vice versa. Well, nearly 400 years have passed since then but responsible practitioners are still battling the same kind of bigotry. If you want to become an astrologer, you'll have to face up to it too!

CHAPTER SEVEN

Preparing Your Integrated Map of the Future—Outer Events Plus Inner Changes

First, we'll put our theories we've been studying to the test by examining the natal charts of two world-famous Edwards—'Teddy' Kennedy, youngest brother of the murdered US President. And HRH Edward, Duke of Windsor, the oldest brother of King George VI and uncle of Queen Elizabeth II. Then, having scoured the natal charts for all they can tell us about the future lives of these two VIP's, we'll discuss the planetary histories.

For the Pisces-born Teddy—his crisis point years were 1968, 1969 and 1970. For the Cancer-born Duke, they were 1935, 1936 and 1937. And, as we go we'll note how plainly their charts told their tales. Warning of the problem patches/trouble spots which were there at birth and long before they finally showed their teeth in the sixties for Teddy and the thirties for the Duke. Demonstrating how a stitch in time in the fabric of destiny could have saved nine. Revealing that forewarning instead of mere foretelling is the best and greatest benefit astrological science can offer us all in our progress along the obstacle courses of our lives.

At this point, I can hear a chorus of professional sceptics shouting: 'Aha! She picked on these two celebrities just because they do seem to "prove" her theories!' Or 'It's all just chance! Coincidence!' Or 'Bet you, she read up on these people first then made it all fit!'

As to 'coincidence and chance'—these are only words to cover up the otherwise inexplicable. They explain nothing, dodge the issue entirely. As to 'making astrology fit'—this cannot be done. The planetary indicators are there or they are not. In the chart. Large as life. As to 'picking on' Teddy and the Duke—in no way! Believe it or not. I merely spotted the two most recent biographical books (mentioned later) during one of my frequent browsings in the local bookshop. I read them because both celebrities interested me and while they were fresh in my mind decided to work through their astrological patterns for this chapter.

What's more, I have observed the same proofs of astrological theory shown in their stories appearing again and again in my chart work with my own clients. The current and future movements of the planets invariably reflect the major aim, decision or problem which is most significant to clients at a given date. (This is, of course, not always what they *believe* it to be at that time.)

Your own experience should show the same result. And, of course, you cannot 'make' the chart say what your client may or may not wish to hear. The planetary positions are written there in black and white for all to see. That's why I always urge students when they become practitioners to hand the completed chart to clients. Agreed, laymen may not understand the planetary symbols/calculations but it stands as proof of the hours of work you've put in. That you did not pull your answers out of the air or 'tailor' them to please or shock. . .in the manner of fortune-tellers. *If you plan to consult a practitioner yourself, always ask at the outset if he/she supplies the calculated chart with whatever service you're seeking.*

If an astrologer does not supply the chart, take your business to one who does. (Chances are no calculated chart has been prepared at all and you may find you've paid a high price for a mass-produced job. And, further, there is no way of later checking—if you so desire—the mathematical accuracy of the work. Wrong sums supply wrong answers!)

The no-chart-supplied 'astrologer' usually goes in heavily for 'predictions' which may be based on nothing more than your Sun Sign and thus are meaningless. Sometimes, wrongly depressing too. Many are the complaints received by responsible practitioners of this type of operator, who not only exposes astrological science to ridicule by ridiculous 'predictions' but also diminishes its stature in the eyes of laymen. (Which makes life a whole lot harder for those of us who do put hours of work and thought—not to mention years of study—into our work.)

But, now let's pick up our astrological 'microscope' and focus it first on Teddy Kennedy and then on the Duke of Windsor—neither of whom really wanted to play the roles destiny cast them in. Thus, as we saw in an earlier chapter, theirs were both 'don't want' situations. Teddy certainly 'didn't want' the presidential label. The Duke certainly 'didn't want' to be king other than on his own terms. It is, however, patently clear from their life stories that neither knew *exactly* what they 'did want'. And therein lay the rub.

Note: All factual material re events and personal backgrounds has been obtained by me from biographies and encyclopaedias and other reference works. (I especially recommend two detailed but very readable books '*The Kennedys. An American Drama*' by Peter Collier and David Horowitz, (726 pages) published in 1984. And '*The Windsor Story*' by J. Bryan III and Charles J.V. Murphy, (751 pages) published in 1981. Both are in paperback but should also be available in public libraries.)

The Sad Astrological History of Edward Kennedy—Last Knight Of the Camelot Rank

Hands up all those Pisceans who'd like to be President of 'God's Own Country?' What, so few of you? All right. Hands up all those Pisceans who'd like to be US President after *three* of their older brothers had been killed—en route to or installed in the Oval Office? What, no takers at all?

I ask those questions because they encapsulate the sad dilemma of Teddy—last male survivor of the 'presidential' Kennedy generation of what US authors have tagged America's Star-Crossed Dynasty. Or, it's closest equivalent to a 'Royal Family'. Variously known as 'Kid Brother' . . .'Fat Rich Kid'. . .'Society Bridegroom'. . .'US Senator'. . .'Star Witness at Drowning Inquest'. . .'Presidential Candidate'. . .Teddy's Piscean pilgrim's progress along the hard and bumpy road his Virgoan father mapped out for his sons has made world headlines more often than not and never been an easy ride. Kennedy biographers and commentators have retraversed it endlessly. On reading any one of these, I think you'd have to say with me as Hamlet did of his childhood friend: 'Alas, poor Teddy!'

What *could* a plump, peaceable, pleasure-loving Piscean (saddled with an ambitious Capricorn Ascendant and dutiful Virgo Moon) do when he knew only too well he was the last 'knight' left in the magical world of Camelot his murdered brother had devised and enshrined in the American Dream? Worse still, how *would* any unassuming Piscean have felt when he read in his school lesson books as a child that he had been born on the very same day as George Washington himself—*exactly* 200 years later? George 'I cannot tell a lie' Washington: Commander-in-Chief of the revolutionary army which routed the British: Father of his country: *and* first President of the United States. Now there *was* an act to follow.

With a family as resolutely 'presidency-minded' as Teddy's, he must have digested this terrible news even in kindergarten with mounting dismay. Then, as he grew up and fate picked on, cast in the role of martyrs to the cause and despatched one older brother after another to their blood-drenched deaths, his apprehensions must have shot up like a runaway elevator.

By the time he was 36, all three of those 'buffers' who had protected him for so long from possible presidential striving were gone. Young, suddenly and in dreadful ways he could never have thought possible. His powerful father was virtually gone too—aged 81, totally incapacitated and in the last few months of his life. Teddy was on his own. There was no-one left. In a sense, it must all have seemed a macabre re-enactment of the old nursery rhyme. . .'First there were four young Kennedy boys, then there were three, then there were two and then there was one'. Would it end, too, like the rhyme? Would one day there be *none*?

Had Teddy known what his natal chart contained, he may have been comforted. Pluto, having embedded the hook at birth on his line of destiny in the gills of this Fish, was just slowly and steadily reeling it in. Still, what *could* Teddy do but soldier on? Run for President eventually, but hope to high heaven in his heart of hearts, that he'd never make it. And, of course, he never did make it. The many and tortuous political *and* family reasons why are set out at length in the most recent of a long line of Kennedy family biographies I've read—

the massive, 726 page work entitled, *'The Kennedys. An American Drama'* by Peter Collier and David Horowitz, published in 1984.

Assuredly, hindsight is easier to apply than foresight. But, I think even the greatest sceptic must agree—after reading Edward Kennedy's natal chart plus the tale told by planetary patterns current around 18 July, 1969—that this 20th century Piscean did *not* want to follow in the footsteps of his brothers *or* his 18th century 'twin'. Was most definitely not in search of a niche in the Presidential Hall of Fame. And any chart analyst, skilled enough in his/her trade, could have said so from the time Teddy opened his eyes on the world at 3.58 a.m. on 22 February 1932, the ninth and youngest child of an American multimillionaire. *Two hundred years to the day* after George Washington, also born into a wealthy family, arrived on the American scene at around 10.05 a.m. on 22 February 1732. More intriguingly still, Teddy shared more than a moneyed background and a Pisces Sun with his illustrious 'twin'.

Washington's Moon was in Capricorn: Kennedy's Ascendant is Capricorn. Washington's Ascendant was Taurus: Kennedy's Moon is Virgo. Thus both men's charts show the water sign of Pisces, sandwiched between two earth signs. . .one of which in each case is the cardinal earth sign of Capricorn. Tough, uncompromising, punctilious, 'make-it-or-else' Capricorn. *But*—Washington's Capricorn thrust was linked to the deep, emotional urge of the Moon and his birth chart shows the majority of planets *above* the horizon with the added perseverance flowing in from his Taurus Ascendant.

Kennedy's Capricorn drive lies on the surface only, is part of the masking quality of the Ascendant. And the majority of his planets are *below* the horizon. Not to mention the clashing demands of the Pisces Sun and Virgo Moon, forcing him into the role of a man divided against himself. Added to all the above, Washington was the first son of his father by a second wife. Kennedy was the ninth and last child. Psychologically—apart from astrologically—the birth order of children has been proved to have marked effects on their adult behaviour. The oldest child, being obliged to 'grow up fast', usually handles responsibility more confidently for instance. The youngest, feeling itself 'the baby of the family', stays 'young' and hence somewhat irresponsible throughout adult life.

Thus, we begin to see why Washington did make it to the peak of

America's political structure and Teddy did not. Bearing in mind, too, that the world in which America's Declaration of Independence was proclaimed on 4 July 1776 was a very different one from that in which Teddy campaigned 200 years later. Nevertheless, (as far as I know and I'm not an expert on American political history), astrological 'twinship' such as that of these two runners in the Presidential stakes has never occurred before or since. That fact in itself makes it both extraordinary and intriguing.

Further, as we've observed in earlier chapters, accurate future trend forecasting is a matter of examining the past and the family situations which set events in train—sometimes years upon years before they actually occur. So before we pass on to examining Teddy's Life Data, Personality Profile and Future Trend Analysis, let's inspect the birth dates and personal planets of his immediate relatives as all have astrological significance and bearing on his story—past, present and future.

FATHER: Joseph Kennedy: Born 6 September 1888: Died 19 November 1969. Patriarch, architect of the Kennedy presidential ambitions, and father of four sons and five daughters.

....	Sun	= Virgo
	Moon	= Virgo
	Mercury	= Virgo
	Venus	= Virgo
	Mars	= Scorpio

MOTHER: Rose Kennedy: Born 22 July 1890. Daughter of a rich and rumbustious politician of Irish extraction like the Kennedys themselves. Considered herself 'the prettiest girl in Boston'. Married at 24. Mother of nine. Outlived nearly all her contemporaries and four of her own children. By July 1986, she was 96 years old.

....	Sun	= Cancer, near Leo cusp
	Moon	= Virgo
	Mercury	= Cancer, near Leo cusp
	Venus	= Cancer
	Mars	= Sagittarius

OLDEST BROTHER: Joseph Kennedy junior: Born 25 July 1915:

Killed on 12 August 1944 during World War II after undertaking a flight mission so dangerous it was considered close to suicidal. This was the son his father intended to be President. Died a few days after his 29th birthday as transiting Saturn was within 3 degrees of his return to his natal position. Fellow pilots in his squadron believed his stubborn determination to fly the plane—experimentally loaded with ten tons of TNT—amounted to a death wish or a belief in his own invulnerability. Twenty-eight minutes after take-off it exploded into a huge fireball in mid-air. As he climbed into the cockpit, Joe junior had said: 'If I don't come back, tell my dad—despite our differences—I love him very much.'

.... Sun = Leo, near Cancer cusp
Moon = Capricorn
Mercury = Cancer
Venus = Cancer
Mars = Gemini

SECOND BROTHER: John Kennedy: Born 29 May 1917: Assassinated on campaign in Dallas, Texas on 22 November 1963 after being warned by leading American astrologers *not* to go to Dallas during 1963. This was the son his father turned to and began grooming for President after Joseph's wartime death. He was elected US President on 8 November 1960.

.... Sun = Gemini
Moon = Virgo
Mercury = Taurus
Venus = Gemini
Mars = Taurus

THIRD BROTHER: Robert Kennedy: Born 20 November 1925: Assassinated during his own presidential campaign at Los Angeles on 6 June 1968. His father's directing hand was not visible behind this son as Joseph senior had by then suffered an incapacitating stroke and could neither move nor speak intelligibly. Nevertheless, Bobby still sought to make him understand and gain his moral support.

.... Sun = Scorpio
Moon = Capricorn
Mercury = Sagittarius
Venus = Aries
Mars = Scorpio

WIFE: Joan Kennedy: Born 9 September 1936: Married Edward on 29 November 1958. Later became severely afflicted with weight and drinking problems. Mother of two sons and one daughter.

....	Sun	= Virgo
	Moon	= Cancer
	Mercury	= Libra
	Venus	= Libra
	Mars	= Leo

CHILDREN: Kara: Born 27 February 1960: Edward junior: Born 26 September 1961: Patrick: Born 14 July 1967. Edward junior became seriously ill with a form of cancer and had a leg amputated on 17 November 1973 a few weeks after his 12th birthday.

Kara	Sun	= Pisces
	Moon	= Pisces
	Mercury	= Pisces
	Venus	= Aquarius
	Mars =	Aquarius
Edward junior	Sun	= Libra
	Moon	= Taurus
	Mercury	= Libra
	Venus	= Virgo
	Mars	= Libra
Patrick	Sun	= Cancer
	Moon	= Libra
	Mercury	= Cancer
	Venus	= Virgo
	Mars	= Libra

EDWARD HIMSELF: Born 22 February 1932. Married at age 26. Previously did army service overseas. Obtained law degree. Elected US senator 6 November 1962. Helped manage John Kennedy's presidential campaign first. Later did same for Robert Kennedy. Wrote book on health, published 19 June 1972. Considered a leading Democratic presidential candidate but on 23 September 1974 announced he would not run for president in 1976. Did run in 1980, was defeated by Aquarian Ronald Reagan but supporters urged him to run again in 1984.

.... Sun = Pisces
Moon = Virgo
Mercury = Aquarius
Venus = Aries
Mars = Aquarius

CRISIS POINT IN EDWARD'S LIFE: Drowning accident at Chappaquiddick, USA on 18 July 1969. Car driven by him, ran off a bridge into deep water. Even now, decades later, mystery surrounds precisely how his passenger—a blonde secretary attached to the Kennedy staff, named Mary Jo Kopechne—came to drown in the submerged vehicle. The accident occurred after a party with Kennedy aides and girl employees.

Biographers state that even on Teddy's own account, his response to the situation was both incredible and irresponsible. Instead of calling the police and rescue teams, he returned to the party, collected his cousin and both drove back to the scene together to make repeated but unsuccessful dives in search of the car. He then swam alone across the inlet at Chappaquiddick to his motel at Edgartown where he changed his clothes and appeared in the lobby at 2.30 a.m. to make seventeen phone calls. None of them were to report the accident to the police. After going to bed, he got up in the morning and boarded a ferry for Chappaquiddick to discover the body had been found. He then made a report. At the date of the accident, he was 37 years old and had been notable for 'drinking like a true Irishman' and driving recklessly since early adulthood.

Biographers further state that due to Teddy's drinking habits and driving style, 'this was an accident which had been waiting to happen for years.' (He is the only Kennedy male of his generation who drank other than abstemiously.)

He later testified at the inquest into Mary Jo Kopechne's death on 5 January 1970. His wife suffered a miscarriage a month after the Chappaquiddick incident. In his subsequent political campaigns, the drowning story and his peculiar response were regularly resurrected and used as ammunition against him by his opponents.

Teddy is the only male Kennedy of his generation to survive past middle age. Joseph junior died at 29, John at 46 and Robert at 42.

Pausing at this point for a moment, let's assess what we have now gleaned from the foregoing family birthdates and scraps of family history. Readers who also have my companion book *Astro-Pick Your Perfect Partner* will observe that two highly significant pointers discussed therein have shown up here. These indicate the astrological reflection of family background and conditioning on life choices.

1. Signs tend to repeat—especially at level of Ascendant, Sun and Moon through many generations, thus showing how inherited characteristics are passed on to influence the future through repeating chart patterns. . .Here Joseph senior, Rose, John and Teddy all have Moon in Virgo. Teddy's late sister, Kathleen and his only daughter were both born under Pisces like himself. Teddy's younger son has his grandmother's Sun sign of Cancer.
2. Individuals often tend to marry the sign or element of one of the parents. . .Here Teddy married a Virgoan, the same sign as his dominating father. John married Jacqueline, born 28 July 1929, and John's mother, Rose was born very close to the cusp of Leo.

If you read up Kennedy biographies, you'll note some interesting similarities appear between Rose's cool handling of her nine children and Jacqueline's of her two, John junior and Caroline. Jacqueline's second son lived only two days after he was born on 7 August 1963, yet repeated again the Leo Sun sign of his mother, his late uncle Joseph junior and part Leo Sun sign of his paternal grandmother.

From this, we see the trip through Teddy's family annals was worth it. We spot that both he and brother John were particularly susceptible to their father's conditioning. His numerous Virgo planets opened a clear channel to both his sons' emotional make-up via their Virgo Moons. We further see that with Teddy, the father's influence hit home hard and permanently as he later chose a Virgoan wife. And the result of that union appears to have been as ambivalent and unsatisfying as his relationship with his father had been. Virgo and Pisces rarely handle each other easily, in any event. For Teddy the conflict was greater still. His Pisces Sun had the same struggle with his Virgo intimates as it had with his Virgo Moon.

We also note from his family history that Joseph junior was killed in action at the time of the Saturn Return. Not through the expected hazards of war but because he undertook a flight mission that was 'close to suicidally dangerous'. Was that evidence of the Leo-type's natural courage and flamboyance? Or was it his subconscious mind presenting a way out of ever becoming US President?

We further perceive that John Kennedy refused to listen to numerous warnings (astrological *and* political) which advised solidly against his fatal visit to Dallas in November 1963. Why did he ignore the warnings? He reportedly stated to the media that he 'put his faith in God and not in the stars'. But no answer came to the next question. 'Who, Mr President, do you think made the stars?' And, supposing he had heeded the warnings which the planets were writing in letters of fire around November 1963, what then? Most leading American commentators on his chart consider he would not have died at only 46.

After his death, it was learned he had been ill and in constant pain from a back ailment since childhood. Not as a result of war injuries as had been formerly given out. It was also not made public—lest it damage his political ambitions—that following his collapse in London in the 1940's he was diagnosed as suffering from Addison's disease—a malfunction of the adrenal glands—and that this was responsible for his frequent illnesses and weight losses in his earlier years. Later in his life, the disease had been controlled by medication but he still suffered great pain and difficulty in walking at times.

In the light of this information, it speaks highly of John Kennedy's personal courage and proven ability to present the perfect image of a youthful, vigorous American male to the world cameras. But what part did continuing and painful illness play in his decision to ignore all warnings and go to Dallas that fateful day in 1963?

Now, we're ready to examine Teddy's natal chart on the next page. Inspect it slowly and thoroughly. Then read through his Personality Profile and Future Life Trend Summary for the years around the Chappaquaddick crisis. . .i.e. 1968, 1969 and 1970. These are set out in a style which could have been used if Teddy had sought advice from a chart analyst in 1968.

Make your own commentary—in brief—then compare it to the one which you'll find at the end. If you don't perceive at once how the

NATAL CHART

Cardinal signs 4+Asc
Fixed signs 3+MC
Mutable signs 3+☉+☽
Positive signs 5
Negative signs 5+☉+☽+Asc+MC

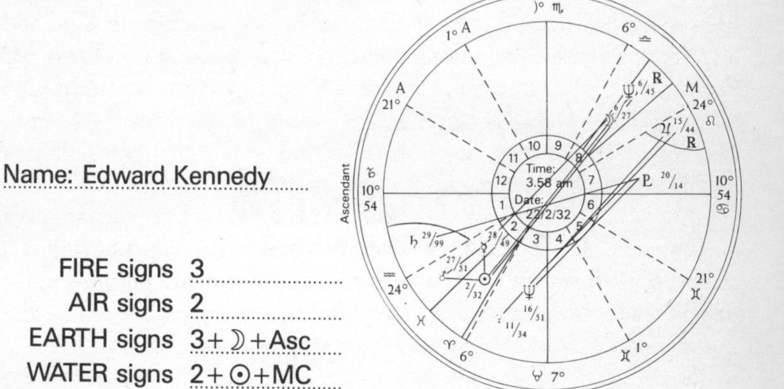

Name: Edward Kennedy

FIRE signs 3
AIR signs 2
EARTH signs 3+☽+Asc
WATER signs 2+☉+MC

B.T.O.	PLANET	NATAL	ASPECTS
NME	8 ♆ Neptune	6.45 ♍ R	
PCF	3 ♅ Uranus	16.51 ♈	□♇
NCE	1 ♄ Saturn	29.49. ♑	☍♇ (wide)
PFF	7 ♃ Jupiter	15.44. ♌ R	△♅
PFA	2 ♂ Mars	27.51. ♒	
NMW	2 ☉ Sun	2.32 ♓	☍☽☌☿☌♂☍♆
PCF	3 ♀ Venus	11.34 ♈	△♃☌♅
PFA	2 ☿ Mercury	28.49 ♒	☌♂
NME	8 ☽ Moon	6.27 ♍	☍☿☌♆
NCW	7 ♇ Pluto	20.14. ♋ R	

various conclusions were reached, you need to brush up on analytical technique. Please refer in that case to my companion book—*How to Astro-Analyse Yourself and Others* or any reliable astrology text, which discusses chart indicators from the points of view of their psychological significance. *No form of future forecasting should be attempted by students unless and until they have acquired a thorough working knowledge of natal chart analysis and interpretation.*

In working through Teddy's natal chart, new students should make careful note of how much information about each individual's future life can be assembled merely by natal chart study and observation of its psychological implications.

Note: It is not known to me or stated in any biography I've read if any Kennedy sought astrological advice. Nevertheless, the horrifyingly accurate 1963 warning to his brother John must have settled itself somewhere in the deep recesses of Teddy's mind. In his later campaigns, after brother Bobby had also been murdered, biographers state he usually travelled surrounded by armed guards in bullet-proof vehicles. Two biographers refer to his saying: 'They're going to shoot my ass off the way they shot Bobby'.

Prepared For Senator Edward Kennedy

NATAL CHART PERSONALITY PROFILE

PERSONALITY PROFILE

PLEASE NOTE: Boxes marked on profile sheets with TICKS point to personality traits as indicated by the natal chart. These profiles are designed for quick reference to significant chart pointers.

1. HEMISPHERE EMPHASIS: Planets Above Horizon: ......4......
Planets Below Horison: ......6......

Above Horizon Stress = Greater involvement in outer world experiences/activities — career, occupation, public affairs. ☑

Below Horizon Stress = Greater involvement in inner world experiences/activities — home, emotional life, private affairs. ☑

Equal Stress = Better balance between outer world activities and inner world experiences. Not likely to pursue success at expense of private life. ☐

2. POLARITIES: Planets in Positive Signs: ....5........
Planets in Negative Signs: ....5........

Positive Stress = Added tendencies towards extroversion — stronger assertion of the self and own aims. ☐

Negative Stress = Added tendencies towards introversion — greater suppression of the self and own desires. ☐

Equal Stress = Good balance between extroversion/introversion — able to assert or compromise as necessary. ☑

3. TRIPLICITIES: Planets in Fire Signs: ....3........
Planets in Air Signs: ....2........
Planets in Earth Signs: ....3........
Planets in Water Signs: ....2........

Fire Signs Dominant = Increased vitality, warmth, spontaneity — but rashness and impatience possible. ☑

Air Signs Dominant = Increased intellectuality, lightness, objectivity — but over-detachment and unreliability possible. ☐

Earth Signs Dominant = Increased supportiveness, strength and dependability — but unresponsiveness and addiction to routine possible. ☑

Water Signs Dominant = Increased intuition, subtlety, depth — but over-emotionalism and moodiness possible. ☐

4. QUADRUPLICITIES: Planets in Cardinal Signs: ......4......
Planets in Fixed Signs: ......3......
Planets in Mutable Signs: ......3......

Cardinal Sign Stress = More forceful pursuit of own aims and needs — but over-energetic thrust for objectives likely. ☑

Fixed Sign Stress = More persevering pursuit of own aims and needs — but rigidity and stubborn adherence to ideas likely. ☐

Mutable Sign Stress = More flexible, adaptable pursuit of own aims and needs — but uncertainty as to life direction likely. ☐

5. ANGULAR PLANETS:

Planets in First House: ......1 — ♄......
Planets in Fourth House: ......0......
Planets in Seventh House: ..2 — ♃ + ♇..
Planets in Tenth House: ......0......

First House Emphasis = Itensified concern with impressions made on others. Desire to excite notice — but egotistical propensities usually manifest. ☑

Fourth House Emphasis = Intensified effects from early home conditioning. Heavier concentration on domestic/family issues — but home problems usually magnified. ☐

Seventh House Emphasis = Intensified expectations of marriage/unions/partnerships. Relationships assume paramount importance — but hopes usually set too high. ☑

Tenth House Emphasis = Intensified demand for career/ occupation supremacy. Search for successes lifelong — but achievement thrust usually overrides private satisfactions. ☐

6. POWER POINT CHARACTER PATTERN:

Ascendant: Capricorn — ♑ — Symbol=The Goat
Sun Sign: Pisces — ♓ — Symbol=The Fish
Moon Sign Virgo — ♍ — Symbol=The Virgin

Compatible Sign Blend = All three personality levels exhibit a generally congruent response. The self finds it relatively easy to satisfy reconcilable needs. ☐

Incompatible Sign Blend = All three personality levels exhibit a generally conflicting response. The self has to struggle continually to satisfy contrary needs. ☐

Partially Compatible Sign Blend = Two personality levels combine easily, one conflicts. The self feels partly at ease, partly at odds with own needs. ☑

7. LOVE AND SEX NATURE: Moon Sign: ♍ House: 8th
Venus Sign: ♈ House: 3rd
Mars Sign: ♒ House: 2nd

Consistent Sign Sequence = Planets specifically affecting love/sexual behaviour work well together. Reactions more predictable — but usually less stimulating to others. ☐

Inconsistent Sign Sequence = Planets specifically affecting love/sexual behaviour clash with each other. Reactions less predictable — but usually more disconcerting to others. ☐

Partially Consistent Sign Sequence = Planets specifically affecting love/sexual behaviour are partly in line with each other, partly out of line. Reactions mix the predictable with the unexpected — but usually puzzling to others. ☑

Appropriate House Emphasis = House location of planets particularly related to private affairs centralizes effort on gaining emotional gratification. ☐

Inappropriate House Emphasis = House location of planets involved in emotional decisions diverts attention to outside, less personal activities. ☑

8. SUCCESS DRIVES: Mercury Sign: ♒ House: 2nd
Jupiter Sign: ♒ House: 2nd
Saturn Sign: ♑ House: 1st

Consistent Sign Sequence = Planets specifically affecting individual achievement combine well together. Sustained progress towards fulfilment of ambitions — but over-concern with own performance likely. ☐

Inconsistent Sign Sequence = Planets specifically affecting individual achievement point to contradictory goals. Broader spread of effort to attain — but periods of frustration likely. ☑

Partially Consistent Sign Sequence = Planets specifically affecting individual achievement partly support, partly negate each other. Progress goes by stops and starts — but periods of self-dissatisfaction likely. ☐

Appropriate House Emphasis = House location of planets particularly related to career/occupation concentrates endeavours on gaining recognition. ☑

Inappropriate House Emphasis = House location of planets involved in career/occupation decisions infers competing activities in other spheres of interest. ☐

9. IMPORTANT PLANETARY ASPECTS:

(i) Sun Aspects:

Should benefit from:

- Increased inner harmony ☐
- Easier attainment of life goals ☐
- Added avenues of self expression ☑
- Better self-control and discipline ☐
- More vigorous approach to problems ☑

Needs to control tendencies towards:

- Restlessness and inner frustration ☑
- Waste of energy in use of physical strengths ☐
- Erratic, self-willed behaviour ☐
- Escapist, self-deceptive attitudes ☑
- Pessimism and overly conservative reactions ☐

(ii) Moon Aspects:

Should benefit from:

- More satisfying emotional life ☐
- Improved capacity to verbalize feelings ☐
- Greater warmth and speed in reactions ☐
- Better judgement in intimate liaisons ☐
- Added personal charisma and sensitivity ☑

Needs to control tendencies towards:

- Awkwardness in expressing feelings ☑
- Intolerant, over-impulsive responses ☐
- Impracticality and fantasizing ☑
- Repression of feelings and over-sensitivity ☐
- Unduly demanding, extremist behaviour ☐

(iii) Mercury Aspects:

Should benefit from:

- Boosted powers of communication in speech/writing ☑
- Cogent, disciplined expression of ideas ☐
- Mental optimism and more broadly-based thinking ☐

- Improved imagination and subtlety of thought ☐
- Faster, more enterprising approach to intellectual matters ☐

Needs to control tendencies towards:
- Caustic, harsh methods of communication ☐
- Careless, over-optimistic decisions ☐
- Impatience and contempt for fools ☐
- Obsessive doubts/fears in mental skills ☐
- Lack of confidence and narrow thinking ☐

(iv) Venus Aspects:
Should benefit from:
- Improved capacity to relate well to others in all personal/friendship/family contacts ☐
- Added ability to show warmth in love/affections ☐
- Greater independence and unconventionality in all types of intimate relationships ☐
- Better discipline and discretion plus supportiveness ☐
- Boosted ability to attract others and achieve popularity ☑

Needs to control tendencies towards:
- Over-forceful, hasty dashing into relationships/ friendships ☐
- Too much demonstrativeness and extravagant displays of affection ☐
- Attraction to unreliable, unstable associates ☐
- Overstress on personal space and freedom in all contacts with lovers/friends/family ☐
- Expectations of unduly high and exacting standards from intimates ☐

(v) Mars Aspects:
Should benefit from:
- More vigorous, enthusiastic response to all types of physical stimuli ☑

- Lessened risk of repressions and doubts as to personal capacities ☐
- Increased magnetic appeal and ability to avoid possessive behaviour ☐
- Greater sensitivity and intuitive understanding of partner's needs ☐
- Added generosity and sense of adventure ☐

Needs to control tendencies towards:

- Inconsistent interest in sexual life and all forms of physical activities ☐
- Extreme self-will and high-handed behaviour ☐
- Deep-seated repressions of sexual needs/energies causing obsessive, demanding attitudes ☐
- Fantasizing about sex and inability to face reality in relationships ☐
- Overstatement, over-expectation and over-give towards others ☐

In the following Future Life Trend Summary for Senator Edward Kennedy, we are examining the years surrounding *the major crisis point in his life* . . . i.e. the drowning accident on 18 July, 1969 in which Mary Jo Kopechne died in a submerged car at Chappaquiddick, USA.

FUTURE LIFE TREND SUMMARY

PLEASE NOTE: *Dates* set out in this section indicate *periods* when major planetary cycles and transits — affecting future events — make the greatest impact on each life. These periods therefore require subjects to make their greatest efforts to achieve beneficial, constructive changes in the life sectors specified in following pages.

If unsure of interpretation, refer back to Chapters 3, 4 and 5.

I. THE CYCLES OF SATURN

★ The Saturn Withdrawal Cycle:
This cycle covers the transits of Saturn from the cusp of first house, through second and third houses to the cusp of fourth house.

Relevant Time Spans:

Commencement of Withdrawal Cycle .... December 1959 ....

Conclusion of Withdrawal Cycle .... March 1970 ....

★ The Saturn Development Cycle:
This cycle covers the transits of Saturn from the cusp of fourth house, through fifth and sixth houses to the cusp of seventh house.

Relevant Time Spans:

Commencement of Development Cycle .... March 1970 ....

Conclusion of Development Cycle .... June 1974 ....

★ The Saturn Achievement Cycle:
This cycle covers the transits of Saturn from the cusp of seventh house, through eighth and ninth houses to the cusp of tenth house.

Relevant Time Spans:

Commencement of Achievement Cycle .... June 1974 ....

Conclusion of Achievement Cycle .... November 1983 ....

★ **The Saturn Stabilization Cycle:**
This cycle covers the transits of Saturn from the cusp of tenth house, through eleventh and twelfth houses to the cusp of first house.

Relevant Time Spans:

Commencement of Stabilization Cycle .... November 1983

Conclusion of Stabilization Cycle .... November 1989

The name of this cycle gives the clue to its effect.

TRANSITING SATURN ASPECTS

1968	1969	1970
t♄^{3} ♂ ♀^{3} April 1968 t♄^{3} ☌ ♅^{3} April 1968 t♄^{3} △ ♃^{7} April 1968	t♄^{3} △ ☽^{8} June 1969 – March 1970	NIL MAJOR FURTHER

II. PLUTO TRANSITS

(a) Long-Range Pluto Effect:

Transit House Position .... 8th House

Relevant Time Spans:

Commencement of Pluto House Transit 1953

Conclusion of Pluto House Transit 1974

Note: Pluto's transits of above named house/houses in each chart focus on events and decisions of a fundamental and transformative nature in following life sectors: ....

All 8th House matters which include involvement with ....

deaths, shared moneys, deceased estates, secret dealings ......

Positive Responses to All Pluto Transits Promote:
*Added resourcefulness in handling events.
*Greater independence and individuality.
*Regeneration of objectives through irrevocable changes.

Negative Responses to All Pluto Transits Invite:
*Errors based on obsessive, compulsive behaviour.
*Dictatorial attitudes and refusal to take advice.
*Severe reversals through actions emanating from egotism.

(b) Current Pluto Effect:
As Pluto transits the house of each chart discussed in the preceding paragraph, life sectors set out therein will be notably activated by aspects occurring in the periods.

TRANSITING PLUTO ASPECTS

1968	1969	1970
Nil major	Nil major	t♇ [8]△♄ [1] December 1970 – All 1971 to Mid 1972

III. NEPTUNE TRANSITS

(a) Long-range Neptune Effect:

Transit House Position .... 10th House ....

Relevant Time Spans:

Commencement of Neptune House Transit .... 1959 ....

Conclusion of Neptune House Transit .... 1971 ....

Note: Neptune's transits of above-named house/houses in each chart focus on events and decisions of a sensitive and intuitive nature in the following life sectors: All 10th House matters which include new career directions, professional status changes and attainments ....

Positive Responses to All Neptune Transits Promote:
*Increased intuition and imagination in handling events
*Boosted creative/artistic abilities and opportunities to apply them
*Heightened appreciation of the needs of others.

Negative Responses to All Neptune Transits Invite:
*Escapist behaviour and pursuit of fantasies
*Self-absorption and attraction to false goals/philosophies
*Evasion of responsibility and psychosomatic disorders.

(b) Current Neptune Effect:
As Neptune transits the house of each chart discussed in the preceding paragraph, life sectors set out therein will be notably activated by aspects occurring in the periods.

TRANSITING NEPTUNE ASPECTS

1968	1969	1970
Nil major	t♆ 10 □ ♂ 2 All 1969 and All 1970	Nil major

IV. URANUS TRANSITS

(a) Long-range Uranus Effect:

Transit House Position .... 1. 8th House 2. 9th House ....

Relevant Time Spans:

Commencement of Uranus House Transit 1. 1960 2. 1969

Conclusion of Uranus House Transit .... 1. 1969 2. 1976 ....

Note: Uranus' transits of above-named house/houses in each chart focus on events and decisions OF A SUDDEN AND UNEXPECTED NATURE in the following life sectors: ......

1. All 8th House matters. These were further stressed after Uranus joined Neptune in that house in 1960. 2. All 9th House matters, which include travel, dealing with foreigners, higher learning and publishing ....

Positive Responses to All Uranus Transits Promote:

*Boosted independence and inventiveness in handling events

*Ability to break free of hampering restrictions

*Willingness to make total changes in life style/ideas.

Negative Responses to All Uranus Transits Invite:
*Erratic, rash and ill-considered actions through over-demand for freedom
*Sudden losses, resulting from thoughtless severance of ties/partnerships
*Perverse, wilful behaviour without thought of consequences.

(b) Current Uranus Effect:
As Uranus transits the house of each chart discussed in the preceding paragraph, life sectors set out therein will be notably activated by aspects occuring in the periods.

TRANSITING URANUS ASPECTS

1968	1969	1970
Nil major	Nil major	t♅^{9} ☍ ♀^{3} November and All 1971

Commentary and Synthesis of Natal Traits:

Profile Point 1
Slight emphasis below horizon. See-saw pattern between bottom left and upper right quadrants. Thus rather more concerned with private life issues but feels constant pull between going own way and relying on own intuition versus public life, co-operative effort and involvement with money of others.

Profit Points 2, 3 and 4
Slightly more assertive overall than typical Piscean personality (2). Also more energetic and capable of better pre-planning (3). Added sense of goal and direction very useful to Piscean (4).

Profile Point 5

Only two angular houses stressed by planets. Thus greatest private life choices lie between individual action/self image and effects of relationships/public image (4).

Profile Point 6

Conflict here between easy-living 'floating' attitudes of Pisces as against tough, work-oriented attitudes of Virgo. Sun sign feels overborne, forced to conform. Drinking and pleasure-seeking may be used as escape valves at times.

Profile Point 7

Not a comfortable mix. Perfectionism, sudden bursts of feeling and intellectualized passions create a confusing impression on the self and intimates. House positions direct energies away from private life concerns.

Profile Point 8

Problematical blend. Harder-line thinking but humanitarian and forward-looking. Restrains Piscean drifting. Such traits attract opportunities. Ambitions are planted in earthy soil but may expect chances to come too easily.

Profile Point 9

Mixed bag of goods and bads.

Hidden Sun Aspects

Emotional conflicts between parents divide own sense of self. More communicative and forceful in life thrust. But inclined to escapism through little real encouragement to develop skills and talents from father in childhood.

Moon Aspects

Again tendency to drift into dream worlds. Finds it harder to express emotions.

Mercury Aspects

Greater vigour and energy in expressing thoughts/ideas in speech or writing. Thinking is not emotionally-directed.

Venus Aspects

Kinder, warmer, more helpful to those cared about. Not the clinging type and rejects clinging by friends/intimates. Attracted to unusual individuals.

Mars Aspects

Nil further. However, Mercury/Mars pattern suggests better ability to discuss private needs with intimates.

Additional Pointers

1. *First house Saturn in wide-orb opposition to seventh house Pluto:*
Here Teddy's birth into a family in obvious pursuit of power, high-status public image and great wealth ensured enormous conflict would ensue between a deeply-felt desire for privacy and fear of exposure of self (first) and the presentation of the right type of public image and appeal (seventh). Thus a 9 degree orb for this opposition is permissible. An opposition as powerful as this one promises a deadly and lifelong struggle between Saturn (fate) and Pluto (destiny)—a battle which Pluto usually wins. While Saturn urges a hiding away behind an impregnable defensive wall, Pluto inexorably forces marital confrontations and appearances in the public arena.

2. *Small Stellium in second house with oppositions to eighth house:*
Thus far more involved with financial matters—own moneys and those of others—than average Pisces type. A see-sawing swing between money from both sources. Stellium itself focuses mind, will and energies on earning powers and material possessions. Possible gain from writing. (Published book on health *'In Critical Condition'* 1972, a likely interest with Aquarius and Pisces influence here.)

3. *Only Sun in Pisces:*
With no back-up from other water sign planets except Pluto, the ego traits symbolized by Pisces feel isolated by contrasting drives and urges. This problem is exacerbated by one hard aspect to Pisces' ruler, Neptune and one controversial aspect to him. Also stronger earth stress implies a demand for practicality within the self which the Pisces ego dislikes.

4. *Third house planets:*
As well as intellectual concerns, this is the house of siblings. Teddy had no less than eight of them. Venus there implies generally good relations with them as was the case. Uranus, linking as he does by hard aspect to the seventh house, infers startling, dramatic events connected with them which will push him further into the public arena and affect him greatly. One sister Kathleen, born 20 Feburary 1920, died in a plane crash in France in 1948. Her wartime marriage to the English Marquess of Hartington, a Protestant, on 6 May 1944 caused consternation and vociferous disapproval within her solidly Roman Catholic family. Her husband died in an army assault action only 4 months after their marriage. She then became deeply involved with the eighth Earl of Fitzwilliam, who was already married and also a Protestant. They planned to marry but died together when a small plane in which they were travelling crashed in a storm *en route* to Cannes. This love affair caused even greater explosions within the family than had her marriage. The assassinations of brothers John and Robert following the death of brother Joseph in World War II ensured Teddy could not escape a role in the limelight.

The tremendous and lifelong effect of the quite remarkable sense of brotherhood felt by all the Kennedy sons is also reflected in both John and Robert's natal charts—as well as Teddy's. (You can check these in any book of charts of famous persons.) John has the North Node of the Moon in the third house, thereby signifying (among other pointers) the vital role his brothers would play in his destiny.

Robert had Pluto there—retrograde and in hard aspect to Jupiter in his tenth house of career. Again, the destiny role of his brothers is stressed *and* the danger of following in their footsteps. Mercury, ruler of both Gemini (John) and Virgo (father Joseph senior) is posited in the eight house. This again suggests both may play a role in the events leading to his assassination.

One more odd fact about the Kennedy brothers. All three are listed together in encyclopaedias, which is something I have never observed before. The inclusion of John and Robert could be expected as both achieved world fame in their lifetimes, through their efforts and attainments. Other than being the last of the Kennedy sons, Teddy's claim to fame seems to rest on little more than that simple fact of brotherhood.

The life story, revealed in the natal charts of the three Kennedy sons further underlines the anguished sense of being bereft of fraternal support that Teddy experienced when he was left to go it alone. He frequently remarked how indefatigably he and Robert had helped John's campaigns. How he backed up constantly Robert's presidential ambitions after John was dead. And how—when it came to his turn—there was no-one left to turn to but ghosts. And ghosts who refused to lie down at that. He often said he felt he was expected to become the kind of men they were and couldn't.

In his later life, the fraternal comparisons continued. Those who envied and hated the Kennedys often referred to him as 'F.R.K.'—an abbreviation of their unpleasant 'nickname' for him of 'Fat, rich kid', as well as a derogatory playing on the title of 'J.F.K.' by which the President was known.

5. *Eighth house planets:*
This is the house of the money of others, a matter by which Teddy was heavily affected due to his family's great wealth. Moon there infers some emotional manipulation over family moneys and Neptune suggests added vulnerability in this life sector. Both Moon and Neptune in hard aspect to the Sun in second house throw further light on Teddy's desire to go his own way financially yet be forever hauled back into family financial dealings. The eighth is also a house which has much to do with deaths. With his Sun ruler Neptune here, deaths of those close to him would assuredly alter his financial affairs and life direction, as they assuredly did.

Lastly, hard natal aspects to Neptune often hint at future danger from water/the sea/drowning. Like most water sign types, Teddy was a keen swimmer and did not drown on the night of Chappaquiddick. But the death by drowning of his passenger shows Neptune's hand in the grim story as did Teddy's strange, confused and secretive behaviour after the accident.

6. *Seventh house planets:*
Pluto here, already mentioned, speaks of crises, power struggles and problems in all permanent relationships—marital or other. The planet's hard aspects tighten the knots of trouble. Still, nearby retrograde Jupiter but with helpful aspects does infer the seventh house scene should not be so crisis-prone in his later years. Biographers stress Teddy's wife

worries and her poor public image through alcoholism, yet agree that he managed to survive all his vicissitudes and continued to attract warm support—despite Chappaquiddick and everything else!

Commentary and Synthesis of Future Life Trends in Years 1968, 1969 and 1970.

Saturn Summary Point 1

Saturn had dropped down into the hard-to-handle Withdrawal Cycle in December 1959 and stayed there until 1970. This period encompassed the occurrence of nearly all of Teddy's toughest trials and tribulations. The early years of his difficult marriage, the deaths of John and Robert, the severe illness and death of his father, Chappaquiddick and its aftermath.

Saturn Summary Point 2

As Saturn began to move upwards again, in March 1970, Teddy's life took an upwards turn too and his past problems began to assume a less threatening perspective. The tumult and the shouting had died: the captains and the kings had departed. Perhaps, for the first time in his life—as he turned 38—he felt he could be himself. No family males left to compete with. No-one to spur him on to achievements he did not seek. Certainly, his refusal of candidacy for the presidency occurred at the end of this cycle but that could be expected too. If it was not part of his own personal development, Saturn would neither have encouraged it nor pushed it as the Achievement Cycle began in 1974.

For anyone to attract support from Saturn, the game must be played by his rules. That is: to select your most important and worthwhile goal and pursue it with unrelenting determination. And, while so doing, to apply tolerance, patience, tact, forbearance and reflection. Although the later movements through the later cycles of Saturn shown in Teddy's Future Life Trend Summary do not so much concern us now, I think it can safely be said that in his middle-age years, Teddy's life became rather more tranquil and far less demanding. . .even allowing for his loss to Ronald Reagan in 1980. At last he was being allowed to do what he did best—most of the time. Write, travel, attend to his duties as a US senator, pursue his humanitarian concerns.

Once having taught Teddy his hard-knock lessons during the Withdrawal Cycle, Saturn's energy would have favoured Teddy more than some Piscean types. The strong earth stress in the natal chart gave Teddy rather better chances of applying the tough Saturn-style demands listed above.

Saturn Aspects 1968 – 1970

Between March and April 1968, transiting Saturn linked Teddy's third house fairly comfortably with three other natal third house planets plus a planet in his seventh house. . .two of them conjunctions.

In March, a Saturn/Venus conjunction in Teddy's third, saw him working hard to back Robert's presidential campaign to the hilt, effort that was still in progress at the time of the June 1968 assassination. The third, being the house of siblings, these circumstances again reflected his close ties with this older brother and the genuine caring he felt. The age difference between them was almost 7 years, but both were born under water signs and in childhood Robert had often been the one who helped and encouraged the last of the Kennedy clan. This aspect gave Teddy the chance to repay the debt.

It will also be recalled that both older brothers, Joseph junior and John were already teenagers at the time of Teddy's birth—Leo-born Joseph approaching 17 and Gemini-born John almost 15. Thus their ages, their attitudes and lifestyles were far removed both from his childhood world. While each served in the armed services during World War II, Teddy was only a 13-year-old schoolboy when peace came in 1945.

The Saturn/Uranus conjunction in April 1968, arriving two months before brother Robert's fatal shooting clearly began to trigger the natal Uranus promise of sudden, drastic events affecting siblings which would throw Teddy further into the public arena. Since Robert's death removed the last buffer Teddy had against his family's presidential ambitions, this transiting aspect overturned his life planning, obliged him to think about undertaking a drastically different type of occupation. Certainly, it happened before the assassination but family fears of Robert's being murdered like John were well to the fore.

The other transiting Saturn link—this time with natal Jupiter in Teddy's seventh house also arrived in April 1968. It too paved the way to political opportunities and injected a more optimistic use of them.

The last transiting Saturn links—this time with Teddy's Natal Moon and Natal Neptune in his eighth house,—arrived between June 1969 and March 1970, Saturn retrograding briefly during that period. On 18 July 1969—the day of the Chappaquiddick drowning accident—Saturn was still within 2 degrees of the exact trine aspect to both the Moon and Neptune. Although Teddy's behaviour at the time of the tragedy could hardly be called realistic, help certainly came from his surviving relatives and his mother to extricate him from its terrible aftermath.

Although such matters as spiritual enlightenment are not discussed in biographies of politicians, it could be justifiably surmised too that Teddy's view of the meaning of life and death must have changed at the deepest possible level following the accident.

It should be noted well that since both Teddy's Natal Moon and Natal Neptune are posited in his eighth, danger and death connected with water could be expected to send him into a kind of emotional collapse where reason temporarily vanished.

Pluto Summary—House Position (1) 1953 – 1974

Pluto's pressure on any house is always radical, slow but finally life-transforming and so it was for Teddy. The pressure on his eighth House began to be applied as far back as 1953—when he was only 21. By then, brother Joseph was dead but the father was still a directing force and John and Robert were still just getting started in their careers.

Pluto continued travelling through Teddy's eighth for a full 21 years until 1974—a period in which most of the heaviest events in Teddy's life happened. The quite cataclysmic disasters which led to the deaths of first his brothers and then Mary Jo Kopechne at Chappaquiddick. Plus the slow deterioration of his father's health, also ending in death on 18 November 1969. All crowding in on Teddy in the short space of a few days less than six years. . .John (1963), Robert (1968), Mary Jo (1969) Father Joseph (1969). Thus, it is obvious that death, financial changes governed his life and life choices with characteristic Plutonic force as he developed from a young man of 21 to a mature 37-year-old.

Pluto, however, had not quite finished changing Teddy through traumatic events. In 1973, his eldest son, Edward Junior became seriously ill with cancer and had his leg amputated on 17 November 1973. At the time, it was feared the 12-year-old boy would die.

Anyone who has envied the Kennedy wealth and power would think twice about changing places with Teddy between November 1963 and November 1973! Interesting to note, too, that John and his father both died in November and Teddy's son came close to death in the same month. Lastly—and this says much for the caring side of Teddy's nature—he tried hard to take over a father role for Robert's eleven children—comforting his sister-in-law when her last daughter was born on 12 December 1968—six months after Robert's assassination.

Pluto-Summary—House Position (2) 1974 – 1987

As Pluto began to depart from Teddy's eighth in December 1973, retrograding briefly in mid-1974 and finally settling into his ninth by October 1974, the grim picture began to lighten. Teddy must have instinctively followed the pull towards travel of the ninth for from 1974 onwards he undertook many overseas trips—not for pleasure but to visit countries which were causing great concern to the US—Russia, Persian Gulf countries to mention only a couple. With the peace-oriented sign of Libra on Teddy's ninth, the urge to help ease problems that could lead to war would be strong and continue to express itself through his position as a US Senator for 13 years.

Pluto Aspects 1968 – 1970

In Teddy's fateful years of 1968, 1969 and 1970, Pluto made no major aspects to any natal planet until December 1970. Then the planet moved towards a trine to natal Saturn, which continued on and off (through retrograding) during 1971 and again during mid-1972. This favourably linked Teddy's eighth house Pluto transit with his natal first house Saturn. Fair-minded thinking, increased discipline, purposeful actions in handling the problems which had beset him helped him over the hurdles.

Neptune Summary—House Position (1) 1959 – 1971

Whatever house Neptune is transiting, there is always a sense of uncertainty, vagueness, even delusion. Teddy was no exception. Neptune entered his tenth house when he was only 27 and did not depart from it till November 1971 when he was approaching 40. Once again, this transit reflected the tumultuous career-changing events of his life *and* the Chappaquiddick troubles. As the ruler of his Pisces Sun, Neptune in this period would have touched Teddy at the core of his being. At its 1959 beginning, he had just been admitted to the Massachusetts bar as a lawyer, by 1962 he had been elected as a US senator, in 1965 he was initiating amendment bills and in 1965 and 1968 he was visiting Vietnam.

Thus, until Robert's death in 1968, his life would have looked as if it was sailing along its appointed course. Then, suddenly events drove it into storms of magnum force. When they were over by 1971, Teddy was no longer just a wealthy US senator. The thought of the presidency was hanging over him like a massive, impenetrable cloud of doubts and uncertainties with the unanswered mysteries of Chappaquiddick making it heavier still.

Neptune Summary—House Position (2) 1971 – 1980

In 1971, Neptune moved on to Teddy's eleventh house. The events, as the eleventh is not an angular house, became considerably less dramatic in changing his life direction. During this period, campaigns towards the presidency were set in train but were not successful. A result which could have been anticipated as Neptune began in 1980—the year when Teddy finally challenged Ronald Reagan—to enter the dark door of the twelfth.

Neptune Aspects: 1968 – 1970

Only one major transiting Neptune link-up in these years and it struck in 1968 – 1969, linking Teddy's tenth with his natal second. The aspect was a square and became exact in December 1968. On the fateful day of 18 July 1969 Neptune was retrograding at 26 degrees of Scorpio and so stood within one degree of Teddy's natal Mars in 27 degrees of Aquarius.

The warning to tread very warily indeed was being sounded—loud and clear—for seven months *before* the night of Chappaquiddick. Dangers, which would affect both his career ambitions and his financial affairs, were outlined also like black clouds on the horizon. They would become more dangerous still if he indulged himself in physical excesses of any kind. Biographers note that just before the accident, Teddy and a group of Kennedy aides and relatives were at a wild party with drinking and girls. While no-one would blame him for trying to forget the horror of Robert's death only a year before and his numerous other troubles, one glance at his chart would have told him the 1968 - 69 years were certainly *not* the time to give in to any form of self-indulgence.

Uranus Summary—House Position (1) 1960 – 1969

Six years after Pluto entered Teddy's eighth house, Uranus followed—on 28 September 1960, retrograding back into the seventh from February to July 1961, then establishing finally in the eighth from 14 July 1961. (Teddy had married his Virgoan wife, Joan, on 29 November 1958. Since at that wedding date, Uranus was still in Teddy's seventh, it did not augur too brightly for his marital future.) But once Uranus was well settled in the eighth, the planet began to create explosive events in the life sector Pluto had been working on since 1953.

On 8 November 1960, brother John was elected President, assassinated three years and two weeks later on 22 November 1963, with Robert's shooting occurring on 6 June 1968. Teddy delivered the funeral oration yet rejected moves to nominate him for presidential or vice-presidential candidate in August 1968. But, Uranus had not yet played all his shock cards.

Four months after Robert's death, the widowed queen of President Kennedy's Camelot shattered her in-laws and startled the entire world by turning her back on America and all it stood for. On 10 October 1968 she married a Greek, old enough to be her father and of such fabulous wealth, he could have bought and sold the entire clan. A fact well evidenced by her ring which was valued at 1.2 million dollars.

Born under Capricorn on 15 January 1906, Aristotle Onassis was more than 23 years older than his new wife and the marriage was short-lived. She had left him long before his death in 1975. Teddy remarked bitterly at the time of the wedding that he now had to carry Jacqueline's load as well as that of his brothers. An odd sidelight on the Onassis marriage was that like Joseph senior, John and Teddy Kennedy, Aristotle too had the Moon in Virgo. *And* Rose, her mother-in-law, which should have warned the bride of trouble to come!

On 25 June 1969, Uranus changed signs from Virgo into Libra, but was still travelling through Teddy's eighth house at the time of Chappaquiddick. It was, of course, the Uranian energy which brought the succession of three deaths into his life in such sudden, violent, unexpected forms. It was Pluto, however, who, while sharing the eighth with Uranus, had ensured these deaths would totally transform Teddy's life. Forever. Now, there was no going back. The ghosts of John and Robert, already deified by many of the surviving Kennedys and a large section of the American populace, would not be laid to rest. They would remain to haunt his thinking, urge Teddy to take on the challenges ever after.

Though the shadows had long fallen over Camelot, its king slain, its queen fled, its dreaming spires still glimmered tantalizing through the mists of time to coax the last knight of them all to raise up the fallen standard and sally forth again into the fray.

Uranus Summary—House Position (2) 1969 – 1976

By October 1969, Uranus had moved on into Teddy's ninth house, retrograding back into the eighth from April to August 1970, then travelling on through the ninth until October 1976. When Pluto joined Uranus there in 1974, Teddy's travelling and negotiating in foreign countries took on a deeper significance. After Uranus finally left Teddy's ninth for the tenth, in August 1977, two more family deaths were to touch his life in the 1980's—both from drug abuse.

They too, would remind him once again that the price of fame comes high. One death was that of his former brother-in-law, English actor Peter Lawford, ex-husband of Patricia Kennedy, father of one of Teddy's fifteen nephews and three of his ten nieces. Lawford, himself, was yet another Virgo. So are Lawford's eldest daughter and four of Teddy's other nieces and nephews. The sign of the Virgin continued to haunt his life too. Many were the troubles which pursued the new generation of Kennedys, some linked heavily with drugs—the cause of death at the age of 27, on 25 April 1983 of Robert's son David, born like his dead uncle John, under Gemini. As ever, Teddy offered his kindly Piscean shoulder to the family to lean on, accepting the paternal role with younger Kennedy offspring whose fathers were dead.

On 19 July 1986, when John's Sagittarian daughter Caroline (born 27 November 1957) married and held the reception at the home of the 96-year-old Kennedy matriarch, Rose, Teddy was on duty as usual to give the bride away as oldest and only surviving male Kennedy of his generation. At 54, his thick hair had turned to silver but that gently wistful Piscean smile was still in place. Little 'Kid Brother' had come a long way and been taught some terrible lessons.

Happening as it did, a few days before Britain's Prince Andrew wed, reporters dubbed it 'America's Royal Wedding', once more resurrecting memories of the bygone days of Camelot. Like her mother Jacqueline, Caroline married a man considerably older than she. He is Edwin Schlossberg, 41, a New York artist and author. The age difference between him and Caroline is close to identical with the 12-year age difference between her mother and father. When they wed on 12 September 1953, John was 36 and Jacqueline was 24. The odd repetitions in the family story continue.

Uranus Aspects: 1968 – 1970

No major aspects appeared for Teddy in 1968 and 1969 while Uranus remained in his eighth house. However, on 2 November 1970 the transiting planet made an exact opposition from the ninth to natal Venus in the third. This remained within a 2-degree orb until 12 September 1971. According to biographers, nothing notably traumatic happened but—to quote journalistic comment at the time—Teddy's marriage 'had become a shambles. Some blamed his playing around, others blamed her heavy drinking!' This aspect would have certainly tempted him into pursuing independence, pleasure and excitement at all costs but also warned that in so doing existing troubles in family affections would be magnified. And they were.

Transits of Faster-Moving Planets for the night of Chappaquiddick: 18 July 1969

Sun = Transiting the seventh
Moon = Transiting eighth
Mercury = Transiting seventh
Venus = Transiting fifth
Mars = Transiting eleventh
Jupiter = Transiting eighth

Merely from a single glance at this list, we see that all the life sectors likely to be pulled into the tragic events of that day and night were being pressured. The ominuous stress on the eighth. . .the seventh . . .the fifth. . .and the eleventh. Dangers likely to affect public affairs, increased pursuit of pleasures, involvement in group activities. Mix them perilously and the story of a fun party which led to a death and seriously damaged Teddy's public image unfolds.

Planetary Switch-points for the ages 40 – 50 years

As discussed in Chapter 2, every human being faces powerful and demanding aspects between the heavy planets in the above age groupings. For Teddy, the Uranus opposition Uranus aspect arrived in late 1971 and continued through to late 1972 as he approached and passed age 40, striking his ninth and third houses. The Neptune square Neptune aspect partially coincided, coming into orb in March 1972 and continuing through to the end of 1973, striking his eleventh and eighth houses. The Pluto Square Pluto aspect followed several years later, arriving in orb in November 1979 and continuing through retrograding until late 1981. This struck his tenth and seventh houses.

Thus Teddy was obliged to avoid plunging over the precipice in his search for freedom: to steer his way through the fogs which obscured his path: to break free of the shackles of the past and start again. As are all of us in those years when we must come to terms with the fact that youth is gone and the weight of age begins to sit more heavily on our shoulders.

Crisis Point Progressions: 1968, 1969, 1970

Up to this stage in our examination of Teddy's crisis point years, we have looked only at the planetary transits which set and sparked the fuse of events and marked the intervention of others in his life story. Now, we must check the progressions current in 1968, 1969 and 1970 to observe their effect on his inner states.

Early in 1968—the Moon, the channel of each individual's emotional energy—had moved by progression into Teddy's first house, remaining there through 1969 and 1970 until mid-1971. This Moon position would have helped his emotional equilibrium to some extent, although stressing changes in self-image—his private view of himself—and so creating fluctuations between confidence and uncertainty.

Progressed Moon Aspects:
Through 1968, Teddy's progressed Moon began a sequence of three awkward links with natal Venus, Uranus and Pluto as the movement through his first house continued. All three aspects tied in important houses with the first—the third for Venus and Uranus: the seventh for Pluto.

Hence, by the beginning of 1969, Teddy's inner state had been much shaken and some of the obsessive fears about his brothers' fates and the dread that bullets might end his life too took root.

The next major progressed Moon link appeared in mid-1969 and is a link by conjunction to Teddy's first house Saturn. This one can be heavy, depressing to the emotions so that troubles are felt more painfully and obstacles look insurmountable. Thus the aftermath of Chappaquiddick was likely to bear weightily on Teddy's spirit.

The final major Moon link occured in late 1970, dragging in Teddy's seventh house Jupiter. The warning, here, was that although Chappaquaddick was fading into the past, over-optimism about its effect on his life should be restrained. Some effort must have been exerted in this direction as he was re-elected to the US Senate in November 1970.

Conclusions

When assessing the effect of the major planetary influences on Teddy's life, do not think of them in relation to him alone. Use them as guidelines. For, in less spectacularly tragic ways, the tragic events and reactions they provoked could happen to anyone. The difference is that they would not have made world headlines. What the famous do and say is public property. But their strengths and weaknesses are as ordinary and as varied as those of the man next to you on the bus. He could, too, have lost brothers, made perilous mistakes in times of crisis but no-one but his nearest would ever hear about them.

And, as you can see, we haven't needed to have recourse to any additional calculations or forecasting techniques to chart Teddy's story. We haven't even included sextile aspects. The more powerful conjunctions, trines, squares and oppositions were quite enough to reveal the path ahead and—had he known of them—to encourage or warn him as he went his increasingly lonely way.

One word of caution to beginners in future forecasting. *Do not assume* that planets transiting the eighth house bring death and disaster in their wake—inevitably and to everyone. They may but then they may not. The eight has other less direful meanings, too. *Do not ever forecast death under any circumstances.*

In my view, it is never possible to make cast-iron 'predictions' about anything indicated by the chart. Only the possibilities or perhaps probabilities. *And* the way to handle the tests and trials of life. If you foolishly forecast deaths, you will cause needless misery and recrimination later should you be wrong, which is very likely. Or if your client is suggestible, you may actually put him/her into a deeply depressive state that will actually court danger.

As we saw in earlier chapters where clients had been told by fortune-tellers of imminent car accidents, a negative, impressionable person will allow the fear to prey on the mind till judgement is impaired and accidents/injuries follow. The self-fulfilling prophecy syndrome. If some clients ask about death—and the more morbidly inclined occasionally do—refuse to answer. As the great Hippocrates said: 'Astrology is not designed to satisfy the morbid cravings of the curious.'

But now the time has come to close our book on Teddy Kennedy with our last 1986 glimpse of him at the wedding of brother John's Princess of Camelot—Miss Caroline Kennedy. As he walked down the aisle to give his niece away he must have felt he was yet again a 'stand-in' for his long-dead sibling—that he was the last knight left standing alone among the ruins of Camelot, his shining armour turning rusty, his helmet dented by the blows of fate, his time past but his head unbowed. Or, as one Hyannis Port neighbour of the Kennedys who watched the wedding put it: 'It's so nice to be able to share something happy with this family, I'm so tired of always going past all those Kennedy memorials.' Teddy must have thought so too. Often.

For our last VIP discussion, we must turn our microscope away from the 'swinging sixties' which swung too far and too hard for Teddy. And swivel it back to what we might call the 'dangerous thirties'—that far-off, frenetic period between two world wars—when the idle rich idled in a style that seems beyond imagining now. When champagne corks popped from dawn to dawn, jewels were scattered like confetti and the music never stopped playing for those who could afford to pay their pipers. For those who could not, for those who stood outside that charmed circle there was only darkness and want.

World War I's ex-heroes stood sullenly in job lines or sold matches in the streets. The Great Depression hung over both victors and vanquished. Tanks and armaments were again rolling off Germany's production lines. Communism was triumphant in Russia. The Aquarian Age of the Common Man was coming. But—for just a short while longer—in the Ritz and Savoy the bands played on. And the song they often played—a tinkling hit tune of the Thirties—was 'I Danced With A Man, Who Danced With A Girl, Who Danced With The Prince of Wales'. The song itself offers an inkling of the extraordinary, film-star-style glamour which surrounded another Edward, whose slight figure, rumpled fair hair and oddly wistful expression had earned him the title of 'England's Fairy Prince' in the ladies' home journals of the day. The same man who would soon shock his Empire and rock the British Monarchy to its 1,000-year-old foundations by vacating his throne at the age of 42 for the love of a twice-wed, 40-year-old divorcee from Baltimore, USA.

Why did he do it? No English king had ever voluntarily abdicated before. None had even so much as dared to contemplate marrying a woman with two husbands still living. But, both his lover and he, himself were around the dangerous age of the Uranus/Uranus opposition and the illusion-generating Neptune/Neptune square. And that was far from all. Newly-discovered Pluto—(official date of discovery: 13 March 1930) had begun to loom larger and larger on world horizons, pressuring mass consciousness, setting in train events which would shortly explode into hitherto undreamed of violence and cataclysmic change. Life, as Edward and his contemporaries knew it, would soon be gone with the wind. And so would he.

An Over-Supply of Geminis—The Bitter Tale of the Doomed Duke—HRH Edward, Duke of Windsor

Geminis to the left of him,
Geminis to the right of him,
Geminis in front of him
Threatened and thundered.'

If we adjust the words of a famous poem from Queen Victoria's reign—itself immortalizing a disastrous British defeat—we can picture the awesome predicament in which Cancer-born Prince Edward, King of England for 325 days and Duke of Windsor for the rest of his life, found himself embroiled during his crisis point years of 1935, 1936 and 1937. A predicament he would have at least understood better and perhaps extricated himself from *if* he had been aware of what his natal chart contained.

As we have seen throughout this book, forewarned is forearmed. And the Duke's chart cried out the loudest, the most urgent warnings of what would follow.

If he set his feet upon a path which could lead in the end to scandal, loneliness and exile.

If he tangled his life with yet another Gemini—in the shape of the five-feet-tall, 'no-one can be too thin', Mrs Wallis Warfield Simpson.

If he stubbornly persisted in repeating the conditions of the 'wretched childhood' he often complained of. Presided over and supervised as it was by a Gemini great-grandmother, the redoubtable Queen Victoria. By a Gemini father, the gruff—'My sons are all dolts'—King George V. By a Gemini mother, the whale-boned epitome of maternal rectitude, Queen Mary.

Among this formidable group, the Prince's only genuine comfort had come from his Scorpio grandfather, Edward VII, also a former Prince of Wales, a water sign like himself and a royal rager who well into old age continued to cut a swathe through the reigning beauties of Great Britain and Europe. But he vanished from Edward's scene all too soon. On 6 May 1910, a few weeks before his grandson's 16th birthday and after having reigned for only 9½ years, he died in his 69th year. The Prince's father was King and the Prince, himself, became heir to the throne.

Very little that Edward did ever—from infancy to adulthood—met with approval in the two parental pairs of sharp Geminian eyes which watched his less than punctilious progress towards the throne of England and her Empire. He took alarming risks on the battlefields of France. He meddled in governmental preserves. He said things to the proletariat that he shouldn't have. He courted married ladies. He fiddled and would continue to do so—so his parents feared—while 'Rome was burning'.

He was photographed wearing nothing but a pair of shorts on playboy-style luxury cruises. He stubbornly refused to be coaxed or coerced into matrimony with any one of a procession of princesses. He bid fair to outdo the dangerous precedent of fast living set by his grandfather.

And—perhaps worst of all—was still unwed and without an heir at the age of 36 when he attended an aristocratic weekend house party and was introduced to two Americans, resident in England Mr and Mrs Ernest Simpson. The meeting took place in November 1930 and was anything but love at first sight. Neither Edward himself nor his later-to-be-bride record in their memoirs that the earth moved under their feet. It should have done. The 'earthquake' which later followed that introduction shook the crockery in every corner of the then Empire. The 'whys' and 'wherefores' of this century's most famous love affair must be sought (as with Teddy Kennedy) in Edward's family history, commencing as far back as 10 February 1840 when German Prince Albert married the young Queen Victoria and a new style of British monarch was born under his earnest, Virgoan tutelage.

So, in setting up the scenery for Edward's short stay on the world stage, we must collect some of it from as far back as the day of his great-grandparents, Albert and Victoria, then add more—via the personal planets— of those of his other forebears and intimates.

GREAT-GRANDFATHER: Prince Albert: Born 25 August 1819. Died 14 December 1861. Reformer and progressive thinker. Architect of the ideal of propriety and dedication in monarchy. Father of four sons and five daughters. Known to his family as 'Dearest Papa'. To his wife as 'My Beloved Angel'. Child of broken marriage. Father was a hard-drinking, woman-chasing libertine, as was elder brother. Very young mother consoled herself with handsome courtiers and soon ran off with one, deserting both small children. This later led to unfounded rumours of Albert's illegitimacy, fuelled by his lack of resemblance in tastes or appearance to his dissolute father and brother. As a result of such childhood experiences, deplored self-indulgence and sexual immorality. Since mother's lover and later husband was of Jewish background, the illegitimacy rumour was resurrected by Hitler more than 100 years later to infer the British Royals had Jewish blood. Worked and worried himself to death at 42 over affairs of state and the unmistakable sensuality of his eldest son. Disliked for his stiff German

ways by the English aristocracy. Posthumously titled 'Albert the Good'.
Sun = Virgo
Moon = Scorpio
Mercury = Virgo
Venus = Leo
Mars = Gemini

GREAT-GRANDMOTHER: Queen Victoria: Born 24 May 1819. Died 22 January 1901. Married Prince Albert on 10 February 1840.

Only child of ageing Royal Duke who died in her early infancy, but had much older half-brother and half-sister from her mother's previous marriage. Reared in impoverished circumstances, considering family status. Loved to dance and socialize all night in youth. Passionate and never a prude. Fell madly in love with Albert, mourning and worshipping his memory for the 40 years she lived on after his death. Always strongly influenced by men closest to her.

Became Queen on 18 June 1837, a few days after her 18th birthday. Ruled Britain and the Empire for 63 years. Frequently despaired of the escapades of her eldest son, Edward, known as 'Bertie', Prince of Wales and finally King of England. Through her own skills and charisma, became the leader of nineteenth century monarchs—the 'doyenne of sovereigns'. At the end of her very long life, her numerous descendants had married into almost every royal house in Europe. So many were called Albert or Victoria, nicknames had to be coined for them. One daughter married Kaiser Frederick of Germany. Her great-grandson, Edward, admitted he was always afraid of her in childhood. He was approaching 7 years old when she died.

Three of Queen Victoria's nine children were still living in 1936—year of the Abdication Crisis. Princess Beatrice, aged 79, Prince Arthur, aged 86, and Princess Louise aged 88, with Arthur living on until 1944. The events of the time must have been beyond belief to those born in Victorian England.
Sun = Gemini
Moon = Gemini
Mercury = Taurus
Venus = Aries
Mars = Aries

GRANDFATHER: King Edward VII: Born 9 November 1841. Died 6 May 1910. Married Princess Alexandra of Denmark (born 1 December 1844) at Windsor on 10 March 1863. As the wedding took place only 15 months after his father's death, the ceremony—in accordance with Queen Victoria's determination to remain in perpetual mourning for her 'Beloved Angel'—was carried out in funereal gloom, much against the bridegroom's wishes. Pre-nuptial festivities included a visit to Prince Albert's mausoleum to receive his blessing.

Edward VII lived for fun, females, and food—all in every large helpings. Smoked a minimum of twenty cigarettes and eight huge cigars every day. Had just turned 20 when his own father expired. Was 59 before his mother died. Felt her disapproval of his life style keenly but did not deviate from it. Father of two sons and three daughters. Death from pneumonia of his eldest son and heir, Prince Albert Victor—born 8 January 1864, (nicknamed 'Collars and Cuffs' because of his long Capricorn neck and skinny arms) shortly before his marriage to Princess Mary and a few days after his 28th birthday—meant his second son, George must succeed him. Indefatiguable traveller, lover and gourmet. Carried on his amorous dalliances with such panache, the aristocratic husband of his last mistress was as broken-hearted at the news of the old King's death as was the lady herself.

At the time of the Abdication Crisis—26 years after her own royal lover's death—she, too, was still alive and professed herself horrified, saying: 'We knew how to do things better in my time'.

Sun = Scorpio
Moon = Virgo
Mercury = Sagittarius, close to Scorpio cusp
Venus = Libra
Mars = Capricorn

FATHER: King George V. Born 3 June 1865. Died 20 January 1936. Married Princess Mary of Teck on 6 July 1893. She had formerly been engaged to his recently dead brother, Prince Albert Victor. Reported to have kissed only one girl in his life before his marriage and none thereafter. Ascended the throne on 6 May 1910 and reigned for 25 years before and after World War I. Father of six—five sons and one daughter, the oldest of whom was Edward, Prince of Wales, later King Edward VIII. The second son become Duke of York and later King

George VI. Was first cousin of the last Tsar of Russia, Nicholas II (born 18 May 1868 near Gemini cusp) and resembled him so closely that when at court together, one was often mistaken for the other. Historians have suggested George could have helped Nicholas and family escape execution by the Communists in 1918 but did not. Was also first cousin of Kaiser Wilhelm, (born 27 January 1859) whose country and the King's were the main protagonists in World War I. Gemini George did not enjoy the Aquarian condescension and eccentric behaviour of his relative.

Repeated in his domestic life the model of propriety established by grandfather Albert. Loved his own father but stood in awe of him. Unable to communicate with his children and extremely critical of them. All were afraid of him. At the end of his life, speaking of his eldest made this uncannily accurate prophecy to his Prime Minister, Stanley Baldwin. 'After I am dead, the boy will ruin himself in twelve months.' His estimate was out only by forty days!

Sun = Gemini
Moon = Libra
Mercury = Taurus
Venus = Taurus
Mars = Leo

MOTHER: Queen Mary: Born 26 May 1867. Died 24 March 1953 aged 85. Only girl and eldest child in a family of boys. Mother, a massive woman weighing nineteen stone. Born in same room in Kensington Palace as Queen Victoria, Mary's future husband's grandmother—48 years before, their birth dates being only two days apart. Victoria admired her as baby—'I think she is rather like me' and enjoyed her company when adult. Mary grew to be very tall for girls of her time—five feet seven inches as compared to her royal Gemini relative's five feet. Lived on continent 'in polite poverty' as girl.

Like Victoria, largely self-educated. Widely-travelled before marriage. Read eight hours per day as young woman to improve her knowledge. Accepted with equanimity proposed marriage to Prince Albert Victor and after his sudden death, marriage to his brother, George.

Welcomed the brides of three of her sons and the husband of her daughter. Refused to meet or recognize Mrs Wallis Simpson, despite her son's pleas, before and after she (Wallis) became Duchess of Windsor, describing her as an adventuress.

Like her husband, she remained remote from her children in their growing up years. At the time of the Abdication Crisis, she frequently stated it was inconceivable that a man born to be king could put love before duty. To this stern admonition, her son replied that all that mattered to him was his happiness. Although some of the Royal Family unbent enough to visit the Duke and his Duchess in later years, neither Queen Mary nor her Leo-born daughter-in-law Queen Elizabeth (later Queen Mother) ever did. Queen Mary blamed her son for flagrant and unforgivable dereliction of his duty. Queen Elizabeth blamed her brother-in-law for obliging her own shy and self-conscious husband to take the throne.

Queen Mary is described as Britain's greatest Queen Consort ever.

Sun = Gemini
Moon = Pisces
Mercury = Taurus
Venus = Taurus
Mars = Leo

WIFE: Born 19 June 1896. Christened Bessie-Wallis Warfield. Died 24 April 1986, shortly before her 90th birthday.

Only child, whose father died soon after she was born. Mother married again twice later in life. Though childhood was improverished, described herself as belonging to the best families in Baltimore. As small girl insisted on red party dress 'so the boys will notice me'. Married Earl Winfield Spencer on 8 November 1916 at age 20. Divorced and remarried—this time to Ernest Simpson on 21 July 1928 in London. Divorced again and remarried for the third time to Edward, Duke of Windsor on 3 June 1937 just sixteen days before she turned 41. Variously described in memoirs and diaries as 'adventuress', 'sorceress', and 'jolly, plain, intelligent, unpretentious and unprepossessing little woman'.

After marriage to Duke was named in the list of the world's best-dressed women for 40 years. Became fashion-leader, noted for her elegance, fabulous jewels and wit. Had no children from any of her three marriages. Some biographers suggest though two years younger than he, she filled a 'mother' role for the Duke. Dominated him in later years. Liked cafe society and danced till dawn well past middle age. Claimed she never wished to be Queen but did not believe the King would be forced to abdicate to marry her. Had little understanding of English attitudes or their politics. Was refused the title of Her Royal Highness by King George VI, a fact which remained a bitter pill for her to swallow ever afterwards.

Though rejected in life by the British Royals, permission was granted for her to be buried beside her husband in the family mausoleum at Frogmore, near Windsor Castle.

Sun = Gemini
Moon = Libra
Mercury = Gemini
Venus = Gemini
Mars = Aries

YOUNGER BROTHER: King George VI. Born 14 December 1895. Died 6 February 1952.

Married Lady Elizabeth Bowes-Lyon, born 4 August 1900, daughter of Scottish Earl, on 26 April 1923. Succeeded to throne following brother's abdication on 11 December 1936, three days before his 41st birthday. Had misfortune to be born on his great-grandfather Prince Albert's death-day and also the death-day of his great-aunt Princess Alice—a problem which made both his parents fearful of announcing his arrival to Queen Victoria.

Was visibly shy, diffident and stammered badly when agitated. Father of two daughters, Princess Elizabeth (now Queen) and Princess Margaret. Was so appalled at thought of becoming King, sobbed on his mother's shoulder for a full hour after hearing the news. Very close fraternal bond with Edward until Mrs Simpson arrived on the family scene. Broke contact with his brother soon after the Abdication Crisis. Again, followed model of domestic propriety upheld by his own parents and his great-grandparents, Albert and Victoria. Was himself called 'Bertie' by family. Full name was Albert Frederick Arthur George.

His accession to the throne was a strange instance of history repeating itself. His father and he were trained for the Navy, both were Dukes of York. Neither had trained for nor expected to be king, nor wanted the job. Death removed the older brother and heir to throne in George V's case, abdication in George VI's. Historians suggest both made better monarchs than their older siblings would have done.

Sun = Sagittarius
Moon = Scorpio
Mercury = Sagittarius
Venus = Scorpio
Mars = Sagittarius but near Scorpio cusp

THE DUKE HIMSELF: Born 23 June 1894. Died 28 May 1972 less than a month before his 78th birthday. Christened Edward Albert Christian Andrew Patrick David. Always known as David to his family and later to Wallis. Was considered a problem child by both parents. Distinguished himself in World War I in France. After war engaged in several royal tours, thereby increasing both his own popularity and the British Monarchy's.

Became the leader of London's post-war society. Was lengthily involved with two married socialites before Wallis, one another American—sister of Gloria Vanderbilt. Between January 1932 and mid-1934, both Wallis and husband Ernest found the Prince moving further and further into their lives until he was almost daily on their doorstep. By mid-1935, his infatuation with her and her hold over him was obvious to all within his social circle. Became King of England on 20 January 1936 but was never crowned. Insisted he would not be crowned without the still-married Wallis at his side. In the face of total opposition to such a marriage from his family and the Governments of England and the Dominions, finally he could do nothing but abdicate in favour of his younger brother. Did so on 11 December 1936.

Was created Duke of Windsor and went into exile in Europe. When his bride-to-be's second divorce decree became absolute in May 1937, he married in France on 3 June 1937—the birthday of his late father. Except for a brief stint as Governor-General of the Bahamas during World War II, he spent the rest of life, biographers state, in jobless exile, his only real interests being gardening, playing golf, looking after his family of dogs, and guarding his money. Despite his vast fortune, he rarely paid bills if someone else was willing. Prior to his marriage, he ran up a bill of 900 pounds for his international calls to Wallis from Schloss Enzefeld on his host's phone.

Some historical sources state the Duke quickly fell into the habit of doing exactly what—and only what—his Duchess told him. He was never invited to return permanently in England and died, still cold-shouldered by his royal relatives, in France. He had no children.

Sun = Cancer
Moon = Pisces
Mercury = Cancer
Venus = Taurus
Mars = Aries but near Pisces cusp.

Crisis Point in the Duke's Life:

Abdication as uncrowned King of England on 11 December 1936. As in the case of Teddy Kennedy, the day of reckoning had been long foreshadowed but with events more historically documented.

The feeling of family rejection in childhood: his post-World War I emergence as 'Prince Charming': his unorthodox social life: his affairs with married women: his ever-present sense of loneliness and isolation: his pursuit of pleasure: his fear of his gruff and critical father: his dislike of the dull, solid respectability of the court. . .one by one they stacked up like sticks of dynamite, ready and waiting for someone to light the fuse.

Malcolm Muggeridge, British author and commentator described the Duke thus: 'His position demanded of him that he suffer pomposity gladly and bear the dull burden of authority without the delight of exercising it; whereas his inclination was to dispense with ceremonial respect and make his own will felt: to be both less and more than the King who ruled before him.' Think over that quote and you'll observe how well it illustrates the Duke's complex personality. It is a perfect astrological portrait of the contrary mix of Ascendant, Sun and Moon although its author would not have known it to be.

The reformist zeal of Aquarius but with the 'damn-the-rules, I'll-do-it-my-way' stance of the sign: the emotional appeal of the Cancer male but with the search for love at any price and any cost of the sign: the vulnerable romanticism of Pisces but with the drift into dream-worlds of pleasure of the sign. For a man born to be king in the more tightly conventional world of the thirties, together they added up to trouble. Plenty of it. Often have biographers, diarists and commentators documented the stubborn steering along collision courses with tradition that invited disaster. Often too, have they recorded disbelief at the Prince-King-Duke's conviction that love really would conquer all things.

Often again, at the dimension of his fantasy that he could charm or manoeuvre his government and subjects into accepting a twice-divorced, American commoner at the end of her child-bearing years as Queen.

How could he have deluded himself that—assuming he did manage to sell the 'Wallis package' to his people at large the Church would also buy it? One of the numerous titles of British monarchs is 'Defender of the Faith' and nominal head of the Church of England. Edward's actions showed him to be—as one Palace official of the time put it: 'A faithless Defender of the Faith!'

Imagine—to gain the full impact of the proposed marriage—the international uproar which would have ensued if the next Prince of Wales—Charles—had announced his intention, nearly 50 years later, of marrying a middle-aged, twice-divorced, foreign-born commoner? Instead of a 19-year-old virgin of aristocratic background and unassailable virtue? World reaction, even in the permissive 1980's, would have been equally condemnatory. Looked at in these terms, Edward's decision becomes both outrageous (Uranus/Aquarius) and bizarre (Neptune/Pisces). The Aquarian Ascendant and Piscean Moon together produced high-handed attitudes plus impractical imaginings.

The house position of Uranus in the Duke's ninth implied sudden, disruptive events related to foreigners and foreign countries. Wallis was an American and after marriage, the couple were obliged to live abroad for the rest of their lives.

The house position of Neptune in the Duke's fourth postulated that his deepest illusions would emanate from his home and those he shared it with. His childhood environment was, in his own words, 'wretched' but wasn't this something of a delusion too? He was reared in royal luxury, wanted for nothing and neither Gemini parent could have been called neglectful.

His adult marital environment was hence based on similar illusions. He proclaimed himself happy and contented with the Duchess but was he? Biographers assert that he was not. As, indeed, his subsequent actions/behaviour suggest. He endlessly badgered his brother King George VI for jobs suitable to his royal status, to no avail. He endlessly pressed for the HRH title for his Duchess again to no avail. He endlessly drifted and wandered through Europe and America, doing nothing much more than socializing and tangled with individuals which, though wealthy, were considered suspect or undesirable. Yet—as we saw with Teddy Kennedy—his choice of a life partner was yet another case of marrying the sign of a parent. Both parents in the Duke's case. Plus that of his Gemini great-grandmother, Queen Victoria. All three of whom he maintained he feared and felt ill at ease with.

Significantly too, we observe the sign of Gemini on the Duke's fifth house cusp thus sparking attraction in romantic affairs to the Gemini type. And the Gemini qualities of sophistication, wittiness, modernity and eternal youthfulness Wallis assuredly possessed in good measure. Many are the reports of her quick and slick retorts, her amusing parties, her ability to entertain. One author even notes that the super-slim, diminutive Duchess was photographed wearing very brief shorts at the age of 57 and did not look ridiculous!

Therefore, she further entranced her Duke by supplying the bright, people-oriented qualities he, himself lacked. Few water types are entirely comfortable in the social hurly-burly and Edward, although his air ascendant disguised this wariness, was no exception. His social nervousness was clearly exhibited by his excessive smoking throughout his life. During World War I, the troops christened him 'Teddy Woodbine', the name of cigarettes which he rarely had out of his mouth and thereby repeating the smoking habits of his water-sign predecessor on the throne and grandfather, Edward VII.

Once again, as previously noted in the Kennedy story, we see that our rummaging through the family cupboards of history has paid off. Rewarding us with information and explanations of conduct that would otherwise have been inexplicable.

Again, we see the repetition of particular signs through the generations of the Royal Family.

* Prince Albert's Virgo Sun and Scorpio Moon were exactly reversed in his son's (King Edward VII's) Scorpio Sun and Virgo Moon, thus revealing how intensely felt were the paternal/filial links between them. As could be expected from these patterns, their relationship was fraught with paradoxes. They both understood and misunderstood each other's precepts and actions. Generations later the sign of Scorpio reappeared again in Prince Charles's Sun sign and also his grandfather's (George VI) Ascendant and Moon sign.

* Queen Alexandra, the Duke's grandmother, was born under Sagittarius. The same sign reappeared in the birth patterns of the grandson who became King George VI. (See chart in this chapter.) His father records in his diary a birth time of 3.40 a.m. which produces a Scorpio Ascendant. Four planets are in Scorpio, three in Sagittarius.

Here's an example of how certain signs repeated and reversed themselves down the generations in the Duke's family.

Great-grandfather Prince Albert. . .	Ascendant/Virgo: Sun/Virgo: Moon/Scorpio:
Grandfather King Edward VII	Ascendant/Sagittarius: Sun/Scorpio: Moon/Virgo:
Brother King George VI	Ascendant Scorpio: Sun/Sagittarius: Moon/Scorpio:

Royal historians record that George VI as a child was much happier and far less nervous in the company of his Scorpio and Sagittarius grandparents than with his own father and mother. The Duke himself was—psychologically and astrologically—odd man out. No planets whatsoever in Sagittarius or Virgo, only the generation planet of Uranus in Scorpio.

* King George V, Queen Mary and Queen Victoria all shared the same Sun sign of Gemini which yet again repeated in young Prince William, eldest child of Prince Charles, and born on 21 June 1982—the Gemini/Cancer cusp. This Sun position also picks up the Cancer Sun sign of two of the boy's great-granduncles: the Duke of Windsor and his youngest brother, Prince John, who died of a mysterious illness, (believed to be epilepsy) in 1919 at age 13.

* The first two children of Prince Charles—one Gemini cusp and one Virgo—bring back thereby the same traits as their 19th century ancestors, Virgo Prince Albert and Gemini Queen Victoria. Gemini is also the Sun sign of their own grandfather, Prince Philip, Duke of Edinburgh.

* Queen Mary's Pisces Moon showed up again in her eldest son's Moon, thus pointing to the underlay of understanding between them.

Further, a royal relative, who was present at her birth, gives a time of 11.59 p.m. which produces an Aquarian Ascendant as the Duke's. Her strong sense of duty and her air-sign rationality forced her to condemn his conduct but she remained to the end of her life emotionally concerned with his happiness or lack of it.

* King George V and Queen Mary shared the same Sun, Mercury, Venus and Mars signs hence indicating their similarity of attitude in most life choices. However, the somewhat conflicting Moon positions would have created their well-documented lack of emotional rapport. Plus, the King's Libra Moon—a sign which intensely dislikes any behaviour likely to rock the standards of civilized living—would have ensured he would never forgive his son for allowing emotion to triumph over reason. It also explains the Duke's fear of admitting to his austere parent that his affair with Mrs Simpson (whose 'brassy American repartee' so disconcerted the English aristocrats) had gone beyond the point of no return. King George died without his son saying one word to him about his marriage plans. It's worth noting, too, that the old King often stated with satisfaction that he'd 'never set foot in America'. Thus, even had Mrs Simpson been an unsullied virgin instead of a double divorcee, she would have had much trouble in endearing herself to her future father-in-law.

Once again, as we saw with Teddy Kennedy, the Duke chose to marry a woman of the same Sun sign as a parent. Both of them, this time. Not to mention, his feared great-grandmother Victoria, visits to whom in early childhood reduced both Edward and his brother George to fits of hysterical weeping. The inevitable result of this wife choice was that precisely the same troubles he had experienced in childhood—that same, cool air-sign detachment—returned to plague his life anew.

Worse, his bride also showed exactly the same Sun/Moon positions as his father: Sun in Gemini, Moon in Libra. Later, predictably after the first flush of romance had worn off, he found himself subjugated to her will as he had been to his father's. Resentment once more began to erode his self-esteem.

Note: The present Queen, who had spent much childhood time with King George and Queen Mary, also chose the sign of her forebears—Gemini—in her husband. As the present Queen was born on 21 April

1926 with Capricorn on the Ascendant, Sun on Aries/Taurus cusp and Moon in Leo, she displayed from her earliest years the sense of royal duty and dignity which so entranced her grandparents. She was almost 10 when King George died in 1936 and almost 27 when Queen Mary died in early 1953. Her Venus in Pisces would also have forged a strong emotional/affectional link with Queen Mary's Pisces Moon.

This Pisces influence suggests why as a crowned monarch she was far less hostile towards her uncle, the Duke and his Duchess than were her parents. Once again her Venus linked with his Pisces Moon. When he became seriously ill in Paris, she took the trouble to visit him with her husband, Prince Phillip.

As ever, from all the foregoing, we perceive how the sins and virtues of the fathers (and mothers and even more distant forebears) are visited on the children unto the third and fourth generation. The Duke himself was in many senses a victim of the strict moral code of royal living and regal propriety laid down by his long-departed ancestor—the Virgoan Prince Albert who had died almost 33 years before Edward's birth.

Until Prince Albert took over and remade the royal rules in the mid-19th century, the British Monarchy had been close to toppling through the wild and dissolute living of the Hanoverian kings and their brothers who preceded Queen Victoria. Perhaps, therefore, if the Duke had lived in the pre-Albert years of the nineteenth century instead of the post-Albert years of the twentieth, his chequered love life—before and after Mrs Simpson—may have appeared less monumentally shocking.

Interesting to spot as well through both historical records and the chart patterns that Prince Albert's son, an earlier Prince of Wales who became King Edward VII, was equally inclined to amorous and often unwise dalliances as was the Duke. But in that case, his Virgo Moon applied a brake on emotional excesses. He too often skated on thin ice, and came close to becoming inextricably entangled in scandalous divorces, but always pulled back from the brink of total disaster. Despite his Scorpio-style sexual appetites, Virgo demanded that he did not let his feet stray too far from the straight and narrow path of propriety.

Our next step is to work through the Duke's natal chart on the next page, and then his Future Life Trend Summary for the years around the Abdication Crisis. . .1935, 1936 and 1937. Again, we'll set these out as if the Duke had sought advice from a chart analyst in 1935. Again, we'll check how much information about the Duke's future life/attitudes/intentions can be gleaned merely from the natal chart itself.

Note: I have recently read that at least one UK practitioner *claims* to be astrologer to the present Royal Family. Whether this is true or not, there is no way of knowing. Nor is there any record of the Duke's interest in astrological science.

However, in biographies of his Duchess, it is stated that she consulted a 'clairvoyant' astrologer after her divorce from her American airman husband, Earl Winfield Spencer and before her marriage to Ernest Simpson. Commentators state the 'horoscope was pretty conventional though the clairvoyant did suggest there would be two more marriages in her life'. . .and that 'between the ages of 40 and 50, she would exercise considerable power of some kind'. . .'not connected with a job' according to the seer 'but the power that is come to you will be related to a man'.

The fact that these 'predictions' have survived from the 1920's indicate the Duchess had certainly not forgotten them. They are couched in the fortune-teller phraseology of those days yet it would be intriguing to see the chart on which they were based. To date, I have been unable to find in any biography the Duchess's birth time.

However, I have recently noted one English astrologer states she was born at about 7.00 a.m. She does not give the source of this information but, if correct, it would indicate a Cancer Ascendant for the Duchess and thus supply a strong attracting link to the Duke's Cancer Sun and Mercury. This Ascendant also promises the home-making skills she undoubtedly possessed.

NATAL CHART

Cardinal signs 4+☉
Fixed signs 2+Asc
Mutable signs 4+☽+MC
Positive signs 5+Asc+MC
Negative signs 5+☉+☽

Name: HRH Edward, Duke of Windsor

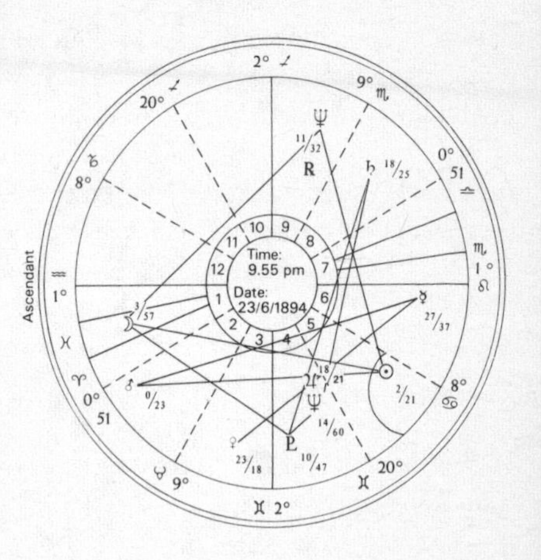

FIRE signs 1+MC
AIR signs 4+Asc
EARTH signs 1
WATER signs 4+☉+☽

B.T.Q.	PLANET	NATAL	ASPECTS
PMA	4 ♆ Neptune	14.00 ♊	☌ ♇
NFW	9 ♅ Uranus	11.32 ♏ ℞	
PCA	8 ♄ Saturn	18.25 ♎	△♇△♆
PMA	4 ♃ Jupiter	18.21 ♊	△♄☌♆
PCF	2 ♂ Mars	0.23 ♈	
NCW	5 ☉ Sun	2.21 ♋	△☽□♂△♅ wide
NFE	3 ♀ Venus	23.18 ♉	
NCW	6 ☿ Mercury	27.37 ♋	*♀△♂
NMW	1 ☽ Moon	3.53 ♓	□♇△♅
PMA	4 ♇ Pluto	10.47 ♊	

Prepared For HRH Edward, Duke of Windsor

NATAL CHART PERSONALITY PROFILE

PERSONALITY PROFILE

PLEASE NOTE: Boxes marked on profile sheets with TICKS point to personality traits as indicated by the natal chart. These profiles are designed for quick reference to significant chart pointers.

1. HEMISPHERE EMPHASIS: Planets Above Horizon: 2
Planets Below Horison: 8

Above Horizon Stress = Greater involvement in outer world experiences/activities — career, occupation, public affairs. ☐

Below Horizon Stress = Greater involvement in inner world experiences/activities — home, emotional life, private affairs. ☑

Equal Stress = Better balance between outer world activities and inner world experiences. Not likely to pursue success at expense of private life. ☐

2. POLARITIES: Planets in Positive Signs: ....5........
Planets in Negative Signs: ....5........

Positive Stress = Added tendencies towards extroversion — stronger assertion of the self and own aims. ☐

Negative Stress = Added tendencies towards introversion — greater suppression of the self and own desires. ☐

Equal Stress = Good balance between extroversion/introversion — able to assert or compromise as necessary. ☑

3. TRIPLICITIES: Planets in Fire Signs: ....1........
Planets in Air Signs: ....4........
Planets in Earth Signs: ....1........
Planets in Water Signs: ....4........

Fire Signs Dominant = Increased vitality, warmth, spontaneity — but rashness and impatience possible. ☐

Air Signs Dominant = Increased intellectuality, lightness, objectivity — but over-detachment and unreliability possible. ☑

Earth Signs Dominant = Increased supportiveness, strength and dependability — but unresponsiveness and addiction to routine possible. ☐

Water Signs Dominant = Increased intuition, subtlety, depth — but over-emotionalism and moodiness possible. ☑

4. QUADRUPLICITIES: Planets in Cardinal Signs: 4
Planets in Fixed Signs: 2
Planets in Mutable Signs: 4

Cardinal Sign Stress = More forceful pursuit of own aims and needs — but over-energetic thrust for objectives likely. ☑

Fixed Sign Stress = More persevering pursuit of own aims and needs — but rigidity and stubborn adherence to ideas likely. ☐

Mutable Sign Stress = More flexible, adaptable pursuit of own aims and needs — but uncertainty as to life direction likely. ☑

5. ANGULAR PLANETS:

Planets in First House: 1 — ☽
Planets in Fourth House: 3 — ♃ + ♆ + ♇
Planets in Seventh House: 0
Planets in Tenth House: 0

First House Emphasis = Itensified concern with impressions made on others. Desire to excite notice — but egotistical propensities usually manifest. ☑

Fourth House Emphasis = Intensified effects from early home conditioning. Heavier concentration on domestic/family issues — but home problems usually magnified. ☑

Seventh House Emphasis = Intensified expectations of marriage/unions/partnerships. Relationships assume paramount importance — but hopes usually set too high. ☐

Tenth House Emphasis = Intensified demand for career/occupation supremacy. Search for successes lifelong — but achievement thrust usually overrides private satisfactions. ☐

6. POWER POINT CHARACTER PATTERN:

Ascendant: Aquarius ♒ Symbol=The Water-Bearer
Sun Sign: Cancer ♋ Symbol=The Crab
Moon Sign Pisces ♓ Symbol=The Fish

Compatible Sign Blend = All three personality levels exhibit a generally congruent response. The self finds it relatively easy to satisfy reconcilable needs. ☐

Incompatible Sign Blend = All three personality levels exhibit a generally conflicting response. The self has to struggle continually to satisfy contrary needs. ☐

Partially Compatible Sign Blend = Two personality levels combine easily, one conflicts. The self feels partly at ease, partly at odds with own needs. ☑

7. LOVE AND SEX NATURE: Moon Sign: ♓ House: 1st
Venus Sign: ♉ House: 3rd
Mars Sign: ♈ House: 2nd

Consistent Sign Sequence = Planets specifically affecting love/sexual behaviour work well together. Reactions more predictable — but usually less stimulating to others. ☐

Inconsistent Sign Sequence = Planets specifically affecting love/sexual behaviour clash with each other. Reactions less predictable — but usually more disconcerting to others. ☐

Partially Consistent Sign Sequence = Planets specifically affecting love/sexual behaviour are partly in line with each other, partly out of line. Reactions mix the predictable with the unexpected — but usually puzzling to others. ☑

Appropriate House Emphasis = House location of planets particularly related to private affairs centralizes effort on gaining emotional gratification. ☐

Inappropriate House Emphasis = House location of planets involved in emotional decisions diverts attention to outside, less personal activities. ☑

8. SUCCESS DRIVES: Mercury Sign: ♋ House: 6th
Jupiter Sign: ♊ House: 4th
Saturn Sign: ♎ House: 8th

Consistent Sign Sequence = Planets specifically affecting individual achievement combine well together. Sustained progress towards fulfilment of ambitions — but over-concern with own performance likely. ☐

Inconsistent Sign Sequence = Planets specifically affecting individual achievement point to contradictory goals. Broader spread of effort to attain — but periods of frustration likely. ☐

Partially Consistent Sign Sequence = Planets specifically affecting individual achievement partly support, partly negate each other. Progress goes by stops and starts — but periods of self-dissatisfaction likely. ☑

Appropriate House Emphasis = House location of planets particularly related to career/occupation concentrates endeavours on gaining recognition. ☑

Inappropriate House Emphasis = House location of planets involved in career/occupation decisions infers competing activities in other spheres of interest. ☐

9. IMPORTANT PLANETARY ASPECTS:

(i) Sun Aspects:

Should benefit from:

- Increased inner harmony ☑

- Easier attainment of life goals ☐
- Added avenues of self-expression ☐
- Better self-control and discipline ☐
- More vigorous approach to problems ☐

Needs to control tendencies towards:

- Restlessness and inner frustration ☐
- Waste of energy in use of physical strengths ☑
- Erratic, self-willed behaviour ☐
- Escapist, self-deceptive attitudes ☐
- Pessimism and overly conservative reactions ☐

(ii) Moon Aspects:

Should benefit from:

- More satisfying emotional life ☑
- Improved capacity to verbalize feelings ☐
- Greater warmth and speed in reactions ☐
- Better judgement in intimate liaisons ☐
- Added personal charisma and sensitivity ☐

Needs to control tendencies towards:

- Awkwardness in expressing feelings ☐
- Intolerant, over-impulsive responses ☐
- Over-indulgence and excitability ☐
- Repression of feelings and over-sensitivity ☐
- Unduly demanding, extremist behaviour ☑

(iii) Mercury Aspects:

Should benefit from:

- Boosted powers of communication in speech/writing ☑
- Cogent, disciplined expression of ideas ☐
- Mental optimism and more broadly-based thinking ☐
- Improved imagination and subtlety of thought ☐
- Faster, more enterprising approach to intellectual matters ☑

Needs to control tendencies towards:

- Caustic, harsh methods of communication ☐
- Careless, over-optimistic decisions ☐
- Impatience and contempt for fools ☐
- Obsessive doubts/fears in mental skills ☐
- Lack of confidence and narrow thinking ☐

(iv) Venus Aspects:

Should benefit from:

- Improved capacity to relate well to others in all personal/friendship/family contacts ☑
- Added ability to show warmth in love/affections ☐
- Greater subtlety and idealism in all types of intimate relationships ☐
- Better discipline and discretion plus supportiveness ☐
- Boosted ability to attract others and achieve popularity ☐

Needs to control tendencies towards:

- Over-forceful, hasty dashing into relationships/ friendships ☐
- Too much demonstrativeness and extravagant displays of affection ☐
- Attraction to unreliable, unstable associates ☐
- Overstress on personal space and freedom in all contacts with lovers/friends/family ☐
- Expectations of unduly high and exacting standards from intimates ☐

(v) Mars Aspects:

Should benefit from:

- More vigorous, enthusiastic response to all types of physical stimuli ☐
- Lessened risk of repressions and doubts as to personal capacities ☑
- Increased magnetic appeal and ability to avoid possessive behaviour ☐

- Greater sensitivity and intuitive understanding of partner's needs ☐
- Added generosity and sense of adventure ☐

Needs to control tendencies towards:

- Inconsistent interest in sexual life and all forms of physical activities ☑
- Extreme self-will and high-handed behaviour ☐
- Deep-seated repressions of sexual needs/energies causing obsessive, demanding attitudes ☐
- Fantasizing about sex and inability to face reality in relationships ☐
- Overstatement, over-expectation and over-give toward others ☐

In the following Future Life Trend Summary for HRH Edward Duke of Windsor, we are examining the years surrounding *the major crisis point in his life* . . . i.e. the Abdication on 11 December, 1936.

FUTURE LIFE TREND SUMMARY

PLEASE NOTE: *Dates* set out in this section indicate *periods* when major planetary cycles and transits — affecting future events — make the greatest impact on each life. These periods therefore require subjects to make their greatest efforts to achieve beneficial, constructive changes in the life sectors specified in following pages.

If unsure of interpretations, please refer to Chapters 3, 4 and 5.

I. THE CYCLES OF SATURN

★ **The Saturn Withdrawal Cycle:**
This cycle covers the transits of Saturn from the cusp of first house, through second and third houses to the cusp of fourth house.

Relevant Time Spans:

Commencement of Withdrawal Cycle March–Dec 1932 (1st cycle) January 1962 (2nd cycle)

Conclusion of Withdrawal Cycle May 1942 (1st cycle) July 1971–April 1972 (2nd cycle)

★ **The Saturn Development Cycle:**
This cycle covers the transits of Saturn from the cusp of fourth house, through fifth and sixth houses to the cusp of seventh house.

Relevant Time Spans:

Commencement of Development Cycle May 1942 (1st cycle) July 1971–April 1972 (2nd cycle)

Conclusion of Development Cycle August 1946 (1st cycle) Died May 28th 1972 (during 2nd cycle)

★ **The Saturn Achievement Cycle:**
This cycle covers the transits of Saturn from the cusp of seventh house, through eighth and ninth houses to the cusp of tenth house.

Relevant Time Spans:

Commencement of Achievement Cycle August 1946

Conclusion of Achievement Cycle February–November 1956

★ **The Saturn Stabilization Cycle:**
This cycle covers the transits of Saturn from the cusp of tenth house, through eleventh and twelfth houses to the cusp of first house.

Relevant Time Spans:

Commencement of Stabilization Cycle February–November 1956

Conclusion of Stabilization Cycle January 1962

TRANSITING SATURN ASPECTS

1935	1936	1937
t♄ 1 ☌ ☽ March-December	t♄ 1 □ ♇ 4 February t♄ 1 □ ♆ 4 March t♄ 1 □ ♃ 4 April	NIL MAJOR

II. PLUTO TRANSITS

(a) Long-Range Pluto Effect:

Transit House Position 1. 6th House 2. 7th House

Relevant Time Spans:

Commencement of Pluto House Transit 1. 1920 2. 1939

Conclusion of Pluto House Transit 1. 1939 2. 1972

Note: Pluto's transits of above named house/houses in each chart focus on events and decisions of a fundamental and transformative nature in following life sectors: 1. All 6th House matters, ie. employment, working environment, health concerns. 2. All 7th House matters, ie. unions, marital affairs, contacts with the public.

Positive Responses to All Pluto Transits Promote:
*Added resourcefulness in handling events.
*Greater independence and individuality.
*Regeneration of objectives through irrevocable changes.

Negative Responses to All Pluto Transits Invite:
*Errors based on obsessive, compulsive behaviour.
*Dictatorial attitudes and refusal to take advice.
*Severe reversals through actions emanating from egotism.

(b) Current Pluto Effect:
As Pluto transits the house of each chart discussed in the preceding paragraph, life sectors set out therein will be notably activated by aspects occurring in the periods.

TRANSITING PLUTO ASPECTS

1935	1936	1937
t♇ 6 ☌ ☿ 6 November and all 1936 and 1937 and mid 1938	NIL MAJOR	NIL MAJOR

III. NEPTUNE TRANSITS

(a) Long-range Neptune Effect:

Transit House Position........................ 7th House

Relevant Time Spans:

Commencement of Neptune House Transit........ 1915

Conclusion of Neptune House Transit........ 1943

Note: Neptune's transits of above-named house/houses in each chart focus on events and decisions of a sensitive and intuitive nature in the following life sectors: All 7th House matters, ie. unions, marital affairs, contacts with the public, all gathered impetus after Pluto followed Neptune into 7th House in 1920.

Positive Responses to All Neptune Transits Promote:
*Increased intuition and imagination in handling events
*Boosted creative/artistic abilities and opportunities to apply them
*Heightened appreciation of the needs of others.

Negative Responses to All Neptune Transits Invite:
*Escapist behaviour and pursuit of fantasies
*Self-absorption and attraction to false goals/philosophies
*Evasion of responsibility and psychosomatic disorders.

(b) Current Neptune Effect:
As Neptune transits the house of each chart discussed in the preceding paragraph, life sectors set out therein will be notably activated by aspects occurring in the periods.

TRANSITING NEPTUNE ASPECTS

1935	1936	1937
t♆ 7 □ ♆ 4 — Late 1934 and all 1935 all 1936. t♆ 7 □ ♇ 4 late 1934. All 1935 and mid 1936	t♆ 7 □ ♃ 4 — Late 1936 and all 1937 and mid 1938	Nil major

IV. URANUS TRANSITS

(a) Long-range Uranus Effect:

Transit House Position .... 1. 2nd House 2. 3rd House ....

Relevant Time Spans:

Commencement of Uranus House Transit 1. 1927 2. 1937

Conclusion of Uranus House Transit .... 1. 1937 2. 1942 ....

Note: Uranus' transits of above-named house/houses in each chart focus on events and decisions OF A SUDDEN AND UNEXPECTED NATURE in the following life sectors: ......

1. All 2nd House matters, ie. income, earning power, possessions 2. All 3rd House matters, ie. educational skills, communications, brothers and sisters.

Positive Responses to All Uranus Transits Promote:
*Boosted independence and inventiveness in handling events
*Ability to break free of hampering restrictions
*Willingness to make total changes in life style/ideas.

Negative Responses to All Uranus Transits Invite:
*Erratic, rash and ill-considered actions through over-demand for freedom
*Sudden losses, resulting from thoughtless severance of ties/partnerships
*Perverse, wilful behaviour without thought of consequences.

(b) Current Uranus Effect:
As Uranus transits the house of each chart discussed in the preceding paragraph, life sectors set out therein will be notably activated by aspects occuring in the periods.

TRANSITING URANUS ASPECTS

1935	1936	1937
t♅ 2 □ ☿ 6 All 1934 and early 1935		t♅ 3 ☍ ♅ 9 All 1937 and early 1938

Commentary and Synthesis of Natal Traits

Profile Point 1
Strong below horizon emphasis. Heavy stress on the bottom left quadrant. Thus private life issues and emotional demands—from the self and others—must dominate life choices. Quite a problem for a man born to be king.

Profile Points 2, 3 and 4
Notably more self-assertive than typical Cancerian personality (2). Also more intellectually detached but weak earth and fire scores show low energy levels and marked impracticality (3). Better sense of goal/direction and improved adaptability but weak on long-term determination and adherence to personal convictions (4).

Profile Point 5

Only two angular houses stressed by planets. Thus private life choices show conflict between early upbringing/home expectations and own fluctuating self-image. Moon in 1st shows capacity and desire to please but clashing aspect to 4th infers heavy subconscious blocks from childhood conditioning.

Profile Point 6

Some conflict again here. The strongly emotional responses of Cancer/ Pisces blend awkwardly with the coolness of the Aquarian Ascendant. This conflict is intensified to some extent by the proximity of the Aquarian ascendant to Capricorn. Thus a nagging sense of duty/ punctiliousness behind the more overt unconventionality of Aquarius and the desire to flow where feelings dictate of Cancer/Pisces.

Profile Point 7

Something of a problem mix here, too. Emotionally-based fantasies, fear of ties, sudden upsurges of passion collide with the search for solid, supportive and sensually satisfying love/and friendship. House positions further divert these needs away from personal issues. Possibly often troubled and perplexed by own reactions. Puzzling to those close also.

Profile Point 8

Not too helpful again. Emotionally-slanted thinking, tradition-based. More alert grasping of opportunities and more adaptable use of them. Ambitions intellectualized too but strong warning of falls from grace if actions based on anything but highest standards of honour/rectitude.

Profile Point 9

Not all that many drastic planetary clashes.

Sun Aspects

Well-integrated Sun/Moon suggest improved inner harmony and satisfactory parental marriage to offer conflict-free example. Wide Sun/Uranus link shows better understanding of father's abrupt manner and his image of male authority. Hard Sun/Mars link implies anger and rashness in face of opposition from men. (This revealed itself graphically in the Duke's clashes with not only his father and later brothers but also with his unsympathetic Prime Minister, Stanley Baldwin.)

Moon Aspects

Better ability to avoid the clinging emotionalism of Cancer/Pisces mix. But, great difficulty in comprehending motivations of females and deep depression in face of domestic disturbances.

Mercury Aspects

Faster, brighter communicator. Added charm in putting own ideas over.

Venus Aspects

Nil further in major aspects. Thus affectional responses have little to channel them effectively. With Venus the only planet in earth, the search for practical support in love/friendship is isolated and spasmodic.

Mars Aspects

Again nil further in major aspects. Again, the only planet in fire and that by only twenty-three minutes so adjacent Pisces influence reappears to influence sexual responses and use of physical energies generally. A mixture of rashness and sentimentality with little to channel direction of either.

Additional Pointers

1. *Grand Trine in Water*

Allowing a 9 degree orb for Sun/Uranus link, the Duke's chart shows a grand trine in water, linking Moon in first, Sun in fifth and Uranus in ninth. Grand trines are not common and act like a closed circuit of self-feeding energy, thus setting off a kind of chain reaction round the points, assisting favourable results from events/responses in the houses or life sectors so linked.

Being in water, it offered the Duke the ability to evoke easily and instantly, emotions in others—a fact visibly exhibited by his early popularity with World War I troops, in London's post-war social scene, in his empire tours and his visits to Britain's poverty-stricken towns and cities. But—and this is a highly relevant 'but' in the Duke's story—

most textbook authors and my own experience point to the sad fact that grand trines encourage the 'Easy Rider' stance. The ease and smoothness of passage they generate often means they are leant on too heavily by their possessors. There is an instinctive feeling of being blessed by the gods—as it were—so that without tougher configurations like t-squares in a chart any form of sustained effort virtually collapses in times of crisis.

And so it happened here. The Duke's chart shows only two major hard aspects. What's more his life history reveals a firm conviction that he would never have to try all that hard to get what he wanted. That his natural charm plus appealing self-presentation (Moon in first) blended with the regal pomp and splendour that surrounded him (Sun in fifth) and topped off with his attractively unorthodox, at times iconoclastic approach (Uranus in ninth) would carry all before him.

Which it did. Until his moment of truth arrived. Even then, right till the last and in the face of public outcry and governmental condemnation which was growing louder by the minute, he flatly refused to believe the battle was lost. In his own words to Wallis: 'Rest assured, I'll manage it somehow'. Meaning, he could keep the throne and seat her upon it.

2. *Small Stellium in Fourth House with Square to First House*
'An Englishman's home is his castle' as the saying goes. And it goes doubly for a Cancer man, who also happened to be English and really did live in castles. The planetary stress from the stellium further intensified the Duke's sensitivity to and concern with his homes at all stages in his life. Jupiter ensured great opportunities/advantages through the home. And these he surely had. But Neptune inferred its foundations would often feel shaky, while Pluto threatened power struggles with those who shared it. This undoubtedly happened—first with his parents, then his brothers, later with his wife. He lost every one of these battles too in the end.

3. *Mars in Second House: Saturn in Eighth House*
Although these two planets are well out of orb, they nevertheless indicate the great significance the two sources of money would assume in the Duke's life. . .that which he earned from his own efforts and that which came to him through others, his royal relatives. After the abdication, he applied himself energetically to investing the income

he continued to command as a royal Duke but later earned a further small fortune by writing his memoirs entitled *A King's Story* published in 1951, which netted a total of £500,000. His wife's version *The Heart Has Its Reasons* appeared in 1956 and gathered another £700,000 for the couple. Both used ghost writers. Saturn produced, as ever, delays and hindrances where royal moneys were concerned. By abdication, the Duke lost much of the vast property assets and income he would otherwise have enjoyed for life.

4. *Mercury in Sixth House*

Good aspects to Venus and Mars in third (ideas/communications) and second (income/moneys) respectively from sixth house Mercury (work/employment) promise that book authorship for the Duke may prove profitable. Which it surely did.

Back in the early 50's world readers were still thirsting for the inside story behind the greatest royal debacle in history and proved it. The vast sums earned by *A King's Story* astronomically exceeded what most authors could dream of in a lifetime of writing. In this endeavour, the Duke was urgently prodded by his Duchess. Not only for the cash returns—the couple were already wealthy—but more to set the Royals, who had so unrelentingly rejected her, back on their heels.

Had she and the Duke looked at his chart, both would have known this course of action was totally alien to his nature. Born under Cancer and with the same sign on his sixth house cusp plus Mercury in Cancer in the sixth, no power on earth—not even the Duchess's—could coerce him into attacking tradition, the crown or those who wore it in anything but a lukewarm way. Thus, in his book, he largely dodged around salient points and skirted biting criticism of his parents, brother and sister-in-law in their response to his conduct. It was partially this underlying reticence, coupled with the Duke's lack of consistent application (Pisces Moon) which drove his ghost writer to desperation as he (the writer) strove to coax his troublesome employer into meeting the publishing deadline. It was touch-and-go from start to finish.

Added to this, the Duke's fifth house Sun, linking by hard aspect to Mars in the second, indicates wasted energy and erratic concentration in the field of creativity. Whereas his third house Venus, though well-aspected, instilled the belief that mental work should come easily . . .which good writing certainly does not. As the great 18th century playwright, Richard Sheridan, once remarked: 'Easy reading is damned hard writing'. The Duke's ghost writer confirms that his employer found it hard to stay at his desk for more than half an hour.

Contrastingly, when it was the Duchess's turn to write her memoirs, biographers note her flow of reminiscence came smoothly. Small wonder with Sun/Mercury/Venus all in Gemini plus Moon in Libra. And the fact that she did not suffer from the same inhibitions concerning revelations about the past as did the Duke. Nevertheless, even she glossed over much about her earlier marriages and other unpleasant or contentious issues her Libran Moon did not wish to recall.

5. *Empty Seventh and Tenth Houses*

The fact that the Duke's tenth house of career/attainment is empty comes as no surprise. In the true sense, he was not career-minded and had few personal attainments, with the Sagittarian cusp suggesting he wanted freedom to roam rather than be tied to the dreary desk-work which afflicts all conscientious monarchs. Biographers note he often left this part of his royal duties undone and secret papers floating about in his residences as casually as if they were visiting cards. The fact that his seventh house of marriage/unions/partnerships is also empty seems odd at first glance. The more so, since it was a contentious marriage which created the uproar that swiftly destroyed him.

But is that empty house so peculiar in terms of his life story? After all, he had studiously avoided any type of permanent commitment to any woman up to the very late age of 43, choosing partners who were invariably already married and thus could demand little from him. And age 43, for a royal heir who is expected to marry early and produce heirs himself, is close to extraordinary in his position. His royal male forebears—Prince Albert (wed at 20 and father of nine), King Edward VII (wed at 23 and father of five), King George V (wed at 28 and father of six), plus brother George VI (wed at 27 and father of 2) had all married in early adulthood to brides of unimpeachable lineage and become fathers soon after.

In the light of the Duke's past love life, it is very possible that had the adventurous, social-climbing Mrs Simpson not first crossed his path as he approached the astrologically and psychologically dangerous age of 40, he may have continued to resist all attempts to marry him off for the rest of his life. No, the chart emphasis clearly implies the fourth, the house of the home, was the true storm centre of troubles, hopes and yearnings. . .not marriage. And in certain ways, through her decorating flair, her interest in exotic cuisine, her skills in entertaining, Mrs Simpson very early in their relationship impressed the then Prince as a homemaker *par excellence*. An irresistible bait for a male of his type.

The Leo cusp on his seventh and the interception of Virgo infers any female with designs upon him would need to be impressive, even commanding as well as taking care with meticulous attention to detail of his creature comforts. Mrs Simpson appeared well endowed with all these attributes. Nor did she ever give any sign of being overawed by his exalted status from the outset. Apart from dropping the essential curtseys and adding the obligatory 'Sir' in conversation, she treated him without ceremony, returning witty, sometimes pert, retorts to his comments. This he enjoyed too.

Finally, the empty seventh plus the heavily stressed fourth reinforces at once the view suggested by biographers that the Duke was not then (or indeed ever was) looking for a wife. He wanted a mother figure. Here, too, she filled the bill. Fellow house guests were aghast when—with her obliging second husband still in tow for the sake of appearances—she began playing hostess at Edward's Fort Belvedere retreat. Taking him over to the point of slapping his wrist and crying 'Naughty! It's bad for you!' when he attempted to put sugar in his tea.

No English friend or lover would have dared to slap the royal wrist. Such liberties and familiarities simply 'weren't done!' Yet the action was unmistakably maternal. And—incredibly to all others present—he appeared to like it.

After their marriage, the censorious mother role grew even more prominent, as this quite dreadful husband-and-wife exchange in the mid-50's, reported by biographers, illustrates:

Duchess: 'David, come here a moment'.
Duke: 'Just a second darling! I have something on my mind'.
Duchess: 'On your *what*?'
Duke: (apologetically) 'I know, darling. I haven't much of a mind'.

A sad commentary on the greatest love affair of the 20th century. Astonishingly too, after the Duke's death from cancer in 1972, the Duchess literally fell apart—mentally, physically and with surprising speed for one who had stayed young, slim and inexhaustibly energetic right into her seventies.

Within a very few years, she was bed-ridden after three serious falls, was suffering from arterioscelerosis and had become a total recluse. A gastric ulcer, which had troubled her most of her maturity, haemorrhaged badly. Her mind wandered back into the past where she continued to live until her lonely death—14 years after the Duke in 1986. From her sad and swift decline, it can be inferred that with the subject of her mothering role gone, her future was empty of purpose, for he was also her passport to fame and high society.

And so the last Gemini performer in a royal drama, which was for the Duke over-supplied with Geminis and rivalled at times the wildest excesses of soap opera, vanished behind the final curtain on 24 April 1986—some 50 years after she first stepped into the spotlight. The part played in the redirection of British history by one perfectly ordinary American woman. . .without status, without rank, without power, without wealth. . .has no parallel. But at the end of the play, there was no applause. For those who had forgotten or barely heard of her, her death meant nothing. For those who did remember, many had never forgiven her.

However, before we move on to examining the planetary indicators affecting Duke's crisis point years of 1935, 1936 and 1937, a quick inspection of the compatibility ratings between him and his chosen bride will be rewarding. (Readers who are unsure of how to assess compatibility between potential or existing love/marriage partners, can learn these techniques from my companion title—*Astro-Pick Your Perfect Partner*). For in Edward's case his infatuation with Mrs Simpson and his determination to wed her lay at the root of the Abdication Crisis.

Look now at the 'Compatibility Rating Table' in this section and watch warning lights at once flash on. More clashes than easy contacts. So let us imagine the couple had come for counselling before the final, irrevocable step was taken and see precisely what their compatibility charts reveal about their future together. In the Duchess's table, her planetary positions are taken direct from the ephemeris on her birth date—19 June 1896—as we have no documented birth time for her.

Duke of Windsor
23/6/1894

Duchess of Windsor
19/6/1896

COMPATIBILITY RATING TABLE

	His Personal Planets by Sign and Degree		Her Personal Planets by Sign
☉	2.21 ♋ (Ego)	☉	28.37 ♊ (Ego)
☽	3.53 ♓ (Emotion)	☽	12.03 ♎ (Emotion)
☿	27.37 ♋ (Mind)	☿	16.13 ♊ ℞ (Mind)
♀	23.18 ♉ (Affections)	♀	23.06 ♊ (Affections)
♂	0.23 ♈ (Sexuality)	♂	21.14 ♈ (Sexuality)

ELEMENTAL STRESS PATTERNS

His Planets

Fire 1
Air 4
Earth 1
Water 4

Her Planets

Fire 2
Air 6
Earth 0
Water 2

N.B. *Broken* _ _ _ _ _ lines above indicate compatible attitudes and easy aspects.
Unbroken ______ lines above indicate incompatible attitudes and challenging aspects.

Planetary Categories (His)

Cardinal signs 4 + ☉
Fixed signs 2

Planetary Categories (Hers)

Cardinal signs 2 + ☽
Fixed signa 3

Planetary Categories (His)		Planetary Categories (Hers)	
Mutable signs	4 + ☽	Mutable signs	5 + ☉
Positive signs	5	Positive signs	8
Negative signs	5	Negative signs	2

Note: One extra point in each above category is added for Sun and Moon. Points for Ascendant and midheaven are not included as the Duchess's birth time is not available.

Direct Planetary Cross-Referencing

1. Some similarity of life styles. (Hidden conjunction between two Suns). (Yes, see biographies.)
2. Differing emotional expectations. (No in-orb aspect but his fantasy-oriented Pisces Moon finds little comfort in intellectualised, cooled response of Libra Moon.) (Yes again, see biographies.)
3. No meeting of minds. (Emotionally-slanted thinking of Mercury in Cancer finds no echo in her Gemini-style duality of mind. Not an in-orb aspect.) (Yes once more. See biographies—little real communication.)
4. Differing affectional expectations. (In-orb semi-sextile. He is slow, possessive in response to love/friendship. She repeats the Gemini-style changefulness.) (See biographies—her flirtations.)
5. Apparently similar sexual responses but not wholly so. His Aries Mars is right on cusp of Pisces and well out of orb with her Aries Mars. She pushes hard for her sexual needs. He sometimes does, sometimes flips back into dream-world fantasy. (See biographies—soon after marriage slept in separate rooms.)

Diagonal Planetary Cross-Referencing

1. Only one major helpful link here. Hidden trine between his Moon and her Sun. Hence, better cohesion between his emotional demand and the manner in which her ego obliges her to behave. Both can switch between emotionalism and reason at these levels. (His emotional dependence on her became total over the years.)
2. Hard aspect between his Mercury and her Mars. Arguments, confrontations flow from this. At times, she would consider his

thinking 'wet' and soggy with feeling. He would feel her physical pushfulness overbearing him. (Many reported incidents of this.)

3. Hard hidden aspect between his Mars and her Sun. Clash of hesitant sexuality and ego thrust here. (He did what she ordered.)
4. Hard hidden aspect between his Mars and her Venus. Troubles again. No meeting ground in expression of sexual urges and demonstration of affection. (This situation, too, is reported in biographies.)

Elemental Stress Patterns Comparison

Fire: Neither show high score on this quality. She, however with Mars well into fire would be the more vigorous and energetic. (Which was so.)

Earth: Both very low score. Practicality and pre-planning not likely to govern decisions. (Which was so.)

Air: Fair score for each. But her air pointers are in four of her Personal Planets. His air pointers stem from the non-personal planets. Hence, detachment/intellectualism/lightness comes much more easily to her than to him. (Which was so.)

Water: Reverse of air pointer picture. He has two of his Personal Planets in water, thus deepening sensitivity/emotionalism. She has none of her Personal Planets in water. She talks about love more than she feels it. (Which was so.)

Planetary Categories Comparison

- He is stronger on pursuit of objectives (cardinals): she is stronger on adherence to convictions (fixeds): both capable of fair degree of adaptability to changes (mutables). (As shown by their actions.)
- She is far more assertive, extroverted and pushful than he is. Strong positive score here implies she takes the lead in a more masculine manner, dislikes domination or taking orders. May steamroll others into submission. (As she did to Edward but not the British establishment.)

Whilst it is far beyond the analyst's authority to veto a marriage between any couple, danger areas or perilous incompatibilities should always be scrupulously but *not* negatively pointed out. And so they could have been by any competent analyst back in 1935 for Edward and Mrs Simpson. Could he resist her dominating tendencies? No, he could not.

He had been conditioned to make obeisance to the sign of Gemini from infancy. Literally with his royal Geminian parents and great-grandmother Victoria. Thus he could not help but go on doing so automatically with his Duchess, an even more strongly Geminian type than his forebears. (Check this out for yourself and your chart subjects. Watch how you and they react to encounters with the birth signs of parents in the loves, friendships or work associations of adult life. Unless the parents were ciphers with minimal influence over their children, you'll note an instinctive tendency to metaphorically 'bow down before them'. To feel faintly inferior or overborne—a psychological carry-over from childhood obedience.) So step warily when the sign of mother or father looms large on your personal horizons or you'll feel a strange sense of being back in the nursery.

Could the Duke cope with the unpredictable mood swings of those born under sign of the Twins? No, again he could not. They had baffled him in adulthood, reduced him to tears in early childhood. His royal Geminian father could switch from alarming jocularity, reminiscent of the quarterdeck of a battleship, to even more alarming, sharply-worded criticisms of his sons in a flash.

Could Edward handle his intended wife's overall personality demand successfully? No, not really. And certainly not, if he wished to retain his own identity.

So was this, after all, the greatest love affair of the twentieth century? A new variation on the ancient themes of Prince Charming and Cinderella, Romeo and Juliet? (Oddly enough, Mrs Simpson's mother's maiden name was Montague, the same family name Shakespeare chose for his Romeo.)

No, most biographers agree it was not. And so say the couple's charts. After all both participants were approaching middle age, a period in life when time has cooled the blood, the wilder passions of youth have been largely left behind, and few are naive enough to believe 'the world well lost for love'. As, at least at the outset, with a push from Uranus, the Duke appeared to do.

Incidentally, one of the most satisfying discoveries for new students, when developing technique through working with famous lives, is the remarkable fact that numerous authors make fascinating astrological comments on their subjects—without apparently realizing it.

Here follows a quote from the last chapter of Richard Garrett's illustrated 1979 book, *Mrs Simpson*. He comments at length on the 'strange affinity' between the Duchess and Queen Victoria from the standpoint of habits and behaviour, but plainly had no idea why such apparently inexplicable affinity existed. 'Strangely enough, if one looks for affinity between Wallis and any member of the British Royal Family, one finds it in Queen Victoria.' He goes on to mention that like the old Queen had done after Prince Albert's death, the Duchess kept her late husband's quarters exactly as he had left them. Clothes, toiletries, even to a packet of pipe cleaners. (This somewhat morbid practice was not uncommon in the nineteenth century. Most unusual in the 1970's.)

Garrett continues:

> There is also the coincidence that they were both of very small stature. But there are other things, too. People are apt to forget that before the sobering, rather prudish influence of Albert came into her life, Queen Victoria was a very gay young lady who enjoyed nothing more than to dance and play games. . .Both Wallis and Victoria were of strong character, given to becoming imperious when the mood took them. Both lost their fathers early in their lives. Both were inclined to base judgements on the verdicts of their hearts rather than their minds.
>
> And both experienced a love that transcended everything else.

One glance at the birth charts of the Queen and Duchess makes those 'coincidences' and 'strange affinity' between them neither inexplicable nor coincidental. Both women were strongly Geminian types. The Queen's chart shows Ascendant, Sun, Moon in Gemini plus Mars in Aries. The Duchess's chart shows Sun, Mercury, Venus, Neptune, Pluto in Gemini plus Mars in Aries. As to their 'inclinations to base judgements on the verdict of their hearts rather than their minds and their experiencing a love that transcended everything else'—this amounts to a misunderstanding of their characters.

The loss of the father in childhood often makes it hard for females to understand male attitudes/behaviour. Purely from the psychological

NATAL CHART

Cardinal signs 0
Fixed signs 5+☽+Asc+MC
Mutable signs 5+☉
Positive signs 6+☉+MC
Negative signs 4+☽+Asc

Name: King George VI

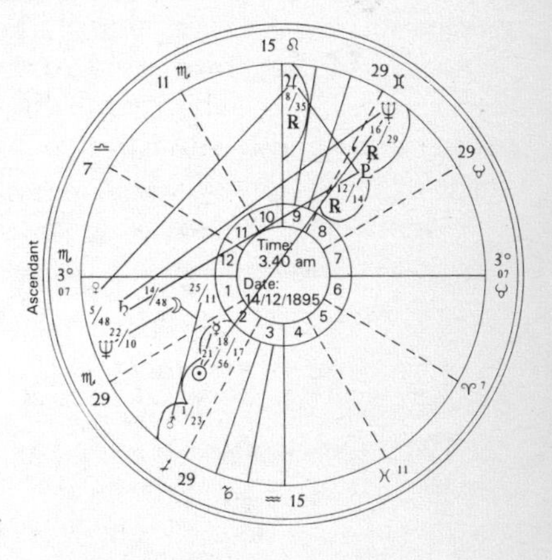

FIRE signs 4+☉+MC
AIR signs 2
EARTH signs 0
WATER signs 4+☽+Asc

Note: Some astrologers assign a 3.05 a.m. time to George VI. Time stated here is as recorded in his father's diary.

B.T.Q.	PLANET	NATAL	ASPECTS
PMA	8 ♆ Neptune	16.29 ♊ R	☌ ♇
NFW	1 ♅ Uranus	22.10 ♏	
NFW	1 ♄ Saturn	14.48 ♏	⊼ ♇ ⊼ ♆
PFF	9 ♃ Jupiter	8.35 ♌ R	* ♇
PMF	2 ♂ Mars	1.23 ♐	
PMF	2 ☉ Sun	21.56 ♐	☌ ☿ ☍ ♆
NFW	1 ♀ Venus	5.48 ♏	□ ♃
PMF	2 ☿ Mercury	18.17 ♐	☍ ♇ ☍ ♆
NFW	1 ☽ Moon	25.11 ♏	☌ ♅ ☌ ♂
PMA	8 ♇ Pluto	12.14 ♊ R	

standpoint. They have no continuing images of masculinity about the house to base judgements upon. Mars in Aries provides the passionate thrust to obtain what one wants in sexual partners, usually rashly, with no regard for consequences. Victoria wanted the handsome Albert the moment she laid eyes on him. Wallis wanted the equally good-looking Edward the moment she perceived what he could offer her. Therefore in both cases, desire—not heart—underlay their judgements.

As for 'love transcending everything else', again this is doubtful. Victoria deified Albert after his early death but their marital battles were many beforehand. He often locked himself in his bedroom while the royal fists pounded furiously on his door. Wallis in their long married life battled and argued equally loudly and often with the Duke. Until his death changed everything too. Then, like Victoria, she also began to set up shrines to his memory and became in many ways 'The Widow of Paris' as her royal astrological counterpart had become 'The Widow of Windsor'—more than a century before.

Fate and Two Younger Brothers

(Chart Links between George VI and Teddy Kennedy)
Although here we are examining the Duke of Windsor's story, the remarkable chart similarities between his younger brother and the US President's younger brother are well worth brief comment. Readers already familiar with chart analysis will spot these pointers at once. Readers who are not can check analytical techniques in my companion title—*How to Astro-Analyze Yourself and Others*.

Compare now King George VI's chart in this chapter and Teddy Kennedy's, bearing in mind that both were younger brothers who, through astonishing twists of fate, each found himself wearing his older brother's shoes.

Here are the similarities which literally leap out of their charts.

* Both charts show Saturn natally in the first. Fear of revealing the self to the world, of coming out from behind the defensive barricade of Saturnian self-doubt. This was present in both personalities.

* Both charts show a see-sawing pattern, linking the second house and the eighth. Both charts show the Sun, Mercury and Mars in the second. Both charts show Neptune in the eighth. Hence both men

would feel the pull between the wish to go their own way in financial affairs and so buck against the equally powerful pull towards involvement with family moneys/business. Quite a problem for each. The Kennedy fortune would not match the royal assets but is still enormous.

* Neptune in the eighth for both men implies some strange, mysterious circumstances affecting their inheritance of power or money or both. For Teddy, it was the tragic deaths of his three brothers, with the mystery of 'who really killed President Kennedy?' still unsolved today. For King George VI, it was the strange, inexplicable obsession of his brother with Mrs Simpson and there too many questions remain unanswered still.

* Both charts show the Natal Sun in opposition to Natal Neptune. Half an hour's perusal of a biography of either man will confirm that neither received much genuine encouragement or understanding from their fathers in childhood. Teddy is a Piscean: his father Joseph was a Virgoan. George VI was a Sagittarian: his father George V was a Geminian. Thus both sons were born under signs which oppose their fathers' signs. Setting aside the numerous other chart indicators concerning the paternal/filial relationships, this fact evidences the fight both sons had to put up to retain their own individuality against their fathers' dictates.

But to return to the crisis point of the Duke's story.

Commentary and Synthesis of Future Life Trends in Years 1935, 1936 *and* 1937.

Saturn Summary Point 1

First transit of Withdrawal Cycle:
March—December 1932 to May 1942. In exactly the same way as in Teddy Kennedy's life, the Duke's time of greatest trial and trouble developed very soon after Saturn sank down into this demanding cycle and continued for as long as the transit period itself did. In the above 10 years, Edward met, become obsessed with and finally married Mrs Simpson. (His youngest brother, the Duke of Kent called him 'besotted with that woman'.) This cycle also saw the death of his father, the loss of own throne, a catastrophically unwise visit to Nazi Germany and

Hitler, and of course, the first years of what were to prove permanent exile.

Second Transit of Withdrawal Cycle:
January 1961—July 1971 to April 1972. Thirty years on from the earlier succession of tests, trials and mistakes, Saturn began to repeat the same kind of pressure. But, now approaching and entering his 70's, the fast ageing Duke found the cycle harder than ever to handle. His physical powers were visibly ebbing, his sense of purpose had long departed. Health ailments, plagued him. . .operations for heart troubles, eye disorders, hernia. Frequent pain from arthritis made walking harder, dancing impossible. He still donned top hat, white tie and tails to ride the social merry-go-round in America and Europe but without heart or energy while his tireless Duchess danced merrily on. A 1970 photograph with President Nixon at the White House shows the ever-youthful Duchess wearing a slit-to-above-knee evening gown at 74, while the obviously aged Duke at 76 walks painfully with a cane.

Saturn Summary Point 2

First Transit of Development Cycle:
May 1942—August 1946. Again, in much the same way as happened with Teddy Kennedy, the Duke's life took on a less problematical pattern once Saturn began to rise upwards in his chart again. He was now moving into his fifties. World War II saw his appointment as Governor of the Bahamas, which was far from being the top-drawer wartime work he'd hoped for but gave him back a small semblance of his former authority. Interestingly, he named a cabin cruiser bought to move around the islands 'Gemini' after his Duchess's Sun sign. By 1945, the war was over and he was bored with Bahamas as was his wife. They resettled themselves in France and became the central figures of a non-stop social whirl which continued for almost thirty years—labelled by one biographer as 'Love in Idleness'.

Second Transit of Development Cycle:
July 1971—April 1972. This cycle was never completed. As Saturn once more crossed the fourth house cusp and began to ascend again peace and release from suffering came at last for the Duke. He died in his home in Paris on 28 May 1972. On 18 May, his niece Queen Elizabeth

II, the Duke of Edinburgh and Prince Charles paid a visit to her dying uncle and his wife. As the Queen did so of her own initiative, it was seen as an act of reconciliation between the Crown and the man who had turned his back on it almost 40 years before.

Saturn Aspects: 1935 – 1937

A group of major aspects between transiting Saturn and the Duke's natal planets arrived in succession, beginning March 1935 and ending in May 1936. One linked with the Duke's first house, the other three with his fourth.

From March to December 1935, Saturn was backing and filling over a conjunction with his natal Moon. This natal Moon position, joined as it was to the natal grand trine in water, was one of the secrets of Edward's personal appeal to all his subjects—high and mighty or small and humble. But the aspect's energy was not used wisely. These months showed his infatuation with Mrs Simpson becoming an obsession and also marked a deterioration of his father, the King's, fast-failing health.

Problems with his royal female relatives piled up. Queen Mary could offer him no sympathy as she saw her son's dereliction of duty looming larger. His sister-in-law, Elizabeth (now Queen Mother) could not hide her disdain of his 'friend' nor her growing anger over where it could lead her own husband and the massive yoke it might one day place on his none-too-confident shoulders. To all this, in line with a negative response to this aspect, Edward appeared insensitive and his attempts to sway opinion in his favour failed.

The Duke's most fateful year—1936—opened with transiting Saturn striking a tough square to natal Pluto from his first to fourth houses. Trouble for certain unless he handled it with kid gloves, which he did not. His natural wilfulness and disregard for the most restrictive forms of protocol hit his home scene hard. Fate and destiny wrestled with each other. Right on cue came threats, fears, family power struggles, nagging anxiety about his love affair. His royal relatives closed ranks against him. Mrs Simpson argued and demanded. Loss of prestige, emotional manipulation followed as night the day.

In March 1936, transiting Saturn increased pressure on the Duke's natal fourth house planets by a square to Neptune. Delusion, fantasy-based plans brought a devastating sense of mental disorientation.

Friends, family and associates all record the weakening of his physical condition through unremitting stress. He retreated more and more into his dream-world where he saw himself and Wallis crowned King and Queen in storybook pageantry.

There was no respite. For in April—May 1936, transiting Saturn produced yet another square from his first to fourth houses—this time to Jupiter. The warning was to tread warily. Not to rush onwards in heedless optimism. Errors of judgement, largely based on his unabated faith that his public popularity would topple opposition, proliferated. The lucky breaks he hoped for and relied on did not come.

It will be remembered that the home, always the area of deepest concern to Cancer personalities, carried even greater import for the Duke through his natal stellium in the fourth house. Saturn's 1936 transits hence struck this bull's eye. They shook Edward to the core of his being. He had never been happy in any of his homes from infancy. Mrs Simpson seemed to promise him a world of everlasting domestic bliss, a bait he could not resist. That it was yet another mistake, another delusion was the sum total of the warnings Saturn offered him through the earlier months of 1936. Had he known or heeded he could have stepped back from the point of no return.

Pluto Summary—House Position (1) 1920—1939

Pluto's life-transforming energy began to concentrate on Edward's sixth house of work/employment within a couple of years of the end of World War I from which the then Prince had emerged a triumphant and charismatic figure. Slowly but surely, for those above-named 19 years, the demand for change was applied to his working life—to his task as Prince of Wales and his preparation to rule as King.

Until he met Mrs Simpson in 1930—the same year Pluto was discovered—the path ahead looked set fair for success. But this planet is never in a hurry. The explosive charge is usually laid long before it blows up. So it happened here. Little appeared to result from the couple's first encounter. But gradually, inexorably they were pushed across each other's paths, riding on the gaily-spinning society merry-go-round of the 1930's. By 1935, the time had come when Edward seemed unable to live through a day or night without seeing Mrs Simpson. Not surprisingly, his work schedules began to lag behind to the mounting irritation of his father. As the King's health continued to worsen, Edward's succession to the throne became increasingly more imminent while the more sensational American newspapers stirred the pot by running page lead gossip stories about the Simpson affair. The behind-the-scenes plotting heated up with Edward and Wallis on one side and the Prime Minister plus the Royal Family on the other. By the time King George V died on 20 January 1936 and Edward became monarch, undercover action between the warring groups intensified, led now by Stanley Baldwin, born 3 August 1867, whose old-fashioned Leo-style concept of kingly behaviour collided headlong with Edward's own. Some biographers maintain it was this Prime Minister's cunning manipulation of the crisis which brought victory for him and defeat for what he regarded as a wilful and recalcitrant ruler. At nearly 70, his aims and beliefs had nothing in common with the Jazz Age generation of which his quarry had long been the leading light. With a low fixed score in his own chart, Edward had little chance of outwitting the unswerving determination of this ancient and wily Lion.

In less than one year—from 20 January 1936 to 11 December 1936—Edward was ousted, sent into exile and his brother installed on the throne. From then on until Pluto completed the sixth house transit in 1939, the former king tried desperately to find a new direction for his long-learned skills but none was forthcoming. His Sagittarian brother, ably directed by his Leo wife (who had neither forgotten nor forgiven the behaviour of the Duke or the erstwhile Mrs Simpson) turned his face sadly but resolutely against them both.

Pluto Summary—House Position (2) 1939 – 1972

Due to the interception of the sign of Virgo in the Duke's seventh house, Pluto's transit this time covered some 33 years—most of his married life. It continued through the early years of the marriage, the troubles that beset it in the 1950's when the Duchess's involvement with a millionaire American playboy raised eyebrows and hit high spots in the more malicious gossip columns. It still had not ended at the date of Edward's death.

Many of the negative results of this transit showed their teeth. Painful power struggles with rivals, (the playboy) indomitable enemies (the Royal Family), compulsion and dictatorial demands from the spouse

(Wallis). Pluto made it clear that having chosen this marriage bed against numerous warnings, the Duke must lie in it—thorns and all.

Pluto Aspects 1935 – 1937

Only one arrived but, due to retrograde movement, it was long-lasting—beginning in late 1935, remaining in orb through most of 1936 and 1937 and ending late May 1938. This was a conjunction between transiting Pluto and Natal Mercury in the Duke's sixth house.

Certainly and in true copybook interpretation style, it opened the Duke's mind to new ways of thinking and offered new persuasive powers to sway others in favour of his views. Prime Minister Baldwin's implacable opposition to Edward's plans did not win easily or hands down. Numerous powerful men, including at least one of the Press Barons, *were* persuaded that a monarch had the right to choose his own wife—whoever and whatever she may be.

The problem here was plain, Pluto will never allow ego to conquer truth. And if the veils of love and romance are stripped away, there is no gain-saying that Edward's choice was based on his own egotistical demand. He said so. 'The only thing that matters to me is my own happiness.'

Not an outrageously egotistical statement for an ordinary man. But Edward was *not* an ordinary man. Nor were his privileges those of ordinary men. All came with his royal rank and if he wished to retain it, he must do his duty and pay the price. But as the last ditch struggle loomed, it was apparent to all around him that his obsession with marrying Mrs Simpson had become fanatical, (Pluto again) blinding him to the true issues of the time.

That he could not or would not see the truth allowed his opponents to brand him as a threat to the monarchy and to the stability of Britain itself. They laid their final plans to rid themselves of this pestilent prince forever.

Neptune Summary—House Position 1915 – 1943

Again, because of the interception of Virgo in the Duke's seventh house, Neptune's transit thereof lasted for some 28 years—taking in the last of his World War I service, his amorous adventures with Mrs Simpson's predecessors, the royal favourites even then being mainly married women, and finally his meeting with and marriage to Wallis himself.

Up until September 1943 when Neptune finally departed from the Duke's seventh house, the planet's negative specialty—in the form of illusions, evasions and fantasies—had been much in evidence throughout his adult years. Indeed, Neptune's entry into the seventh, 5 years before Pluto followed, had begun raising the tidal waves of misplaced emotions which would later engulf Edward. The build-up began when he was a youth of 21 and did not ebb until he was a middle-aged man of 49.

Sadly, again, Edward appeared to make the negative set of responses to Neptune's long-term influence. He was far from being irreligious yet so much of what he did offended deeply the religious convictions of his contemporaries. Not merely the established church but the moral standards of ordinary people throughout the kingdom and empire. Part of Mrs Simpson's attraction for him stemmed from his bitter dwelling on his early life and 'wretched childhood'. From his belief that she could offer him the happy home he had never had. The fact that she must by her very nature—yet another Gemini with similar planetary patterns to his unsympathetic parents—repeat the same glum story was a subtle and typically Neptunian twist to the plot.

Undoubtedly Neptune-inspired too was the decision to choose 3 June as his wedding date—the actual birthday of his later father, who had died 18 months before. Perhaps, there was here one last flash of reprisal and rebellion, unrecognized by the conscious mind yet still the hidden, motivating force behind the deed.

It is of course, all too easy to condemn a man who deserts his duty in the face of challenge but few could stand before the united onslaught of Pluto *and* Neptune over decades of time, striking relentlessly from youth to middle age. Most of us would falter before so much force. The fact that the Duke faltered and then fell from grace so far and so hard was not solely his fault. He had, by birth, been raised to the pinnacles of power. From there it was a very, very long way down.

Neptune Summary: House Position 2 1943—1960

In late 1960, Neptune at last vacated the Duke's eighth house after a 17-year transit thereof. Tragically, just before the planet's entry into that house, Edward's youngest surviving brother—the light-hearted, insouciant Duke of Kent, born like their grandmother Queen Alexandra and brother King George under Sagittarius (date 20 December 1902)—was killed in a RAF plane crash on 25 August 1942 at 39. He was the only member of the Royal Family to die in wartime action. Edward was then in the Bahamas and did not attend the funeral.

After Neptune had settled into the eighth house, two more sad deaths followed. That of his brother, King George VI, of lung cancer at age 56 on 6 February 1952. The following year his mother, Queen Mary, died on 24 March 1953 aged 85. Most Cancer-born individuals take family bereavements very hard as did the Duke. Himself in ill health and alone—the Duchess was still unwelcome with his royal relatives—he travelled to England from France to attend both funerals. Photographs show him walking with downcast eyes in the cortege that followed the coffins.

Although both the fraternal and maternal bonds had long been broken by his unacceptable marriage, his grief was clearly evident, made greater by the fact that (like most Cancer types) he was at heart a family man. With no family of his own to console him, there was now no-one left. Father, mother, two younger brothers all gone.

Little else of significance happened during this transit. As one biographer put it: 'The small, rather empty, somewhat purposeless world of the Windsors continued in its orbit.'

Neptune Aspects: 1935 – 1937

In these years, Neptune produced a pair of tough square aspects, both linking ominously the Duke's seventh and fourth houses. (It will be noted that Saturn had also begun hitting the fourth with squares through 1936). The first—the Neptune square Neptune aspect—arrived in late 1934, remained in orb through 1935, then retrograded back to the aspect in mid-1936 up till August.

This is one of the middle-life crisis aspects which everyone experiences around age 42 (see earlier). It leads into a thick fog of uncertainties, illusions and pursuit of impossible dreams unless a tight hold is kept on reality.

Edward had virtually lost touch with reality from the moment he became infatuated with Mrs Simpson so did nothing to resist Neptune's pull into dark, uncharted waters. The final outcome of his dream love was ignored: fairy tale endings took shape in the mist. Past home and family ties dissolved, suspicions multiplied around him. (Although we are not now looking at the year of 1934 in depth, it should be recorded that as early as late 1934 Neptune had struck a square to Pluto as well, again a seventh to fourth house link. This continued through 1935 and mid 1936 and had hence set up a prior subconscious pull towards gullible thinking and self-deception.)

The next 1936 Neptune square partially overlapped its predecessor. This linked to Jupiter, once more from the seventh to the fourth, continued through 1937 until it finally concluded in July 1938.

If ever anyone was warned of dire and desperate dangers from marriage decisions and home opposition thereto, Edward was. Neptune and Saturn had both switched on red lights beforehand, bright as beacons.

Edward again appeared to respond in the negative manner to the Neptune/Jupiter square. He listened to ill-considered advice, became involved in muddle-headed schemes and steered both the Ship of State and himself on to a reef. The State survived the wreck. He did not.

Uranus Summary: House Position (1)

This planet did not join in the maelstrom surrounding the Duke as directly as did Saturn and Neptune. Here the disruptive energy focused on the Duke's second house from 1927 through to 1937. Income changes, spending, financial affairs were thus stressed through those 10 years. There were the usual swings between losses and gains, typical of Uranus in the second. When the transit began in 1927 Edward was the leader of post-war British society, living and spending accordingly. Although his lifelong parsimony was even then in evidence. He only paid the bills he could not avoid, biographers state.

By 1937, his vast resources as Prince of Wales and then King had evaporated with the titles that created them. The Duke remained a very wealthy man with a regular annual income his brother, the next King, had settled upon him for life in his new role as a royal duke.

No biography states precisely how much his wedding at a French chateau on 3 June 1937 cost or who paid his bride's couturier bills. These were the first of a never-ending succession of expenditures for extravagances in clothes and pleasures that Wallis ran up and Edward never opposed or questioned.

Uranus Summary: House Position (2)

From 1937 to 1942, Uranus continued to move through the Duke's third house. Several travel opportunities connected with his intellectual interests were offered and were taken—one of them the highly-damaging visit to Hitler's Germany in late 1937 from which it was alleged that the Duke was pro-Nazi. Another in 1940, was the couple's race to escape the advancing German armies as they were forced to flee through France and Spain.

The German trip was unquestionably a serious error of judgement. The Governorship of the Bahamas which began in 1940 revealed the Duke as restless, unable to concentrate and at Wallis' demand slipping off for frequent spending sprees in America. This was looked on sourly by the citizens of wartime Britain.

Uranus Aspects: 1935 – 1937

Only one in the above period—the Uranus-opposition-Uranus aspect which is also one of the barrage which strikes all those passing between the ages of roughly 40 and 50 (See earlier).

This aspect moved into orb in May 1937 and remained so until April 1938, linking Edward's third and ninth houses. In typical Uranus style, it drove him to the edge of the precipice, stirring conflict between what he had been trained to be, the skills he had been educated to apply and foreign ideas, foreign life styles and foreigners themselves.

Even before he fell finally under Mrs Simpson's spell, Edward had been strongly attracted to foreigners as a whole, Americans in particular. His previous lover was the American socialite, Lady Thelma Furness. Wallis herself was American, her husband was half-English and half-American. This is consistent with natal Uranus in Edward's ninth and part of the grand trine in water which allowed him earlier emotional empathy with foreign-born individuals.

The surge for freedom and independence of the current transiting aspect carried him forward, eliminating people from his life who no longer mattered, precipitating the search for new and more exciting life directions. The trouble was it went too far.

Transits of Faster-Moving Planets for the day of Abdication: 11 December 1936

Sun = Transiting the tenth
Moon = Transiting the ninth
Mercury = Transiting the eleventh
Venus = Transiting the twelfth
Mars = Transiting the eighth
Jupiter = Transiting the eleventh

Again, as we saw with Teddy Kennedy, highly significant life sectors were being stressed on this sad/happy day, for biographers would note the odd mixture of regret and exhilaration which the departed King appeared to exhibit as he bade his royal world farewell. He was not happy to have been forced to abandon his high position; he was overjoyed at the prospect of being reunited with Mrs Simpson in the not too distant future.

The Sun's transit of the tenth focused his will on career changes and the travel from England which immediately followed. The Moon's transit of the ninth further stressed emotional concern with travel and involvement with foreigners. The Duke went to Europe and remained there to marry Wallis as soon as her divorce decree became absolute. Mercury's transit of the eleventh directed the mind towards achievement of wishes and changed social situations. The Duke was obliged to live with friends in Europe prior to attaining his greatest wish—marriage to his beloved. Venus' transit of the twelfth warned of the self-undoing and sacrifices which would follow in the area of affections/love. His abdication cost him forever the support and affection of his royal relatives as well as his former subjects as a whole.

If Wallis' love really was enough to fill the void, no-one will ever know for certain. The Duke in his memoirs and statements often said so—even as late as 1970 when he humbly proclaimed it to President Nixon's guests at the White House: 'I have had the good fortune to have had a wonderful American girl consent to marry me and thirty years of loving care and devotion and companionship—something I have cherished above all else.'

But. . .But. . .Was that wholly true? Neither the Duke's demeanour in the post-abdication years nor the documented evidence of life on the social wave with Wallis support it. One thing only is certain. Edward *wanted* to believe every word of it. He had to. Otherwise, his world would have been well lost not for love but for nothing at all.

Certainly, Mars' transit of the eighth, also operative on Abdication Day, threatened the conflicts over property/income which were part of the royal assets. What the Duke would retain and what he would forfeit. Biographers agree there is no doubt that his brother, George VI tried hard to be both fair and generous but in the circumstances that wasn't easy. Edward was demanding: the British Government was antagonistic: the other Royals were unforgiving. George did his best—as indeed he always did. Edward was dissatisfied—as indeed he always was.

It should be noted that the Duke's natal chart shows Mars in the second (income/moneys) and Venus in the third (siblings). Thus an odd blend of easy results from dealings with his brother could be foreseen from Venus but arguments when money reared its ugly head. And so it was when the Mars transit stirred up eighth house matters.

Lastly, Jupiter's transit of the eleventh, which had begun in mid-February 1936 (just after the old King's death) and continued until early January 1937 (covering the Abdication Crisis and its immediate aftermath) gave an added lift to the Duke's hopes and would have contributed to the cheerful optimism, which he intermittently displayed throughout those eleven months of trial and decision.

Nevertheless, it's worth recording that on the day of abdication itself, transiting Jupiter was already in orb to an opposition with the Sun in the Duke's fifth house. One more warning that if romantic hopes were allowed to fly too high without a solid basis in reality, they would be doomed to disappointment.

Planetary Switch-Points for the ages 40 to 50 years

Whereas in the case of Teddy Kennedy, all three of the major clashes between the heavy planets arrived much later in his life than his 1969 crisis point, the Duke experienced both the Uranus/Uranus opposition in 1937 (at age 43) and the Neptune/Neptune square in 1935 (at age 41) during his crisis years. (See earlier.) The last of the Duke's trio of heavies—the Pluto/Pluto square did not arrive until late 1961 (at age 67) and continued intermittently through 1962 and 1963 until September.

Thus this switch-point was not directly in evidence at the time of the abdication. The reason it turned up so late in the Duke's life and still in his seventh house is partly due to Pluto's erratic orbit and partly to the interception of Virgo in the seventh. Being born in the last decade of the nineteenth century when Pluto was in the early degrees of Gemini, it had taken the planet nearly 70 years to travel from the fourth house natal position to the seventh house transit position.

Nevertheless, when the Pluto/Pluto square finally arrived, its target was yet again Edward's seventh and fourth houses—the same life sectors which both Saturn and Neptune had hammered with aspects long ago in the mid-1930's. Now, the gauntlet was thrown down for one last time. The unsolved subconscious struggle between home/country versus love/marriage was resurrected. Too late for a man of his type. Too late for drastic change. Too old to try again.

If the Duke allowed himself to look back over almost 70 years of existence through the lens of the inner eye what did he see? Certainly not half a lifetime of 'loving care and devotion and companionship' as his conscious mind kept on insisting. If he looked ahead—no joy either. He died a few months after transiting Pluto had begun to retrograde to and from over the eighth house cusp.

Crisis Point Progressions: 1935, 1936, 1937

Now, we've considered the Duke's crisis point years from the standpoint of the natal chart, the transits and the events they prompted, we must examine how his inner states were being affected during his time of trial.

In 1935, the Moon had already been progressing through Edward's seventh house for a couple of years, remaining there until mid-1936 when a progression through the eighth began and continued well past the end of 1938. The Moon's movement through the seventh invariably turns the emotional drives towards union/relationship, thereby making this life sector one of prime concern. And so it was with the Duke.

Remembering that his natal seventh house is empty, this urgent need to seek happiness in marriage was for him a novel sensation, since it immersed him in deep wells of feeling he had not before experienced. As his emotional dependence on Mrs Simpson intensified, he jettisoned—coldly and abruptly—his two former married lovers, neither of whom (in contrast to Wallis) had ever dreamed of his marrying them.

The wedding itself took place after the Moon had passed on into the eighth, thereby implying the financial problems which would flow from it and his highly emotional concern with them.

Progressed Moon Aspects:
Through 1935, the year that Edward's infatuation with Mrs Simpson became uncontrollable, his progressed Moon set up a series of tough aspects to his fourth house planets, thus pulling inner demands into line with the outer changes brought by the transiting planets.

The progressed Moon reached squares with natal Pluto, Neptune and Jupiter, covering between them the entire 1935 year. At the beginning of 1935, the Duke's inner state had been deeply disturbed as the Pluto link created a struggle between what his royal parents had conditioned him to do and feel and what he now so desperately wanted.

By mid-1935, the Moon/Neptune aspect had stimulated illusions, deceptions by the self and from others. This was the time when Mrs Simpson was still protesting she had no thought of marrying her royal lover, yet showed by her actions she had already cast herself in the role of wife. She was never prepared to remain tucked out of sight as the King's mistress in the way her predecessors would have been.

At the close of 1935, when the old King's life was obviously ebbing fast away, the progressed Moon completed the year with the square to Jupiter. Over-optimism, trusting to his luck and popularity urged Edward into believing he could 'pull it off' and achieve his impossible ambition.

The 1936 year opened with a more helpful progressed Moon aspect—a link with Venus. He would have begun to feel that his plans were running more smoothly than he'd hoped. Despite oppostion from many quarters, there were some loud and powerful voices of encouragement. However, Moon/Venus links in progressions are not of great force and could not prevail against the tougher aspects affecting his life choices.

No further major Moon progressed aspects occurred in 1936. But the early months of 1937—after the Abdication Crisis had passed and the wedding day awaited only Mrs Simpson's divorce decree becoming absolute—the progressed Moon linked again with natal Pluto, this time helpfully. From this one, came the compelling force which enabled the Duke to break down the obstacles and continuing opposition to push his project through to completion.

Disturbingly though, a sinister Pluto-type figure suddenly appeared and took a hand in the wedding plans—in the shape of the owner of the luxurious French chateau where the ceremony took place. The man ingratiated himself with Edward and Wallis as well as organizing their visit to Hitler. His name was Charles Bedaux, a wealthy naturalized French-born, American with undercover links with criminals, who was working (undercover again!) to further the Nazi cause. Later in 1943, he committed suicide after being arrested for treason. The couple's comparatively brief association with Bedaux brought accusations, suspicions of Nazi sympathies and further bad publicity.

Not long after the very quiet wedding, attended by only eight guests and no royals, on 3 June 1937, the Moon moved on to aspect natal Neptune again in the Duke's fourth, this time also helpfully. The duration of the aspect covered the honeymoon travels and three-month stay in an Austrian castle. Biographers state at the very outset of their marital life, on the honeymoon itself (Wallis' third and Edward's first experience of early wedded bliss) bickering began over who had failed to do what and why her meteoric rise towards the crown of England had crashed back to earth in a conflagration of anger and rejection. At this moment, the softening, sympathetic Moon/Neptune pattern came to the Duke's aid. He suddenly said: 'Darling, if we keep this up, we are never going to agree, so let's drop it for good.' And for a time, they did.

As 1938 hovered on the horizon, the progressed Moon made two more contacts—simultaneously. A trine to Jupiter in the fourth, promising pleasurable, expansive opportunities. A conjunction with Saturn in the eighth, threatening bitter disappointments and delays. Both aspects were coming into orb during the late 1937 German tour and both produced a troublesome blend of the above circumstances. The sinister, conniving Bedaux had promised to organize an American tour, immediately following the German visit, a prospect which delighted the Duke. It never came off. The Duchess's home country pulled the welcome mat out peremptorily from under their feet as soon as press pictures of the couple, shaking hands with Hitler appeared in American newspapers. The Duke was despondent and bewildered. The Duchess was furious. Hitler himself made an odd comment to one of his associates referring to the long, private conversation he had

had with the Duke (who spoke fluent German): 'An hour with me and he would never have abdicated'.

One wonders what was said to provoke it. Was Edward already half-regretting his choice?

Progressed Sun Aspects:
At the very beginning of 1934, the progressed Sun began to approach an ominous square to natal Uranus—linking all the more ominously the Duke's seventh house with his ninth. The will to wed a foreigner was colliding with the urge to throw convention to the winds. This aspect came into full force in early 1935 and continued through that year—lending fuel to the flames of Edward's passion for his American-born lover. Progressed Sun aspects do not turn up all that frequently in any chart and—since the Sun represents the very core of being—when tough aspects do appear, they hit hard. This one struck the proverbial nail right on the head!

Read any biography and you'll observe the irritability, the erratic behaviour, the actions always stamped with the 'damn-all-I'll-go-my-way' signature of Uranus. Striking as it did the Duke's seventh, this one amounted to a danger warning as loud as an air raid siren. Any thought of marrying anyone—especially a foreigner—should be abandoned until this separative and disruptive influence was long gone. But the Duke obviously made no attempt to resist it. Upheavals, estrangements, separations of whirlwind magnitude ensued as it pushed him even closer to the edge of the precipice.

Conclusions:

It is of course—as the old saying goes—easy to be wise *after* the event. Yet, from our detailed examination of the Duke's story and the astrological patterns which directed it, we can observe how easy it would have been for him to be wise *before* the event—had he known what his chart contained. And—more importantly still— had he been willing to listen to what his chart was telling him. That second point is the vital one, a problem with which all analysts are sadly familiar.

Whether you're advising ordinary people or those of high estate, you'll always find some clients who resolutely close their ears, particularly if you warn against something they very much want to do. You can take your horse to water. You cannot make him drink of the fountain of wisdom the chart offers.

I, myself, have had cases of clients ringing or writing in a flood of remorse with statements like: 'I didn't take any notice of what my chart said. In fact, I did the opposite. Now, everything's gone wrong for me. Can you help me get out of this mess?' To which I usually reply: 'Only if you listen this time. Otherwise, you'll be wasting both your money and your opportunities.'

In the Duke's case, in just the same way as for all of us, the natal chart revealed the outlines of his future. His personality pluses and minuses which, if wisely handled, could have led on to happiness and fulfillment. If unwisely handled, to sadness and disappointment. The fact that he did turn his back on duty and responsibility in exchange for a life of escalating futility was partially because his royal birth had placed him in the unenviable position of being a square peg in a round hole. But then so placed have been many far less exalted individuals. The only real difference is that their mistakes or evasions do not reverberate around the world nor play a part in changing the course of history.

The source of many of the Duke's problems lay largely with his grand trine in water. Throughout his earlier life, it had encouraged him to believe that his charm, his unconventionality, his royal glamour would sway emotions and give him everything he ever wanted without really trying. Which it did. For almost 40 years. Then came the crunch. He had leant too heavily upon it for too long. When transiting and progressing planets built up peak pressure, the grand trine could not hold fast under the strain. Still, it did not totally give way. It helped to keep him going long after his younger brother, George VI, had succumbed to overwork and over-worry. Edward survived to almost 78: George died at only 56.

Footprints in the Sands of Time

Our studies of the lives of Teddy Kennedy and the Duke of Windsor as well as those of other famous and everyday people discussed in this book, prove the basic tenet of astrological science-timing.

Work in tune with the planetary patterns of the natal chart which stem from the *moment in time* when each birth occurred. Watch the movements of the planets in their transits and progressions as they accentuate or obstruct natal potentials so that decisions/changes are *timed* to bring optimum results. Move when the *time* is right. Pause and reflect when the *time* is wrong. As noted earlier, read and chart the lives of the famous to expand your knowledge of how this concept of timing works for success or failure, for good or ill—depending on how wisely each man or woman responds to it. Some do so instinctively. Others pull against it.

Those who attune their actions to this sense of time, win. Those who do not, lose and hopefully learn not to make the same mistake again. Sometimes the patience of Job is necessary though restraint may be difficult to apply. Sometimes courage—to grasp the chance as it flies past—is vital even in the face of hesitation and doubt.

I remember my actress mother reciting an old poem from which the heading of this final section is a quote. It went something like this:

> Lives of great men all remind us
> We can make our lives sublime
> And, departing, leave behind us
> Footprints in the sands ot time.

Looking at lives from the astrological standpoint, I think we can safely say that the lives of *all* famous personages, whether good or bad, great or tragic, leave 'footprints in the sands of time' for us to study and learn lessons from. With their charts in hand, we can get to know such people better than if we had been their brothers, sisters, parents or partners. We can see what lay ahead for them and remember it when similar (but less news-making) challenges arrive in our own lives and those of people important to us.

We, too, can take the downward path or the upward one. The choice is always yours, mine and everyone else's. But once we learn how to focus our futures through the foreknowledge the chart unerringly offers, the margins of error are narrowed. We can feel surer that the footprints we leave at last in the sands of time will have led in the right direction.

INDEX

Of further interest . . .

ASTRO-PICK YOUR PERFECT PARTNER

A Step-by-step Guide to Compatibility in Relationships

What makes you fall in, and out, of love? How can you tell the difference between brief sexual attraction and long-term affection? Written by university-qualified psychologist and leading astrologer **Mary Coleman,** this book answers these questions – and more – by showing you how to assess your own special needs in a sexual relationship.

The technique used is called astro-analysis, because it blends the interpretation of personality traits shown in the horoscope with modern methods of psychological analysis. As you work with it, you'll discover facets and drives in your own nature that you never knew existed! You'll also begin to see those you care most about in a new and revealing light.

Easy-to-use Compatibility Rating Tables ensure you get the best out of all your relationships, whilst the unique presentation of quick reference data allows the non-astrologer to begin using astro-analysis immediately. *Astro-Pick Your Perfect Partner* covers:

– battling the Elements, yours and your partner's
– marriage or *de facto* liaisons, which do you want?
– are you and your partner 'getting through' to each other?
– how to set up your own Compatibility Rating Table
– analysing your conscious hopes and subconscious blocks

HOW TO ASTRO-ANALYZE YOURSELF AND OTHERS

Making the Most of Yourself and Your Relationships

Wouldn't you like to:

— **understand** yourself, and those you care about, better?
— **discover** why you do the things you do?
— **plan** your life instead of just letting it happen?
— **use** your individual talents and minimize your failings?
— **learn** what makes people fall in and out of love?

In short, do you want to make the most of yourself and your relationships? If so, **astro-analysis** can help provide practical solutions to the conundrums of life, love and sex that puzzle us all.

Astro-analysis — a potent and exciting blend of traditional astrology and modern psychology — is easy to understand and simple to use: there are no complex calculations and the computation procedures are virtually mistake proof. As you master its techniques, you'll begin to discover a more confident 'you' emerging, and the path to a happier, more satisfying future opening out before you.

Author **Mary Coleman,** one of Australia's leading astrologers, qualified first in psychology and then in the law, holding BA and LL.B. degrees from the University of Sydney, before taking up the study of astrology. The author of several books, she is a Professional Member of the Federation of Australian Astrologers and runs a private practice in astro-analytical counselling.